PEAK WHEN IT COUNTS
Periodization for American Track and Field

4th Edition

William H. Freeman

TAFNEWS PRESS

Book Division of Track & field News

FOURTH EDITION

Published by Tafnews Press,
Book Division of Track & Field News,
2570 El Camino Real, Suite 606
Mountain View, CA 94040 USA

Printed in the United States of America

First edition copyright in 1989
Second edition copyright in 1991
Third edition copyright in 1996

Standard Book Number 0-911521-62-3

Design and production: Teresa Tam

Cover photo of 2000 Olympic 400mH gold medalist Angelo Taylor
by Victor Sailor/Photo Run.

Dedicated to

James Bernard Cox III

1947-1990

The runner who made me a coach

and

Bill Bowerman

1911-1999

A coach whose influence lives on

CONTENTS

Acknowledgements

Every coach learns from a long series of athletes, with their varying talents and goals. I have coached athletes from the junior high school level through the Olympic Trials level over the past three decades. I have learned much from them. They have given much to me, and each of them is appreciated for his or her part in my coaching experiences. Coaching is very fulfilling, and I have been fortunate to have the opportunity to work with athletes at many different levels.

Bill Bowerman, coach at Oregon (1948-1973) and 1972 Head U.S. Olympic Coach, provided many opportunities for me during our 30-year association. His training patterns, developed in the 1950s and 1960s, are remarkably close to the periodization theories that are so successful today.[1, 2] He was a coach far ahead of his time.

Bill Dellinger, a former Bowerman NCAA champion and Olympic medalist, his successor at Oregon (1973-1998), and the 1984 U.S. Olympic Distance Coach, also provided insight with his work with Olympic-level athletes. His extension of the Oregon training patterns has also produced many world-class runners.[3]

I am pleased to write for Tafnews Press, having read *Track & Field News* and *Track Technique* (now *Track Coach*) faithfully since my days as a high school runner. *T&FN* has usually been the first American source for the "hot" new training theories from abroad and from other language sources.

I want to acknowledge our nation's middle school and high school coaches. They are the people who are developing our future Olympians. I hope that this book will make their task easier and more productive.

Bill Freeman

REFERENCES

1. William J. Bowerman & William H. Freeman. (1974). *Coaching Track and Field*. Boston: Houghton Mifflin.
2. William J. Bowerman & William H. Freeman. (1991). *High-Performance Training for Track and Field* (2nd ed.). Champaign, IL: Human Kinetics.
3. Bill Dellinger & Bill Freeman. (1984). *The Competitive Runner's Training Book*. New York: Collier.

Preface

Periodization is the most successful method for organizing training for competitive athletes. It can be applied to any event in track and field, to any individual or team sport. It is the reason that a small nation like East Germany could compete head-to-head with the United States in the Olympic medal race. Even so, it sees limited use in the United States.

This book explains periodization and how to use it effectively in the American setting. Applying the theory in the USA is critical, because our national system has peculiarities unlike any other nation. Most of our athletic success comes from our intensive system of organized school athletics, ranging from occasional elementary school teams to organized middle and high school sports, through an essentially semiprofessional sports program at the NCAA Division I collegiate level.

While this system provides widespread opportunities for early exposure to sports, it also emphasizes immediate competitive success over a very short time span, with three major sports seasons in nine months. The emphasis with such a brief schedule is on a quick conditioning period (often as little as two weeks), then plunging into competition. It is conducive primarily to locating natural talent, rather than developing skills for the future.

The most effective training systems require longer developmental periods. However, coaches must compete at home, not in another nation. This book explains how periodization of training is applied, then shows how to use it effectively in the United States at the public school level, at the uni-versity level, and for the post-school elite athlete. Our competitive seasons require a peak during months ranging from April (in collegiate early-semester programs) to September (for elite athletes competing in Europe). This book diagrams the periodized training year and its application to athletes at all levels. It shows how to apply periodization to the different events of track and field, with a detailed discussion of periodization for middle and long distance runners.

Coaches and athletes are always searching for a better training system. A successful system must meet local needs and conditions. Our early colonists tried to develop "American" systems to meet their new conditions of life, rather than copy the systems of their original homes in Europe. At the 1892 convention of America's physical educators, they called for an "American System" of physical education.[1] A 1968 booklet gave a brief explanation of running training that it called the "American System."[2] It was a very 1950s-60s, intensive interval-oriented training system that was popular in the U.S. at that time. Now, we will learn how to apply this no-longer-new "foreign system" of periodization to our best use at home.

REFERENCES

1. William H. Freeman. (2001). *Physical Education and Sport in a Changing Society* (6th ed., p. 124). Boston: Allyn & Bacon.
2. Tom Rosandich, Tom Ward, & Bob Lawson. (1968). *American Training Patterns*. Upson, WI: Olympia.

About the Author

William H. Freeman received his Ph.D. from the University of Oregon in 1972. For 30 years he has coached athletes from the junior high school to the post-collegiate levels. He has directed the decathlon and heptathlon competitions at three U.S. Olympic Trials and four NCAA Championships. Freeman has written extensively on training, and his books include *Coaching Track and Field*, with coaching guru Bill Bowerman (1974), *The Competitive Runner's Training Book*, with former Oregon Coach Bill Dellinger (1984), and the revision of the Bowerman book as *High-Performance Training for Track and Field* (1991). The sixth edition of his textbook, *Physical Education and Sport in a Changing Society* was published by Allyn & Bacon in late 2000. Freeman is currently chairman of the Department of Exercise Science at Campbell University, Buies Creek, North Carolina.

PART 1:
The Basics Of Periodizaton Theory

Regina Jacobs

CHAPTER 1:
The Value Of Periodization

WHAT IS PERIODIZATION IN TRAINING?

The most effective training plans for today's athletes are very detailed plans that divide the year into phases and microcycles. This method of training is called "periodization." It has become the dominant method of training for the world's best athletes in most sports.

Periodization is simply dividing an athlete's training program into a number of periods of time, each with a specific training goal or goals. It is a form of "indexing," developing an objective method of measuring the training load and determining if it meets the athlete's needs. For example, a single year may be broken into three periods, units of time with a small number of specific goals. Each period will prepare the athlete for the next, more advanced training period, until the athlete peaks at the most important competition of the year.

In a sense periodization is like fractals. That is, the training process is a pattern that repeats itself, moving from the small scale to the larger scale. It is similar to what we are learning about the non-linear realities of the human body. We coaches attempt to develop models of elite performance, then train our athletes to duplicate those models. In earlier times, the model for a sprinter was essentially to develop quick reaction time, good drive out of the blocks, and a well-timed dip at the tape. I think Tom Tellez used a considerably more complex model for athletes like Carl Lewis and Leroy Burrell.

James Gleick writes that "traditional education concentrated on systems that were linear. . . A linear system obeys laws of proportionality—the faster you go, the farther you travel. . . Unfortunately, most real world systems are nonlinear." Try to explain that to coaches and athletes who firmly believe that twice the work always means twice the progress.

Researchers studying the human body found that its systems are not as regular, as periodic, as they once believed. Indeed, they discovered that, contrary to medical traditions, "irregularity and unpredictability. . . are important features of health, [while] decreased variability and accentuated periodicities are associated with disease."

We must stop viewing the workings of the human body, and thus the sport training process, as if we can somehow discover some small, single rule that will open all doors to us, make us all-wise, and allow us to prepare perfect athletes. There is order, but we must search through the chaos to find it.

The heart of periodization is very simple: Make training an objective process. From the start this was the major idea behind periodization. We plan our training based on an objective knowledge and analysis of the traits needed for success in the event, then we train the athletes and test them, refine the plan, train again, retest, and continue the process until we achieve our best result. In short, you create a model, plan a training system to replicate the model, then spend your time tweaking the system.

It is an attempt to wed science and efficiency to the art of preparing athletes for competition. Coaching is an art because we must cope with a flexible world. We cannot plan for everything that might happen, because we can never guess everything that might happen. Without flexibility no coach can produce consistently successful athletes.

Periodization does not have to be highly complex. Simply stated, the coach uses it to set specific, measurable goals, along with objective tests of progress. Does this mean that only lab tests should be used? No.

The test effort or competition is as valid a measure. *Objectivity* is the criteria, not laboratory purity.

WHY IS PERIODIZATION AN IMPORTANT TRAINING CONCEPT?

Perhaps the greatest difficulty in achieving athletic goals is planning the training program in an objective, measurable way. If the training is planned subjectively ("That seems like enough mileage"), the result is almost accidental. While coaches rely on a certain amount of instinct or "feel" that arises from their years of experience, the athlete deserves a more reliable measure.

Periodization enables the coach and athlete to measure the work that the athlete does, so it can be compared to earlier training and results and to future needs. The resulting training record gives objective measures for predicting the future performances of the athlete.

Pasquale Bellotti writes about the general needs of an organized training system, noting that "the competing athlete has such a specific psychophysical condition as to require highly sophisticated investigations and responses." He refers to "the complex problem of organizing modern sport training," going on to explain that "to periodize means to state a number of theoretical principles, with respect to: (a) the detailed trend of development of physical workloads in the periods of the training macrostructure, and (b) the orderly distribution of the individual components of training. Periodization should be initially based on the control of the athlete's specific condition and its final goal should be that of checking whether the workload adopted was really effective."

At the same time, coaches and athletes are concerned about the timing of training. The goal of every performer is to peak (achieve the best performance of the year) at the most important competition, whether it is a conference meet, a national championship, or the Olympic Games. At the higher levels of competition, an athlete may need to achieve a peak performance twice a year (usually indoors and outdoors).

Periodization is used to point the training effort toward the major goal, taking into account the competitions along the way. Training is a very complex process, involving both internal and external variables. It is affected by the quantity and quality of the workouts, by rest, and by the competitive experiences of the athlete. At the same time, the major achievements in sport (such as world records and Olympic gold medals) are extremely difficult to achieve. Consequently, the coach and athlete must try to remove (as much as possible) the element of chance from the training process if they hope to achieve such goals. Periodization of training is the best way to do it.

Even with periodization, coaching is still an art. If periodization is treated as an inflexible, unchanging system, then it will not produce optimal results—as is true for *any* training system. At the same time, *no system* succeeds when applied by inexperienced theorists. Theory grows from prior experience, then it is proven by experience gained from application. The coach's art lies in assessing and reacting to the changing state, the condition and needs of the athlete. Is the athlete weak in speed? Endurance? Mental toughness?

This is why we coach: The challenge never ends, because every athlete comes to us with a new combination of strengths and weaknesses. While we can take elements of the training that we have used with other athletes, we can never simply use one athlete's training to develop another athlete to his or her full potential. In short, as trite as it may seem, athletes are like snowflakes—no two are exactly alike.

One difficulty that coaches face in planning an effective training program is the popular saying, "Just do it."

I prefer to use an expanded version of that statement for athletes: "Beginners just do it, but *Olympians plan it, then follow their plan.*" If I am feeling unkind, I might be tempted to add, "That's why they are Olympians, and that's why you are not. Think about it."

IS PERIODIZATION STILL A VALID APPROACH TO TRAINING?

Yes. But why do we ask the question?

In a 1998 article titled "The End of 'Periodisation' of Training in Top Class Sport," Yuri

Verhoshansky, an expert Russian sport scientist, argued that periodization "does not meet the requirements of contemporary sport and. . . does not present a model training system for elite athletes within the demands of modern competition calendars and other international development tendencies."

His arguments assumed that only the pure, fairly rigid system that Matveyev described in the past can define how periodized training works. His positions were strongly criticicized in articles by training experts Klaus Bartonietz, Vladimir Platonov and Peter Tschiene, as well as a limited response by this author, who had seen only an abstract at that time. To understand Verhoshansky's remarks, we need to understand the change in the competitive environment over the last 30 years.

At the time Matveyev first wrote of periodization, track and field competition for most of the world was a relatively simple system with only a small number of truly significant competitions. In most countries an athlete's goal was to perform well at the national championships. We hear little of qualifying standards in the early years.

An American athlete had major competitions at conference championships for school meets, a national championships (for college or open athletes—and many top collegians skipped the open nationals), and every four years the Olympic Trials.

Basically, this meant that the really important meets for high-level performances were only two a year for high school athletes (assuming they made it to their state meet), one or two meets for collegians, and one meet for post-collegiate athletes, except in an Olympic year.

Before 1987 there were no world championships in track. The Olympic Games were designated as the only world championship. Dual meets between two nations were major events.

So how has that changed? For high school and college athletes in the United States—it has not changed. The only major change is at the elite or high-performance level, and the real change was the arrival of professional sport.

During the 1980s elite track and field became professional, and during the same period the IAAF greatly expanded their series of high-level championships. Most years now feature a world championships of some sort, usually following an extensive number of elite competitions. The demands of those meets are not for a peak, but for sustained elite performance over a series of 20-30 competitions, often with three meets a week. Indeed, Helmut Digel argues that we are now oversaturated with high-level competitions, to a degree that has damaged spectator interest in lower-level meets (including national champion-

ships) in most nations around the world.

Such an athlete is no longer training to reach a peak—instead, he or she is training to maximize income. Some performers can make large incomes even if they rarely win a major competition.

This book is not for those people.

High school athletes must peak. Without a peak, you cannot qualify for or try to win a conference or state championship.

College athletes must peak. Without a peak, you cannot qualify or try to win a conference or national collegiate championship.

Most post-college athletes must peak. Without a peak, you cannot qualify or try to win a national championship.

Without a peak, you cannot qualify to represent your nation in international competition. You cannot represent your country in the Olympic Games. Internationally successful American athletes have failed to make the Olympic team because they did not peak properly. Some have made it to the Olympic Games, then performed poorly, because, again, they did not peak properly.

When the championship meets come around, there is only one rule: Show us what you can do right now! Your season record does not matter, your past competitions do not matter, your income and appearance fees do not matter. The rule is to put it on the line—or go home.

The basis of periodization is valid and extremely valuable for all sports, today and in the future. Practically every athlete attempting to win a world or Olympic championship used a training plan based on the principles of periodization as described in this book. That is in part because it is a flexible, changing system, adapted to the growing complexities of sport, not the rigid, creaking, authoritarian system described by Verhoshansky. And in fact Verhoshansky's own writings still describe successful training programs in terms of periodization.

HOW DID PERIODIZED TRAINING DEVELOP?

The pioneering work on periodization was done by L.P. Matveyev of the Soviet Union during the 1960s. After introducing his research in 1962, he published his book *Periodization of Sports Training* (in Russian) in 1965. Matveyev's continuing research into periodization and training effects was translated and used widely in East Germany (GDR) by coaches and researchers, led by Dietrich Harre. Most of the developmental work on periodization was done in the Soviet Union and the GDR, along with other Eastern European nations, though much independent research has also been conducted in Finland.

Early articles on periodized training first appeared in the United States in the late 1960s. For example, a 1967 article in *Track Technique* illustrated the periodization of high jump training in Poland. A translated 1967 Czechoslovakian article showed schedules mixing types of training across the training year, varying the training emphasis depending upon the time of year. An English article on hurdle training from 1968 divided the training year into three macrocycles.

An excellent example of the periodization of elite training in the past is the unique "High Jump Issue" of *Track Technique*, a condensed translation of a 1966 Soviet text by their national high jump coach, V. M. Dyatchkov, who was the great Valeriy Brumel's mentor. A 1967 Czechoslovakian article showed a 12-month "cycle" divided into five "periods," each with a number of "microcycles," based on the work of Polish women's sprint coach Andrezj Piotrowski.

V. Popov introduced the basic principles of periodization in a translated 1967 Russian article, while Arnd Kruger got to the heart of coaches' interests by referring to periodization as "peaking at the right time." Kruger presented figures showing the training emphases through the year for several track events.

While the Russians were experimenting with patterns or cycles in training in the 1960s, they warned against applying their research in too rigid a manner. By the 1970s the Soviet training process was divided into macro-structures of one year, then subdivided into meso-structures or "monthly" cycles of 2-6 weeks, then further divided into micro-structures of one week.

Frank W. Dick gave the first detailed English-language overview of periodization in a series of short articles reprinted in *Track Technique* from 1975 through 1977. He explained the approach of periodization and how units and microcycles were planned, then discussed different aspects of training under the system. In 1978 his British booklet explained the system in more depth, along with general principles of training.

While European coaches were swiftly adopting periodized training, the norm for elite distance training in the United States in the 1960s and 1970s was still the traditional seasonal pattern, as shown in a typical schedule for an elite American distance runner of the time. For those athletes, the pattern was Summer, Fall, Winter, and Spring (competitive season) training, while for others the year was Cross Country or Fall training, Indoor Track, Outdoor Track, and Off Season or Summer.

As you can see, periodization is not new. It is a common technique now used with increasing sophistication throughout the world. However, carefully-planned periodization began to appear as a training structure in the United States only in the mid- to late-1980s.

Andrew McInnis presented a compact, but thorough, overview of periodization in 1981, while Vern Gambetta presented an approach that he called "Planned Performance Training." Chris Walsh's study of the "Oregon School" of training, developed by Bill Bowerman, shows that it was a highly developed form of periodization that evolved from the 1950s to the present day.

The primary English language works on periodization are Frank W. Dick's *Training Theory* and *Sports Training Principles* from Great Britain, Tudor O. Bompa's *Theory and Methodology of Training* from Canada, Thomas Kurz's *Science of Sports Training*, and this book, *Peak When It Counts*.

The next chapter explains the basic terms and concepts of periodization. Then we will show how periodization is applied to sports training.

REFERENCES

1. William H. Freeman. (1994). Factors in planning periodized training in a flexible world. Presented at the 10th Commonwealth and International Scientific Congress, University of Victoria, BC, Canada, 11 August 1994.
2. James Gleick. (1987). New images of chaos that are stirring a science revolution. *Smithsonian*, p. 127.
3. Ary L. Goldberger, David R. Rigney & Bruce J. West. (1990, February). Chaos and fractals in human physiology. *Scientific American*, p. 44.
4. William H. Freeman. (1995). Peaking when it counts. Presented at the Massachusetts Track Coaches Clinic, Mansfield, March 25, 1995.
5. William H. Freeman. (1994). Coaching, periodization, and the battle of artist versus scientist. *Track Technique*, 127 (Spring 1994), 4054-4057; updated in *Modern Athlete and Coach*, 33 (January 1995), 19-23.
6. Pasquale Bellotti. (1987). The control of performance within the framework of the sport training process. *New Studies in Athletics*, 2(4), 7-10.
7. Yuri Verhoshansky. (1999). The end of "periodization" of training in top class sport. *New Studies in Athletics*, 14(1), 47-55.
8. Klaus Bartonietz. (1999). The unavoidable end of periodization or a start of further development of training? [abridged translation]. *Leistungssport*, 29(1).
9. Vladimir N. Platonov. (1999). The concept of "periodisation of training" and the development of a training theory. [abridged translation]. *Leistungssport*, 29(1).
10. Peter Tschiene. (1999). Discussion of "periodisation" comments. [abridged translation]. *Leistungssport*, 29(1).
11. William H. Freeman. (Fall 1999). A reply to Verhoshansky on periodization. *Track Coach*, 149, 4767-4768.
12. Helmut Digel. (1997). International athletics on the threshold of the 21st century. *New Studies in Athletics*, 12(1), 7-14.
13. Yuri Verhoshansky. (1996). Principles for a rational organization of the training process aimed at speed development. *New Studies in Athletics*, 11(2-3), 155-160.
14. Siff, Mel, & Yuri Verhoshansky. (1999). *Supertraining*. (4th ed., pp. 319-336). Denver, CO: Supertraining International.
15. Lev Pavlovich Matveyev. (1981). *Fundamentals of Sports Train-*

ing. Trans. Albert P. Zdornykh. Moscow: Progress.

16. Dietrich Harre, ed. (1982). *Principles of Sports Training: Introduction to the Theory and Methods of Training* (2nd ed.). Berlin: Sportverlag.

17. Adam Bezeg. (1967). Improving spring in the high jump. *Track Technique, 28,* 895-896.

18. Milan Bures. (1969). Training of Czech women middle distance runners. *Track Technique, 35,* 1114-1118.

19. Les Mitchell. (1968). Planning hurdles training. *Track Technique, 31,* 986-988.

20. V.M. Dyatchkov. (1969). High jumping. *Track Technique, 36,* 1123-1157.

21. Pavel Glesk. (1969). Training of Polish women sprinters. *Track Technique, 38,* 1200-1202.

22. V. Popov. (1969). Foundations of training planning. *Track Technique, 38,* 1217-1220.

23. Arnd Kruger. (1973). Periodization, or peaking at the right time. *Track Technique, 54,* 1720-1724.

24. Yevgeniy Kashkalov. (1971). Varying work loads in middle distance training. *Track Technique, 43,* 1375-1377.

25. F.P. Suslov. (1974). Soviet women's middle distance training. *Track Technique, 58,* 1842-1844.

26. Frank W. Dick. (1975). Periodization: An approach to the training year. *Track Technique, 62,* 1968-1969.

27. Frank W. Dick. (1978). *Training Theory.* London: British Amateur Athletic Board.

28. Jerry Smith. (1969). Ken Moore: How he trains. *Track Technique, 35,* 1118-1119.

29. Andrew McInnis. (1981). A research review of systematized approaches to planned performance peaking with relation to the sport of track and field. *Track and Field Quarterly Review, 81*(2), 7-12.

30. Vern Gambetta. (1989). Planned Performance Training: The application of periodization to the American system. In *TAC/USA Track and Field Coaching Manual* (2nd ed., pp. 37-45). Champaign, IL: Human Kinetics.

31. Chris Walsh. (1983). *The Bowerman System.* Mountain View, CA: Tafnews.

32. Christopher M. Walsh. (1990). Bowerman Oregon distance tradition meets Bompa training theory: Periodized Bowerman mile and 5 km training. *Track and Field Quarterly Review, 90*(2), 12-20.

33. Frank W. Dick. (1989). *Sports Training Principles* (2nd ed.). London: A & C Black.

34. Tudor O. Bompa. (1994). *Theory and Methodology of Training: The Key to Athletic Performance* (3rd ed.). Dubuque, IA: Kendall/Hunt.

35. Thomas Kurz. (1991). *Science of Sports Training: How to Plan and Control Training for Peak Performance.* Island Pond, VT: Stadion.

36. William H. Freeman. (1989). *Peak When It Counts: Periodization for American Track and Field.* Mountain View, CA: Tafnews.

CHAPTER 2:
The Language Of Periodization

IMPORTANCE OF LEARNING THE "JARGON"

If you want to communicate with someone, both of you must speak a common language. One difficulty with improving the training of athletes is that coaches and athletes use many non-standard terms. The terms *endurance* and *strength* do not mean the same thing to every coach. As a result, training suggestions may be applied incorrectly.

One of the first goals of any educational system is to develop a common technical language, so discussions of the field will be understandable to anyone in that field. We need to use the same terms, with commonly-accepted meanings, if we want to improve our coaching and understand what other coaches are doing in training. The more advanced writings on training methods and periodization today are coming from European sources that use a common training language. As a result, the European training articles are very usable and quite easy to understand.

Most articles today also use graphics to enhance their clarity. A hallmark of periodization writings is the use of training graphs to illustrate the rise and fall of different training emphases at different times during the training year. Periodization theory is an attempt to quantify training in a meaningful way, so you can summarize an athlete's training in tables and charts. This allows you to see more clearly how the athlete is expected to progress.

We will discuss the use of graphics in planning and recording training in more detail later. We will give examples of charts and tables used to plan and record training, from the overview of a full Olympiad (four years) to the smallest microcycle (the training session, with its individual training units). First, let's explain the terms used in periodization.

PERIODIZATION TERMS

The term *periodization* simply means the division of the training process into *periods*, which are assigned a variety of names depending on their training emphasis and length. We will examine these training periods from the largest unit of training time down to the smallest. The training periods are called *cycles*, which is the origin of the terms:
- Macrocycle (a large or long cycle).
- Mesocycle (an intermediate or medium-length cycle)
- Microcycle (a small or short cycle).

Vern Gambetta suggested *planned performance training* (PPT) as an American name for periodization. However, any organized training system is "planned performance training," while the term "periodization" is specific and indicates how the training is organized. Thus, I prefer to use the term "periodization."

CHANGING TERMINOLOGY IN HIGH PERFORMANCE SPORT

You may encounter conflicting terms in some writings about periodization. This book describes traditional periodization, with training aimed at a major peak. The process used for high performance athletes, particularly those who compete at the international level, is considerably more complex.

As a result, some experts will use the term "macrocycle" for what this book calls a "mesocycle." For an elite athlete, the season may involve a series of minor peaks, instead of a single major one, and each of the cycles of training is called a macrocycle, each containing 2-6 microcycles.

To show the contrast, Matveyev described the traditional meaning of a macrocycle as: "the structure of big training cycles...of the type of semi-annual, annual, and those of many years." For a small group of microcycles he used the term "mesocycles."

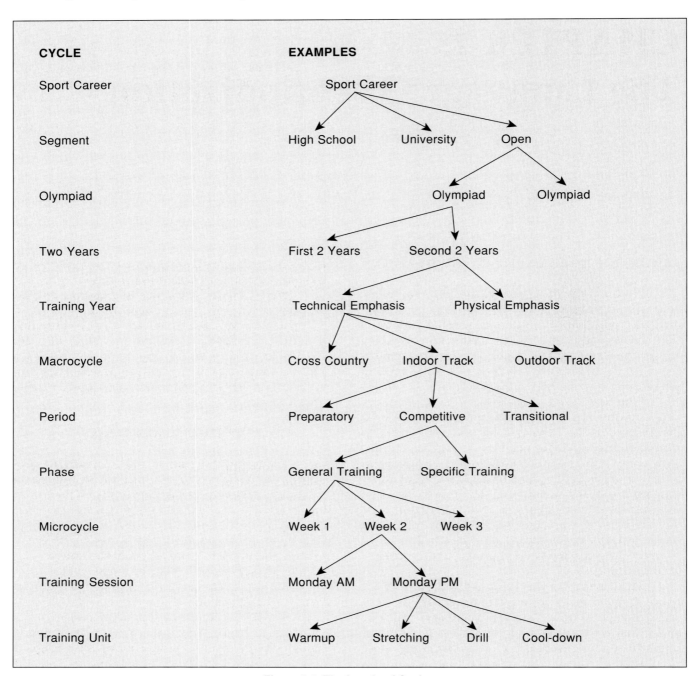

Figure 2.1. The Levels of Cycles

We see the same language in Vladimir Platonov: "the standard parts of the construction of training [are] the formation of typical microcycles into larger mesocycles to finally reach a macrocycle."

Vladimir Zatsiorsky says "macrocycle refers to one entire competition season and includes preparation, competition, and transition periods." Mel Siff and Yuri Verhoshanky use the same terminology, describing a macrocycle as lasting 10-12 months, with the occasional use of "large macrocycle" to refer to a multi-year period.

On the other hand, Tudor Bompa now uses the macrocycle as a portion of the phase, containing a small number of microcycles, while Peter Tschiene comments that "today the fundamental theoretical construction of a training year is based on six or seven cycles. This corresponds to the realistic situation in high performance sport at the end of the 1990s."

Istvan Balyi describes the multi-year plan in terms of three "phases," each lasting about four years: (1) training to train, (2) training to compete, and (3) training to win. In that model, the proportion of competition to preparation increases as the athlete's performance level rises. He defines a macrocycle as 2-4 weeks of microcycles of progressive overloading, followed by 1-2 cycles of unloading and/or restoration. This usage is reflected in other current writing about the highest levels of competition.

This is an unfortunate change in terminology, as it takes a simple term and creates confusion about its meaning. For that reason, this book uses the term macrocycle in its traditional meaning: the full training cycle through the preparation, competition and transition periods.

LONG-TERM CYCLES (ONE OR MORE YEARS)

Sport Career. The longest unit of planning is for the athlete's entire career in sport, from the start of training as a youngster until retirement after reaching a peak as an athlete. While the training process would be more effective if training is planned for the full career, it is not a realistic goal for American athletes at this time, as it requires a more centralized system, which was common in the socialist states. Figure 2.1 shows the levels of cycles.

Most training plans for the full career are theoretical models. They can be very useful if (as was the case in the GDR) they are based on extensive testing of age-group and senior athletes. Such testing allows the development of standards of performance to evaluate young athletes in terms of their future potential. In the GDR those performance models were used to rank young athletes' potential each year. The youths who continued to perform at high levels were strongly encouraged and offered special coaching and training opportunities to aid their development.

Much publicity has been given to the Eastern European practice of sending youths away from home to special boarding schools that combine normal schooling with special sport training opportunities. While the East Germans, Russians, and other Eastern Europeans were criticized for the schools, Western news media and commentators generally overlooked a critical aspect of the schools: They were voluntary. In fact, more detailed articles on the schools have included the complaints of national sport directors that too many parents refused to allow their children to attend, because they did not want them to live away from home.

Segment of career. A segment of a career represents a number of years, usually at a given age or competitive level, such as junior or senior competition, or for an American athlete, age group or middle school, high school, university, and open (senior) competition.

Olympiad. An elite athlete may plan broad goals for an entire Olympiad, either to assure making the Olympic team or to achieve a higher finish in the next Olympic Games after competing in the previous one. The plan might involve focusing on a different area of fitness or technique during each year.

Two years. Athletes in the technical events may benefit from a two-year cycle, with the first year emphasizing improvement in technique, followed by a year emphasizing improvement in physical characteristics (such as strength, speed, or endurance).

Training year. Normally when we think of a long cycle (macrocycle), we think in terms of a training year. In essence, this is a year of training with a single primary goal or training emphasis, leading to a single major competition (*single periodization*, Figure 2.2). While the single training emphasis often holds true, training years will often include two major competitions (peaks), such as indoors and outdoors in American track and field. This is called *double periodization* (Figure 2.3).

While some coaches and athletes may try for three peaks for distance runners (cross country, indoor track, and outdoor track), experience and research show that this is very difficult to achieve against elite competition. Proper preparation for elite competitive efforts requires too much time for an athlete to achieve a true peak three times a year. Most athletes who have been able to perform at that level carry a very high training load, such that they cannot really predict a peak; it is more a matter of chance. Instead, they perform at a fairly stable elite level over a long period of time. This type of athlete

Macrocyle									
Periods	Preparation				Competition			Transition	
Phases	General 1		Specific 2		Precompetition 3	Comp. 4	Peak 5	Transition 6	
Microcyles									

Figure 2.2. Single Periodization

Aug.	Sept.	Oct.	Nov.	Dec.	Jan.	Feb.	March	April	May	June	July
Phase 1			Phase 2		Phase 3		1	2	3	4	5	6
Preparation					Competition		Preparation	Competition			Transi-tion

Figure 2.3. Double Periodization

may set world records, but often does not succeed at the major events that require a peak performance (such as the Olympic Games).

Triple periodization is more appropriate for explosive technical events (jumps, throws, sprints, and hurdles). Indeed, European athletes commonly divide their long summer season into two mesocycles of competition, separated by a mesocycle of transition, regeneration, or modified base training lasting two to four weeks.

In some events a double periodized year will result in better performance improvements than a single periodized year. Early research on the percentage of improvement for a training year is shown in Table 2.1. Results in the endurance events were unknown at the time the table was developed.

Table 2.1. Annual Performance Improvement

Event	Single Periodization	Double Periodization
100m	0.96	1.55
High Jump	2.40	5.05
Long Jump	1.35	1.46
Shot	2.58	3.85
Discus	3.11	3.87

A periodized training year contains five categories of training periods (from the largest unit of time down to the smallest):
- Macrocycle
- Period
- Phase
- Microcycle
- Training Session.

A *macrocycle* is a complete training cycle, from the start of training to a planned major competition, then through the concluding transitional or recovery period. A calendar year consists of 1-3 macrocycles.

COMPONENTS OF A MACROCYCLE

A typical macrocycle includes three *periods*: preparation, competition, and transition or recovery (recovering from the stresses of the macrocycle, while making the transition from the end of one macrocycle to the start of the next macrocycle). Each period is a different training emphasis and load within a macrocycle. A period lasts for 1-6 months.

The *preparation* period is the first part, as it prepares the athlete for competition. In traditional terms, the preparation phase includes what we once called preseason training.

The second period of the cycle is the *competition* period, as it includes the actual meets in the athlete's season. The meets are chosen to prepare the athlete for the single meet selected as the goal of the season, where the athlete expects or desires his or her peak performance.

The third period of the cycle is the *transition* period (sometimes called recuperation or regeneration), as it is a bridge or transition between competition and the start of the next preparation period. It allows the athlete to recover from the physical and psychological stress of competition. While this period does not involve any event-training activities, it is generally a time of active rest, designed as much for the psychological change as for the physical recovery.

Medium-Term Cycles (More Than a Week)

Each training period consists of one or more

20

BRIAN J. MYERS/PHOTO RUN

Pole Vaulter Lawrence Johnson

the track. An athlete might have from zero (on a rest day) to three training sessions in a single day, though one or two sessions are most common. Each session has a single training focus.

Each session includes a number of *training units*. A training unit is a single component of the training session. Usually a training session includes between one and five training units.

TYPES OF TRAINING

Training falls into three categories: general, special (specific), and competition-specific. *General training* (basic conditioning) is "training for the general functioning capacity of the athlete. It is the foundation of endurance, strength and mobility through training units. . . The objective here is to ensure that the athlete will be fit to accept and benefit from special training."

Special or *specific training* is training that develops the conditioning, traits, and technique that are specific to success in the athlete's event. *Competition-specific training* is "training where technique and conditioning are completely rehearsed by applying the fitness acquired through special training to the event itself." It is done either within competition or with special simulations that are similar to competition.

This summarizes the basic terms of periodization. In the next chapter we will look at the training principles that underlie the theory of periodization. Then we will show how the principles are applied to a training plan.

REFERENCES

1. Andrew McInnis. (1981). A research review of systematized approaches to planned performance peaking with relation to the sport of track and field. *Track and Field Quarterly Review, 81*(2), 7-12.
2. Lev Pavlovich Matveyev. (1981). *Fundamentals of Sports Training* (p. 246). Moscow: Progress
3. Vladimir N. Platonov. (1999). The concept of "periodisation of training" and the development of a training theory. *Leistungssport, 29*(1).
4. Vladimir M. Zatsiorsky. (1995). *Science and Practice of Strength Training* (p. 111). Champaign, IL: Human Kinetics.
5. Mel Siff & Yuri Verhoshansky. (1999). *Supertraining* (p. 319). Denver: Supertraining International.
6. Tudor Bompa. (1981). *Periodization: Theory and Methodology of Training* (pp. 186-186). Champaign, IL: Human Kinetics.
7. Peter Tschiene. (1999). Discussion of "periodisation." *Leistungssport, 29*(1).
8. Istvan Balyi. (1995). Long term athlete development model. In *Australian Strength and Conditioning Association 1995 National Conference and Trade Show Proceedings* (pp. 17-35). Gold Coast, Australia: Australian Strength and Conditioning Association.
9. Istvan Balyi. (1995). Planning, periodisation, integration and implementation of annual training programs. In *Australian Strength and Conditioning Association 1995 National Conference and Trade Show Proceedings* (pp. 40-66). Gold Coast,

phases. For example, the preparation period includes two phases. The first phase emphasizes general conditioning, while the second phase emphasizes the more specialized or specific conditioning needed for the event. A phase usually lasts from two weeks to four months. Both periods and phases are *mesocycles*, so to avoid confusion, the term "mesocycle" will not be used again.

Short-Term Cycles

Each phase consists of a number of *microcycles* (usually from two to six). A typical microcycle lasts for one week, though it can be as short as three days.

A *training session* (also called a *lesson*) is a single workout, such as the afternoon workout at

    Australia: Australian Strength and Conditioning Association.

10. Dietrich Harre, ed. (1982). *Principles of Sports Training: Introduction to the Theory and Methods of Training* (2nd ed., pp. 78-87). Berlin: Sportverlag.

11. Bob Myers. (1988). Periodization for the high jump. In Jess Jarver (Ed.), *The Jumps* (3rd ed., pp. 46-49). Mountain View: Tafnews

12. Jose Manuel Ballesteros & Julio Alvarez. (1979). *Track and Field: A Basic Coaching Manual*. London: IAAF.

13. Frank W. Dick. (1978). *Training Theory* (pp 56-81). London: British Amateur Athletic Board.

SOURCES OF TABLES

2.1. Annual Performance Improvement: Dick, p. 59

SOURCES OF FIGURES

2.1-2.3 Author

CHAPTER 3:
The Principles of All Sport Training

Regardless of the training program used by a coach or athlete, it must conform to the same principles of training. They are called principles because they will always hold true. Any effective system must be planned around them. We will look at three types of principles: the physiological, psychological, and pedagogical (teaching).

The physiological principles are the physical effects of training on the athlete; they concern the athlete's physical state. The psychological principles affect the athlete's mental or psychological state more than his or her physiological state. The pedagogical principles relate more to how training is planned and implemented, how skills are taught, than to its physiological effects. When combined, these principles give a holistic approach to training.

THE PHYSIOLOGICAL LAWS OF TRAINING

All training systems are affected by three physiological laws: the Law of Overload, the Law of Specificity, and the Law of Reversibility. Other principles cited by different coaches are aspects of those three laws.

Law of Overload

The Law of Overload is that any improvement in fitness requires an increased training load that challenges the athlete's state of fitness. That training load acts as a stimulus and elicits a response from the athlete's body (Fig. 3.1). If the load is greater than the body's normal load, the body will be fatigued, lowering its level of fitness to below normal. As it recovers from the stimulus during the time that follows, its fitness level rises back to normal. If the loading was optimal (neither too great nor too little), after full recovery the fitness level will rise higher than the original level.

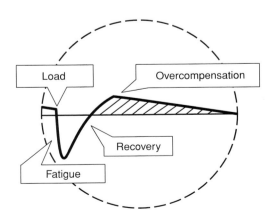

Figure 3.1. Training Effect (Overcompensation Curve)

In short, loading causes fatigue, and when the loading ends, recovery begins. If the training load was optimal, after recovery the athlete will be more fit (as a result of overcompensation) than before the training load was applied.

This *supercompensation* by the body is what training is all about. We try to plan a training load that will result in improved fitness when the athlete has recovered from the session. However, if the training load is too little, the overcompensation (training effect) after recovery will be less than we want (Fig. 3.2). If the training load is too great, the athlete will be fortunate to return even to the original fitness level. An overloading microcycle may be designed with too little rest, followed by a longer recovery that results in supercompensation (Fig. 3.3).

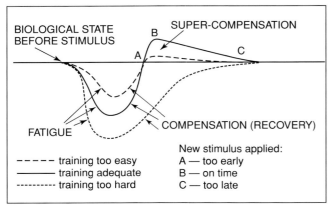

Figure 3.2. Effective and Ineffective Training Effect

A newer two-factor theory of training is challenging the older (and simpler) concept of supercompensation. It assumes that an athlete's fitness is affected by two components, one of which changes slowly, while the other changes quickly. The immediate training effect of a workout is a fitness gain from the training, but it is offset by the fatigue brought on by the workout.

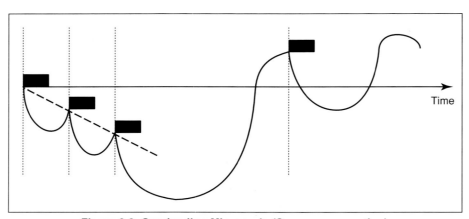

Figure 3.3. Overloading Microcycle (Supercompensation)

Principle of Individualization. Each athlete reacts to a training stimulus in a slightly different way. There are differences by age and by sex. The Principle of Individualization requires that training be planned in terms of the individual's abilities, needs, and potential. No fully effective training program can be simply a copy of another athlete's training, no matter how successful the other athlete was.

The most effective training program will be most appropriate only for the person for whom it was planned. It will change gradually over the years as that athlete's fitness and skill level (and physical maturity) progress. The coach must consider the athlete's chronological and biological (physical maturity) age, experience in the sport, skill level, capacity for effort and performance, training and health status, training load capacity and rate of recovery, body build and nervous system type, and sexual differences (especially during puberty).

Principle of Multilateral Development. The Principle of Multilateral Development calls for developing a base of general skills and fitness as a foundation for developing the more specialized skills of each event. This multilateral development refers to the general motor skills and fitness development that are the major goal of the early part of the training year. Like a forest, the body has its own ecology. All of its functions interrelate. The more balanced its early development is, the greater the performance levels it can attain later. This principle should be the major focus in training children and junior athletes. It is the first step of the sequential approach to sport training.

Law of Specificity

The Law of Specificity is that the nature of the training load determines the training effect. The training must be specific to the desired effect. To train properly for an event, an athlete must use training methods tailored to meet the specific demands of that event. The training load becomes specific when it has the proper training ratio (load to recovery) and structure of loading (intensity to load).

Intensity is the quality or difficulty of the training load. The measure of intensity depends on the specific attribute being developed or tested. Running speed is measured in meters per second (m/sec) or stride rate (s/sec). Strength is measured in pounds, kilograms, or tonnage moved. Jumps and throws are measured by height, distance or number of

Table 3.1. Estimating Intensity of Effort

| Intensity | Percent of Maximum | | | Endurance % VO₂max |
	Work	Strength	Heart Rate*	
Maximum	95-100	90-100	190+	100
Sub-maximum	85-95	80-90	180-190	90
High	75-85		165	75
Medium	65-75	70-80	150	60
Light	50-65	50-70	-	-
Low	30-50	30-50	130	50

* Should be based on a percentage of the athlete's heart rate, as it varies considerably among individuals.

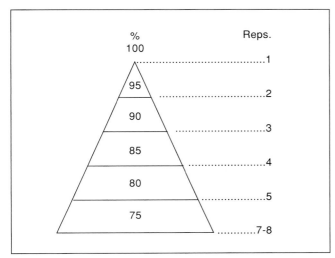

Figure 3.4. Intensity of Effort for Strength

efforts. The intensity of the effort is based on the percentage of the athlete's best effort (Table 3.1). The heart rate can be used as a guide for endurance running. Figure 3.4 shows a scale of intensity for strength activities.

The *extent* of the training load is the sum of all of the training in terms of time, distance, accumulative weight, and so forth, while the *duration* of the load is the portion of the load devoted to a single unit or type of training. An athlete may run for 75 minutes (extent), yet elevate the heart rate over 150 BPM for only 10 minutes (duration) of that time.

Principle of Specialization. Specialization refers to training exercises that develop the capacities and techniques needed for a specific activity or event (Figs. 3.5 & 3.6). A thrower needs strength in specific areas of the body, just as different specific motor skills are needed for each throwing event. A runner needs speed and endurance components, with the mix or ratio of those components depending on the length of the race. A runner must also develop running technique that uses the most efficient running pattern for the racing distance. All of these traits are developed by using specialized training.

Elite training is not purely specialized training, any more than it is all general or multilateral training. Tudor Bompa suggests a gradual change of emphasis from multilateral to specific training as the athlete ages. He recommends that youths first practice track and field between the ages of 10 and 12, begin specializing about ages 13 to 14, and reach high performance levels between the ages of 18 and 23. However, most elite athletes are only beginning to reach international status by age 23. Over the last few decades the average age of the top athletes has risen. In the explosive events, a peak is often reached between the ages of 20 and 25, though it can be carried longer. In endurance events, the peak years are in the late 20s, and can continue well into the 30s.

Principle of Modeling the Training Process. This principle calls for the development of a model of the competitive event. That model is used to develop the training pattern, which closely simulates the competitive requirements of the event. The greatest difficulty of modeling is that it requires years to develop and perfect the model. It begins with the coach's analysis of the competitive event, but from that point onward the emphasis is upon trial and error refinement of the model.

Law of Reversibility

The Law of Reversibility is that the fitness level will fall if the loading does not continue. In essence, the training effect will reverse itself. If the training does not become more challenging, the fitness level will plateau (flatten out). If the training ends, the fitness level will gradually drop until it reaches the level needed to maintain normal daily activities.

Principle of Increasing Demands. The Principle of Increasing Demands (in the training load) is that the training load must continue to increase if the athlete's general and specific fitness are to continue to improve. If the training load remains at the same level, the fitness will rise for a time, then begin to

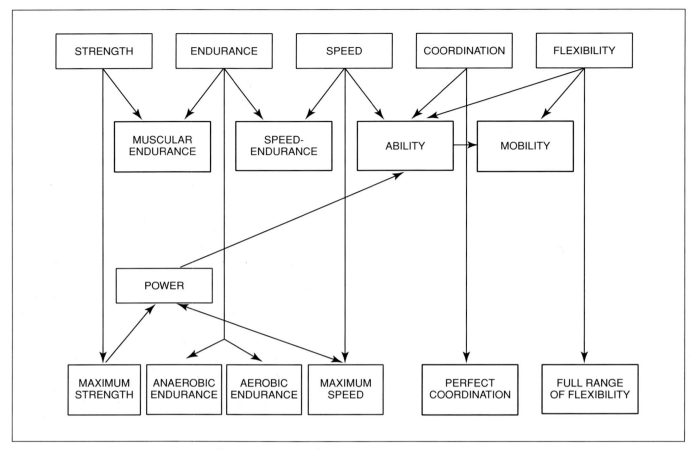

Figure 3.5. Interdependence of Biomotor Abilities

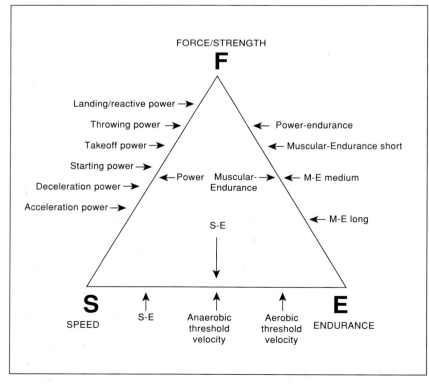

Figure 3.6. Dominant Biomotor Abilities

fall. The training load must increase regularly (*progressive overload*) for the performance level to improve (Fig. 3.7), though the load may rise and fall (allowing recovery and compensation) across the different microcycles (Fig. 3.8). The *training ratio* (load to recovery) is critical. The coach must determine how much recovery is needed within a session and between sessions.

Principle of Continuous Load Demand. This principle requires that the athlete not have long interruptions to training. While tapering is used to reach a peak, too much time spent with low training loads will result in a drop in the fitness level.

Principle of Feasibility. The Principle of Feasibility is that the planned training load must be *realistic*. This is a critical aspect of the Principle of Increasing Demands. The demand should never be beyond the reasonable capability of the athlete, or it will become psychologically (and perhaps physically) de-

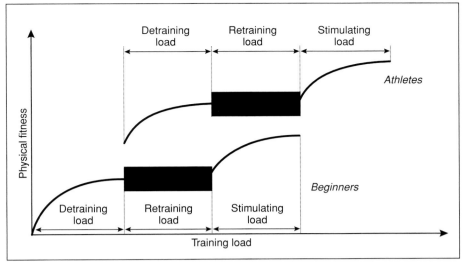

Figure 3.7. Progressive Overload

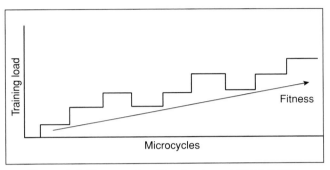

Figure 3.8. Progressive Overload over Microcycles

structive to the athlete's progress. The athlete should not be given a task that is, at best, only marginally possible to complete. The object of training is improvement, not discouragement or defeat.

Restoration. Restoration is recovery from a high training load. Restoration or recovery is just as critical to the training effect as the training load itself. If too little restoration is allowed, the athlete will gradually lose fitness.

Active rest. Active rest is a form of restoration (also used in the transition phase) that includes physical activity of a light nature. It might involve jogging, or it might include participating in other sports. It allows the athlete to recover, yet it helps to maintain a base of general fitness.

THE PSYCHOLOGICAL PRINCIPLES OF TRAINING

Principle of Active, Conscientious Participation. This principle means that for optimal results the athlete must be actively involved in the training process by his or her own choice. The athlete is not a passive participant, simply following the coach's orders and waiting for the coach to motivate him or her.

This principle is too often overlooked by coaches and athletes.

Training is a cooperative venture between the coach and the athlete. The athlete must understand the training objectives and plans set by the coach. Ideally, the athlete should help in planning the training program. The training progress should be assessed regularly by the athlete and coach together. Bompa describes the athlete as having an "independent and creative role" in the training process. No matter how skilled a coach may be, no coach always knows how the athlete's body or mind are reacting to a given training stimulus. The athlete must provide quality feedback, working with the coach to reach for the optimal training effect.

Principle of Awareness. This principle refers to the requirement that the coach always explain to the athlete what the training program involves, what its goals are, and how the goals will be met. As Harre says, "It also implies that they are in a position to participate actively in the planning and evaluation of their training. This includes developing the determination and independence of the athlete" (pp. 87-88).

Principle of Variety. The complex nature of training, and the high loading needed for success, require a variety of training means and methods to avoid boredom or staleness. This factor becomes even more critical in the less complex events, such as distance running, which has limited (in complexity) technical and physiological requirements.

Principle of Psychological Rest. At times the exhaustion of an athlete comes from mental or psychological strain, rather than the physical training load. An athlete benefits from change-of-pace activities that free the mind from training and competition. These may involve a change to an entirely different type of physical activity for a time, or they might involve a change of scene. This factor can be a critical part of the restoration process.

THE PEDAGOGICAL PRINCIPLES OF TRAINING

Principle of Planning and Use of Systems. This principle requires that the training program be designed systematically and efficiently, from the long-term program down to the level of the individual training unit. It requires that planning be thorough, careful, and meet all of the known training needs and effects.

Principle of Periodization. The Principle of Periodization calls for the development of the training program through a series of cycles or training periods. As Harre notes, "It is based on the regularity of the development of the sporting form [standard of performance]... Accordingly, the sporting development and improvement always proceeds in stages of acquisition, relative stabilization and temporary loss of the sporting form. These phases are repeated under the influence of training with an ever higher level in the standard of performance" (p. 78).

Principle of Visual Presentation. The Principle of Visual Presentation is to try to make training information as vivid as possible for the athlete. Whenever possible, audio-visual aids should be used to give information. Videotaping your athletes is an essential teaching tool these days. The feedback provided is invaluable. In addition, commercial videos and films furnish supplemental help.

A variety of presentation methods should be used in teaching and coaching. The athlete should be taught to observe everything as carefully as possible.

TRENDS IN TRAINING THEORY

Coaches and scholars continue to seek the perfect training model. Three examples of recent examinations of training theory are the ecological approach to training of Christine Wells and Muriel Gilman, the Boiko theory of training explained by Peter Tschiene, Robert Lyden's discussion of cycles of acquisition, and Yuri Verhoshansky's principles of training. Because Lyden's study is directed toward training distance runners, it is a comprehensive look at endurance training theory regardless of the sport.

Wells and Gilman call for "a holistic approach to training for the purposes of improving performance and enhancing health" (p. 15). As they say, "current training methods often result in the opposite—less than optimal performance, endangered health, and premature demise of promising athletic careers" (pp. 15-16). They argue that the most effective training program will integrate mind and body, consider the total demands on the body (including the external factors of daily life), and include a concern for optimizing health in the future as well as the present.

They examine the athlete as an ecosystem, declaring that the biological, psychological, and sociological factors of the athlete's ecosystem determine the athlete's potential for adaptation to training (Fig. 3.9). Wells and Gilman argue that the athlete's energy output and input must be carefully

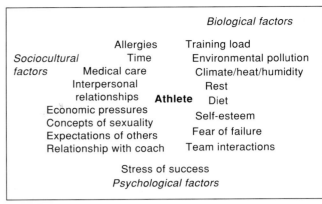

Figure 3.9. The Athlete's Ecosystem

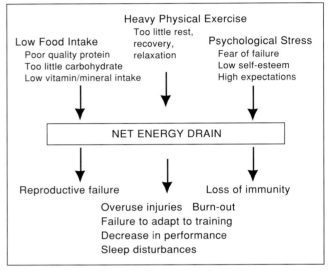

Figure 3.10. Energy Drain

balanced, so it does not stray too far from an equilibrium. If the energy input is too little, the result is an energy drain (Fig. 3.10).

As they summarize their theory, "To achieve peak levels of performance... requires a model in which the training load is applied in sine-wave fashion. This allows the organism to gradually achieve new levels of net energy balance by alternatively applying high levels of stress with periods of recovery and adaptation... [this model should be] envisioned in terms of life-span physical performance" (p. 27).

As Wells and Gilman note, "The primary explanation for age at peak performance and age at retirement from sport appears to relate more to cultural expectations than to scientific principles... one's competitive life span... should be viewed in terms of decades, and not as a brief, highly intensive period of time that often leads to athletic self-destruction" (pp. 27, 29).

Peter Tschiene argues that no comprehensive theory of training has been developed, resulting in the simplistic training pattern of "more is better."

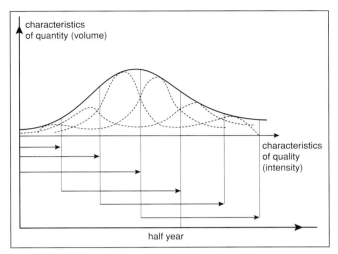

Figure 3.11. Training Structure for Athletes

Table 3.2. Boiko's Principles of Training

1. The wave of a cycle (Fig. 3.11)
   The relation between volume and intensity of load, based on the normal distribution curve.
2. The dynamic asymmetry of a loadwave.
   The share of new and intensive work is dominating in the cycle.
3. The maximum dynamic of the training process.
   Exploiting the athlete's adaptive reserve:
      More dynamically—for new, better results
      Less dynamically—to maintain gained levels and skills.
4. The programmed increase of load quality.
5. Short cycles are better than annual cycles.
   The biogenetical principle. This is the Tschiene model of periodization (discussed later), as contrasted to the Matveyevan model.
6. Variation of load.
   A low cycle is necessary to maneuver the adaptive reserve.
   This principle includes:
      The Impulsive Method of Loading Dose: Use short, intensive work (as in competition), with no large quantities or repetitions.

The result is drug use to enable the body to survive under ever greater training loads, requiring extensive training time. The currently developing theories are in line with Wells and Gilman's call for treating the athlete as an ecosystem.

Tschiene calls for a quality approach to training, a move away from the old quantity-dominated approaches. This approach calls for an increase in specific exercises and competitions, as seen in the training of international athletes (Fig. 3.11). He discusses V. Boiko's training theory (Table 3.2), then uses a figure (Fig. 3.12) to illustrate his view of a future theory of training.

Verhoshansky suggests five principles for organizing the annual training cycle of elite athletes:

a. Methodological concepts must be in accordance with the course of the body's adaptation to an intense muscle activity.

b. Systematization of the training stimuli.
c. Specific orientation of the whole system of training stimuli.
d. Superimposition of work loads having different priorities.
e. Absolute priority of the special physical preparation.

Vern Gambetta suggests that seven trends are visible in current training theory:

1. Synergy: The whole is greater than the sum of its parts.
2. Reevaluation of the concept of periodization.
   Common traits of successful programs:
   (1) Strict control of competitive schedule
   (2) Long-term commitment to the program
   (3) Guidance from the coach planning the program.
3. Validity of the Matveyevan model.
   The Matveyevan (simple) model of training applies best to the earlier years of training. As an athlete reaches higher levels, a more complex model (Tschiene) becomes more appropriate. As Klaus Bartonietz explains, the extensive scientific research that formed the basis for that model was never made available outside the Russian establishment.
4. The effects of drugs.
   Models were developed with athletes using drugs. To assess the programs, Gambetta recommends decreasing the volume by 20% and the intensity by 30-35% for a non-drug setting. This is an area in which our concrete knowledge is very limited.
5. Youth training and early specialization.
   While this leads to earlier success, it also tends to shorten the career. Ideally, the early sport experience should be more informal and play-oriented.
6. The long-term career plan.
   This is the pattern for the most successful athletes, as it encourages patience and commitment, along with a more careful, thorough design of the program.
7. Modeling and quantifying training.
   "The trend will be the modeling of training through the analysis of training records."

Now we will take a look at the larger blocks of periodized training, including how they are planned and what types of records are most useful.

REFERENCES

1. Lev Pavlovich Matveyev. (1981). *Fundamentals of Sports Training* (pp. 29-85). Trans. Albert P. Zdornykh. Moscow: Progress.
2. Tudor O. Bompa. (1990). *Theory and Methodology of Training* (2nd ed., pp. 29-49). Dubuque, IA: Kendall/Hunt.
3. Frank W. Dick. (1978). *Training Theory* (pp. 36-39). London:

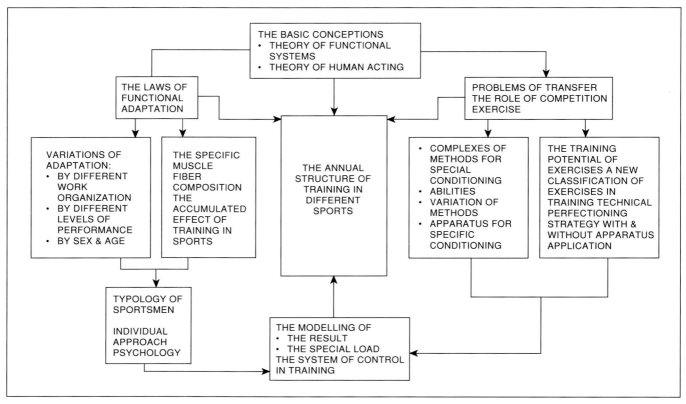

Figure 3.12. Details of a Future Theory of Training

British Amateur Athletic Board.

4. Dietrich Harre, ed. (1982). *Principles of Sports Training* (2nd ed., pp. 73-94). Berlin: Sportverlag.

5. Thomas Kurz. (1991). *Science of Sports Training: How to Plan and Control Training for Peak Performance* (pp. 15-49). Island Pond, VT: Stadion.

6. Peter J.L. Thompson. (1991). *Introduction to Coaching Theory.* London: International Amateur Athletic Federation.

7. Tudor O. Bompa. (1993). *Periodization of Strength: The New Wave in Strength Training.* Toronto: Veritas.

8. Yuri Verhoshansky. (1995). Principles of the organization of training for high performance athletes. In Jess Jarver (Ed.), *Long Distances: Contemporary Theory, Technique and Training* (3rd ed., pp. 11-14). Mountain View, CA: Tafnews.

9. Vladimir M. Zatsiorsky. (1995). *Science and Practice of Strength Training* (pp. 15-16). Champaign, IL: Human Kinetics.

10. Bob Myers. (1991). Restoration for jumpers. *Athletics Science Bulletin, 3*(1), 1-6.

11. M. Zalessky, V. Sobolevsky & L. Khomenov. (1989). Basic restoration procedures. *Track Technique, 106,* 3381-3382, 3396.

12. Ulrich Pahlke & Hans Peters. (1995). Recovery after training loads. In *Long Distances* (3rd ed., pp. 29-33).

13. Christine L. Wells & Muriel Gilman. (1991). An ecological approach to training. *The Academy Papers, 24,* 15-29.

14. Peter Tschiene. (1989). Finally a theory of training to overcome doping. In P. Bellotti, G. Benzi, & A. Ljungqvist (Eds.), *Official Proceedings, IInd World Symposium on Doping in Sport* (pp. 145-153). Monte Carlo: International Athletic Federation.

15. Robert Lyden. (1990). Cycles of acquisition and training periodization. *Track and Field Quarterly Review, 90*(2), 21-42.

16. Yuri Verhoshansky. (1998). Organization of the training process. *New Studies in Athletics, 13*(3), 21-31.

17. Vern Gambetta. (1989). New trends in training theory. *New Studies in Athletics, 4*(3), 7-10.

18. Klaus Bartonietz. (1999). The unavoidable end of periodisation or a start of further development of training? [abridged translation]. *Leistungssport, 29*(1).

OTHER RESOURCES ON SPORT TRAINING PRINCIPLES

Dick, Frank W. (1997). *Sports Training Principles* (3rd ed.). London: A & C Black.

Elliott, Bruce. (Ed.). (1998). *Training in Sport: Applying Sport Science.* New York: John Wiley.

Hargreaves, Mark (Ed.). (1995). *Exercise Metabolism.* Champaign, IL: Human Kinetics.

Hartmann, Jürgen, & Harold Tünnemann. (1995). *Fitness and Strength Training for All Sports: Theory Methods Programs.* Ed. Peter Klavora & Peter Gaskovsku. Toronto: Sports Books.

Hawley, John, & Louise Burke. (1998). *Peak Performance: Training and Nutritional Strategies for Sport.* St. Leonards, N.S.W., Australia: Allen & Unwin.

Huntsman, Stan. (1999). The fourth dimension [zest for life]. *Track and Field Coaches Review, 72*(4), 15-17.

Kreider, Richard B., Andrew C. Fry, & Mary L. O'Toole (Eds.). (1998). *Overtraining in Sport.* Champaign, IL: Human Kinetics.

Lyden, Robert. (1997). *The Way of Athletics.* Beaverton, OR: Author.

Montoye, Henry J., Han C. G. Kemper, Wim H. M. Saris & Richard A. Washburn. (1995). *Measuring Physical Activity and Energy Expenditure.* Champaign, IL: Human Kinetics.

Naughton, Geraldine, Nathalie J. Farpour-Lambert, John Carlson, Michelle Bradley & Emmanual Van Praegh. (2000). Physiological issues surrounding the performance of adolescent athletes. *Sports Medicine, 30*(5), 309-325.

Orlick, Terry. (2000). *In Pursuit of Excellence: How to Win in Sport and Life Through Mental Training* (3rd ed.). Champaign, IL: Human Kinetics.

Reaburn, Peter, & David Jenkins. (Eds.). (1996). *Training for Speed and Endurance*. St. Leonards, Australia: Allen & Unwin.

Schexnayder, Irving. (1998). Applied kinesiological concerns for athletes. *Track Coach, 145*, 4621-4626.

Schiffer, Jürgen. (1998). Selected and annotated bibliography 48: Youth athletics. *New Studies in Athletics, 14*(1), 81-104.

Schiffer, Jürgen. (1998). World list of periodicals relevant to athletics. *New Studies in Athletics, 13*(2), 45-90; Supplement, *NSA, 13*(4), 79-82.

Ungerleider, Steven. (1996). *Mental Training for Peak Performance*. Emmaus, PA: Rodale.

SOURCES OF TABLES

3.1. Estimating Intensity of Effort: Dick, pp. 38-39; Harre, p. 59
3.2. Boiko's principles of training: Tschiene, p. 150

SOURCES OF FIGURES

3.1. Training Effect: *Track Technique, 99*, 3164
3.2. Effective and Ineffective Training Effect: Klavora, p. 6
3.3. Overloading Microcycle (Supercompensation): Zatsiorsky, p. 15.
3.4. Intensity of Effort for Strength: Dick, p. 6
3.5. Interdependence of Biomotor Abilities: Bompa, p. 8.
3.6. Dominant Biomotor Abilities: Bompa, p. 14.
3.7. Progressive Overload: Zatsiorsky, p. 5.
3.8. Adapted from Bompa (2nd ed., p. 47)
3.9. The athlete's ecosystem: Wells & Gilman, p. 23
3.10. Energy drain: Wells & Gilman, p. 26
3.11. Training structure for athletes: Tschiene, p. 150
3.12. Details of a future theory of training: Tschiene, p. 151

CHAPTER 4:
Records—The Heart Of A Successful System

BASIC RECORDS FOR ATHLETES

A major value of the periodized approach to training is the emphasis upon thorough planning and record keeping. The training plan is based on a thorough analysis of the criteria for success in the athlete's event, combined with a comparison of the athlete's performance compared to the model of his or her event. Because of this objective approach to training, the training process can be recorded in great detail.

Too often athletes (and sometimes coaches) fail to realize the value of a thorough system of training records. Such records permit a careful study of the strong and weak points of the athlete's preparation. They can help to predict how well the athlete will perform.

Some basic records are needed regardless of the training plan. For example, for each athlete there should be a personal data record that lists items such as the athlete's:

- Name
- Date of birth
- Age, grade, class, or other designation
- Height
- Weight
- Address and telephone number
- Name and address (if different) of parents or guardian
- Number of years of training in track and field
- Other sports competed in
- Chosen event(s) and best mark(s)
- Results of performance tests.

Both the coach and the athlete should have a copy of this record.

THE VALUE OF DETAILED TRAINING RECORDS

Why should the coach and athlete keep detailed training records? A few reasons include the following uses:

1. Estimate future potential
2. Determine current health and fitness
3. Measure progress toward a goal
4. Provide benchmarks for future training
5. Create a detailed objective and subjective record of the full training process.

Why are those uses important to a coach or athlete? Some of the reasons for their value include the following:

1. *Estimate future potential.* This can help the coach in guiding a young athlete into the event or sport that offers the likeliest chance of future success. Some critical performance traits are hereditary

and cannot be changed significantly through training. Those traits (or their absence) cannot be ignored by the coach.

2. *Determine current health and fitness.* This helps coach and athlete evaluate the impact of the training program on the athlete on a session-to-session and day-to-day basis.

3. *Measure progress toward a goal.* This shows whether the athlete is progressing as planned toward meeting the training and performance goals. It guides the training process and indicates if the plan needs to be modified.

4. *Provide benchmarks for future training.* The training record allows an in-depth evaluation of the training at the end of the year. That evaluation is used in refining the next year's program, building on the strengths of the old plan, while lessening or avoiding its weaknesses.

5. *Create a detailed objective and subjective record of the full training process.* This allows the coach and athlete to compare any given training year to other training years. The comparative data help in evaluating current progress and planning modifications of the current and future training plans.

The idea of the importance of detailed training records is not a new one. However, the computer age has made record keeping and evaluation much easier than in the past. Lee Brown and Richard Knee have demonstrated how a coach can use spreadsheet software to monitor and evaluate different periodization options. Vern Gambetta and Kevin McGill have described some software programs designed for track and field. Training records and analysis systems for sport training are becoming common. An example of a software program that uses detailed periodization and analysis of training is Gary Winckler's *Training Design*, a HyperCard program for Macintosh computers.

Records exist at levels from the long-term plan, as shown in Chapter 5, down through the daily training record. The examples that follow are not exhaustive. The types of records that are useful in coaching an athlete depend upon many factors, including the sport, the event, and the age, experience, and goals of the athlete.

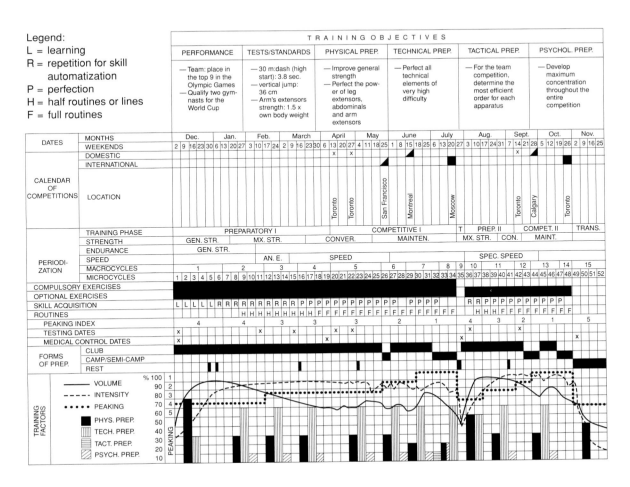

Figure 4.1. Hypothetical Annual Training Plan

RECORDS FOR THE ANNUAL PLAN

The annual planning process begins by planning the year's competition schedule. Figure 6.8 in Chapter 6 shows a planned and actual competition schedule. This gives a starting point to planning the year's training structure. It can be combined with the four-year plan's objectives for the year, which is then modified based on the evaluation of the year of training and competition that has just been completed. Then the annual training plan is developed.

As an example of a completed annual plan, Figure 4.1 shows a theoretical plan for a year of elite-level gymnastics training. Though it is in a different sport, it gives an example of how the year's plans, control tests, and progression are recorded.

Next, detailed exercises and tests are placed into the training plan, as in the following example of a hypothetical high jumper (Fig. 4.2). As the year progresses, the coach keeps a record of the athlete's performances on the control tests and in the meets.

EXAMPLES OF SUMMARY TRAINING RECORDS

The first category of records simply show the training that the athlete actually performed during the year, both in graphical (Fig. 4.3) and tabular (Fig. 4.4) form for intensity, loads, and volume. These examples are from the training of Soviet women middle distance runners.

Another example shows the coach's record for the 1988 women's 800m Olympic champion Sigrun Wodars of East Germany (Fig. 4.5). Figure 4.6 shows how the Soviet coaches planned the use of concentrated strength and speed-strength training during the training cycle of long distance runners.

Training records ideally will include numerical data that indicate the relative loading and intensity of each training session, as well as the accumulative values (and training effects) of the training. Control tests are one valuable type of data. Figure 4.7 is a summary of the control tests and their parameters for Italian sprinters, while Figure 4.8 is

---

Year: _____

Athlete's Name _____
Event: High Jump
Performance Obj.: 2.10 m.　　　　　　　　　　　　　Coach: _____

Calendar / Periodization / Training

Macrocycle	1	2	3	4	5	6	7	8	9	10	11	12	13
Month	Nov.	Dec.	Jan.	Feb.	(T)	March	April	May	June	July	August	(C.)	Sept./Oct.
Weekends	4 11 18 25	2 9 16 23 30	6 13 20 27	3 10 17 24	2	9 16 23 30	6 13 20 27	4 11 18 25	1 8 15 22 29	6 13 20 27	3 10 17 24 31	7	1 2 28 / 5 12 19 26
Domestic				x x ▟				x x	x x	x	□	■	
Location				Toronto / Edmonton / Montreal				Toronto / Toronto	Regina / Quebec City	Vancouver / Toronto	Sudbury		
Training Phase	Preparatory I	Preparatory I	Preparatory I	Compet. I	T	Preparatory II	Preparatory II	Competitive II	Competitive II	Competitive II	Competitive II	Competitive II	Transition
Sub-Phase	Gen. Prep.	Spec. Prep.	Spec. Prep.	Comp.	T	G.P.	S.P.	Pre-C	Competitive	Competitive	Unc.	C.	Transition
Objectives	G.S.	G.S.; P M.S.	M.S.; T.	M.S.; T. P.	T; P; M.S.	G.S. M.S.	M.S.; T.	M.S.; T P.	T.; M.S. P.	T.; P.	T.; P.	T.; P.	G.P.P.
Intensity	M	M	M	H	H	L	M	M	M	H	H	H	L
Performance Objectives				2.06				2.06		2.08	2.10		
Forms of Preparation	Club	Club	Club	Cmp.		Club	Club	Club	Club	Club	Camp	Camp	Holiday

Means of Training

Item	Nov	Dec	Jan	Feb	(T)	Mar	Apr	May	Jun	Jul	Aug	(C.)	Sep/Oct
Jumps 600		15	30	35	60		40	50	100	150	100	20	
Technic. Drill 800		25	70	50	85		60	60	130	200	100	20	
Weight Train. (KGM):													
— Leg Press 342.000	22.000	30.000	60.000	30.000	60.000	20.000	50.000	20.000	30.000	20.000			
— Jump 1/2 Squat 90.000	3.000	6.000	12.000	10.000	15.000	5.000	15.000	5.000	6.000	7.000	5.000		
— Power Lift 266.000	15.000	20.000	45.000	20.000	40.000	15.000	50.000	14.000	14.000	15.000	7.000		
— Ankle Flex. 109.440	4.000	7.220	15.000	10.000	16.220	8.000	20.000	6.500	8.000	10.500	4.000		
Bounding Ex. 35.700		2.200	3.800	3.200	3.400	1.850	5.000	2.400	4.200	5.200	3.600	850	
Exer. Benches 3.340		280	480	360	360	500	800	560					
Exer. Gym Box 1.280		160	200	140	200 2	140	260	180					
Exer. Med. Balls 4660	260	300	1.400	600		200	1.600	300					

Tests and Standards

Item	Nov	Dec	Jan	Feb	(T)	Mar	Apr	May	Jun	Jul	Aug	(C.)	Sep/Oct
— 30 m. dash 3.3 sec	3.7		3.5		3.4		3.5	3.4		3.3	3.3		
— Stand. high j. 62 cm	54		58		60		60	60		62			
— Stand. pent. j. 15.20m	14.00			14.80			14.80			15.20			
— Leg press 260 kg	00	220		240	260	230	250		260				
— Power lift 90 kg	65	70		75	90		90						
— Back flex. 70 cm	60		65			68		70					

Figure 4.2. Hypothetical Plan for a High Jumper

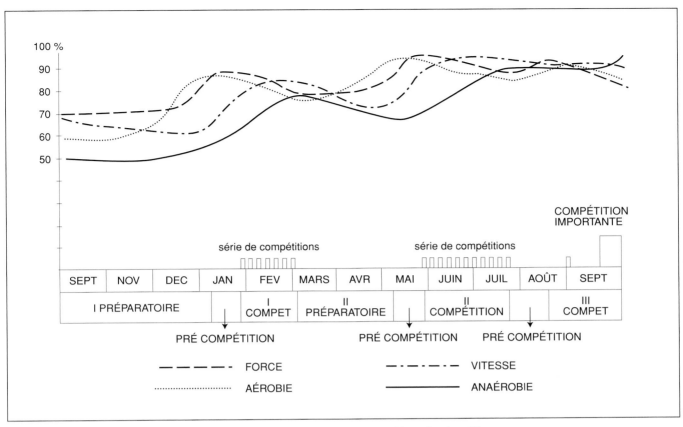

Figure 4.3. Annual Training Plan, Litovchenko, 55

the form used to record the data.

An example of the use of control tests is Table 4.1, which shows the testing norms for Soviet sprinters. It is based on research that shows how performance in the control tests relates to specific times in the sprint races. At the same time, it indicates the ages by which the more talented sprinters should be able to achieve those marks.

Examples of long-term training records include Table 4.2, based on control tests of Sergey Bubka from ages 10-20, and Table 4.3 showing the changes in Bubka's annual training load for each year from ages 15-20. These records give a coach much useful information, not only on how Bubka progressed, but on the training and performance results that produced that progress.

The coach can evaluate the long-term changes in training loads (Fig. 4.9) and the proportional changes of parts of the training load (Fig. 4.10) with graphs and figures that illustrate those loads. These changes may take place over months, but long-term detailed records allow the coach to compare changes in training loads and proportions within a single year, as for the female discus throwers in Figures 4.11 and 4.12, from one year to the next, and even across a 4-year period (Fig. 4.13).

RECORDS FOR THE TRAINING SESSION

A sample training lesson plan for a sprinter (Fig. 4.14) shows how a training session is planned for a group of athletes. It is divided into four parts, beginning with an introduction. It includes notes of points that the coach wants to stress, including points relating to individual athletes. Not only does such a plan help the coach to focus the training session, but it provides a good record for reviewing the training process later in the year or during later years.

A final example is a training diary form that an athlete can use as a record of his or her individual training (Fig. 4.15). The coach and athlete can decide what other information should be included in the diary. Various versions of training diaries have included the morning's resting pulse, details of diet, sleep, fatigue indexes, and other items in addition to the workout details themselves.

Examples of several record forms for planning periodized training are reproduced by Tudor Bompa. Remember that thorough planning, combined with good records of what was actually done, is essential if you are to make the training process optimally effective.

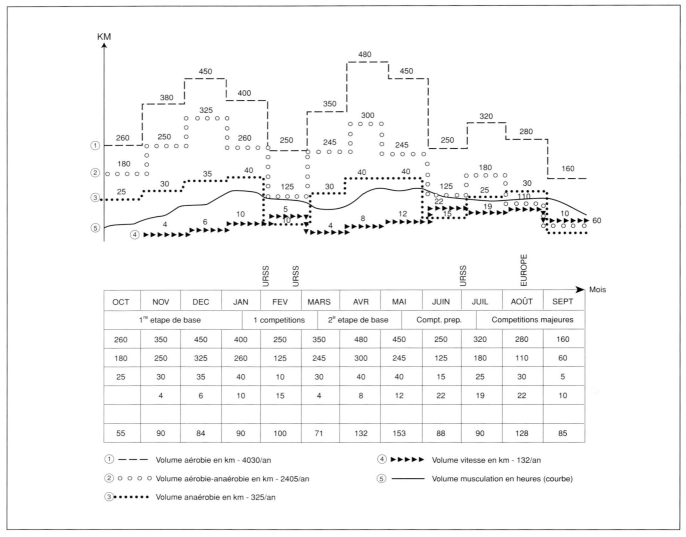

Figure 4.4. Comparative Training Loads, Litovchenko, 55

REFERENCES

1. Kuulo Kutsar. (1991). Hereditary physiological factors in talent identification [abstract]. *Track Technique, 115*, 3681.
2. Stephan Starischka, Hans-Martin Stork, Thomas Friedhoff, Joachim Wargalla, & Klaus Carl. (1992). Computer based documentation and analysis of training and competition data. Presented at the First International Congress on Computer Science and New Technologies in Sport, Torremolinos, Spain, March 23-27, 1992.
3. Lee E. Brown & Richard Knee. (1999). Monitoring periodization with a spreadsheet. *Strength and Conditioning Journal, 21*(6), 45-49.
4. Vern Gambetta. (1990). The computer and the coach. *New Studies in Athletics, 5*(2), 7-15.
5. Kevin McGill. (1993). From the editor.*Track Technique, 124*, 3944, 3972.
6. Kevin McGill. (1995). Hot tips. *Track Coach, 134*, 4291-4292.
7. Gary Winckler. (1991). *Training Design for the Macintosh.* N.p.: n.p.
8. M. Litovchenko. (1991). High level women's training program: 800, 1500, 3000 meters. *Track and Field Quarterly Review, 91*(2), 54-56.
9. Joachim Neuhof. (1990). Structure and yearly training build-up in middle and long distance running. *New Studies in Athletics, 5*(2), 69-81.
10. A. Polunin. (1991). Strength and speed-strength endurance in the training of long-distance runners [abstract]. *New Studies in Athletics, 6*(4), 97-98.
11. Tony Sandoval. (1990). Middle and long distance training load index analysis with the Macintosh computer. *Track Technique, 113*, 3603-3606.
12. Tudor O. Bompa. (1989). Physiological intensity values employed to plan endurance training. *Track Technique, 108*, 3435-3442.
13. Tudor O. Bompa. (1994). *Theory and Methodology of Training: The Key to Athletic Performance* (3rd ed., pp. 358-359, 363-369). Dubuque, IA: Kendall/Hunt.

OTHER SOURCES

Australian Sports Commission. (2000). *Physiological Tests for Elite Athletes.* Champaign, IL: Human Kinetics.
Brunner, Rick, & Ben Tabachnik. (1990). *Soviet Training and Recovery Methods.* Pleasant Hill, CA: Sport Focus.
Dellinger, Bill, & Bill Freeman. (1984). *The Competitive Runner's*

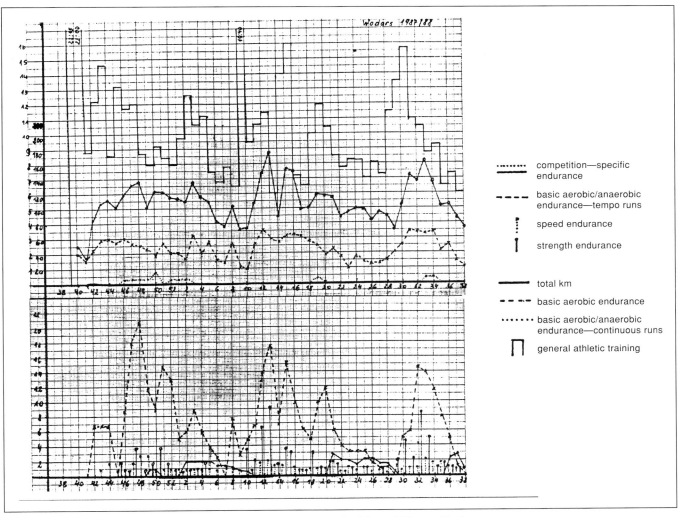

Figure 4.5. Yearly Training Buildup of Sigrun Wodars

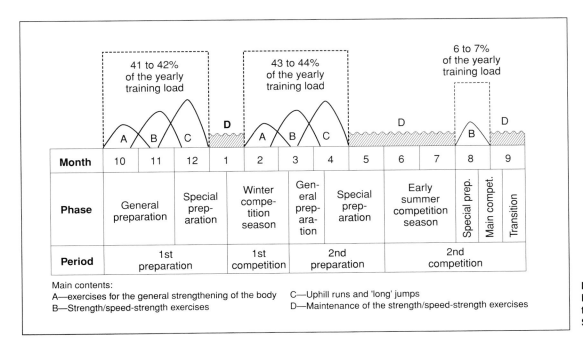

Figure 4.6. Annual Pattern of Concentrated Strength and Speed-Strength

Main contents:
A—exercises for the general strengthening of the body   C—Uphill runs and 'long' jumps
B—Strength/speed-strength exercises   D—Maintenance of the strength/speed-strength exercises

SUMMARY FRAMEWORK OF THE TESTS AND PARAMETERS													
Performance 100m	Squat	Scm cm	Scm cm	Scm cm	Sh	Triple m	5 jumps m	Run with longer strides	Bounding run	Run with shorter strides	Skipping 50 skips	30m standing start	30m running start
10.60/ 19.40		40/45	48/53	60/65		9.00/ 9.50	15.50/ 16.20		22.50/ 23.50			3.70/ 3.60	2.88/ 2.78
10.20/ 10.00		52/58	60/68	72/80		10.00/ 10.50	17.00/ 17.90		24.50/ 255.50			3.50/ 3.40	2.70/ 2.62
	Relative force (ratio of weight lifted to body weight, should be at least 2)				As per model envisaged in the hypothesis			Same height of the Scmb test with contact times between 170-145 milliseconds		As per model envisaged in the hypothesis	Performance with pratically equal to running with short strides		

Figure 4.7. Control Tests and Parameters for Sprinters

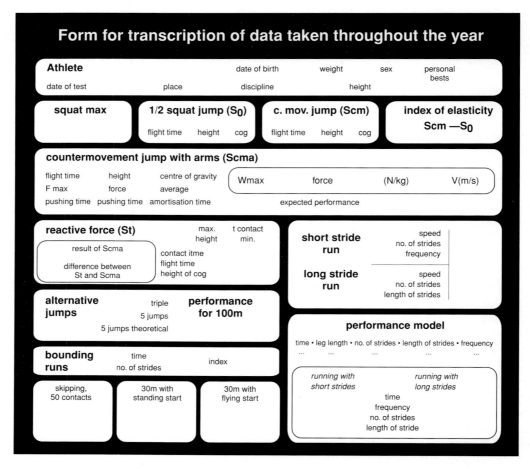

Figure 4.8. Control Test Record Form

Table 4.1. Control Tests for Soviet Sprinters

Tests	Phases/Ages in Years 11-12	15-16	16-17	18-19	20+
60m	8.6-9.0	7.3-7.5	7.0-7.2	6.8-6.9	6.55-6.65
100m	—	11.4-11.6	11.0-11.3	10.5-10.7	10.25-10.35
200m	—	23.0-24.0	22.5-22.8	21.0-21.5	20.4-20.7
30m crouch start	4.8-5.0	4.4-4.6	4.1-4.3	3.8-4.0	3.85-3.95
30m flying start	3.8-4.0	3.1-3.3	3.0-3.1	2.80-2.85	2.70-2.75
150m	—	17.6-18.0	16.7-17.1	15.8-16.8	15.0-15.3
300m	—	38.5-40.0	36.2-37.2	35.2-35.8	32.6-33.4
Standing LJ (cm.)	220-230	250-260	280-285	290-300	300-315
Standing TJ (m.)	6.50-6.80	7.40-7.80	8.00-8.20	8.50-9.00	9.50-10.00
10-step jump (m.)	—	26-28	31-32	34-35	35-36

Table 4.2. Control Tests for Sergey Bubka

YEAR	Age	Height (cm)	Weight (kg)	60m Standing Start From First Movement	100m Stand Start First Movement	Standing Long Jump (cm)	Standing Triple Jump (cm)	Long Jump (cm)	Bench Press (kg)	Snatch (kg)	French Press (kg)
1974	10	145	35	8.6	14.8	230	610	420	-	-	-
1975	11	153	40	8.2	14.0	240	670	500	20	25	-
1976	12	161	47	7.9	13.5	245	715	600	30	35	-
1977	13	169	54	7.7	12.9	255	775	630	40	40	20
1978	14	173	60	7.4	12.3	270	800	657	50	45	25
1979	15	176	65	7.2	1108	285	830	672	65	50	30
1980	16	178	67	7.0	11.6	292	880	685	80	60	35
1981	17	181	72	6.9	11.3	306	912	701	90	70	40
1982	18	182	75	6.7	11.0	310	940	725	95	80	45
1983	19	183	77	6.5	10.6	317	960	750	105	85	50
1984	20	184	77	6.3	10.3	324	990	775	110	90	55

Table 4.3. Long-Term Training Loads for Sergey Bubka

Main Means of Preparation	Age 15	16	17	18	19	20
Number of:						
Training Sessions	215	290	305	345	310	295
Pole Vaults	608	652	739	750	686	672
Weight Training (tons)	61.2	70.5	85	115.7	145	112
Special Gymnastic Exercises (hrs.)	71	80	98	125	113	78
General Jump Preparation Exercises (takeoff)	20,150	25,000	25,800	40,080	35,330	25,200
Run with Pole on Approach (km.)	10.2	12.1	14.2	10.7	15.2	18.5
Special Sprinting and Hurdle Exercises (km.)	25.4	20.1	25.5	34.3	23.5	25.8
Sprinting 60-80m & Sprinting with Pole (km.)	17.3	20.4	30.7	38.2	45.5	51.0
Sprinting more than 100m (km.)	33.8	35.0	35.0	44.2	53.2	40.4
High Jump & Long Jump Takeoffs	580	693	650	785	724	590
Competitions	11	12	19	24	16	17

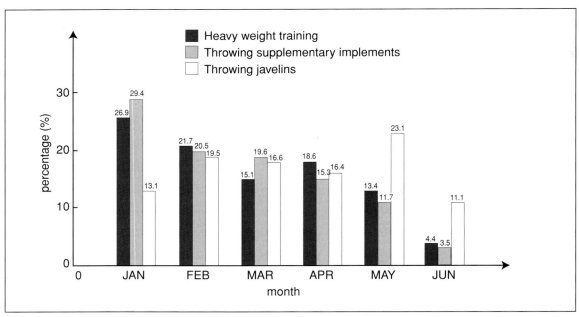

Figure 4.9. Variations of Three Load Volumes

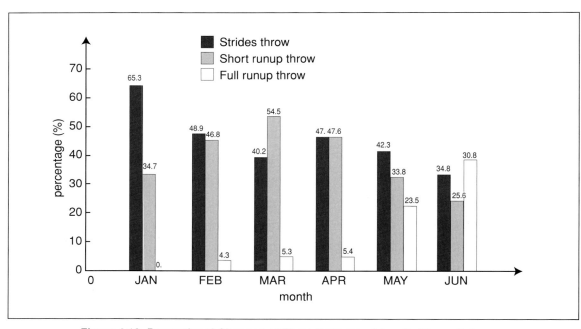

Figure 4.10. Proportional Changes of Three Patterns of Javelin Throw Volumes

Training Book. New York: Collier.

Heyward, Vivian H. (1998). *Advanced Fitness Assessment and Exercise Prescription* (3rd ed.). Champaign, IL: Human Kinetics.

Hopkins, William G. (1995). Quantification of training in competitive sports: Methods and applications. *Sports Medicine, 12*(3), 161-183.

Janssen, Peter. (2001). *Lactate Threshold Training.* Champaign, IL: Human Kinetics.

Jianrong, Chen. (1992). Load variations of elite female javelin throwers in a macrocycle. *Track Technique, 119,* 3788-3792.

NSA Round Table 26: Technology. (1994). *New Studies in Athletics, 9*(4), 13-24. [José Manuel Ballesteros, Neil Craig, Frank W. Dick, Vern Gambetta, Craig Hillyard, Elio Locatelli, Jarmo Mäkelä, Canadian Panel, & Chinese Group].

Rachmanliev, Peter, & Edward Harnes. (1990). Long term preparation for advanced female discus throwers. *New Studies in Athletics, 5*(1), 69-92.

Vittori, Carlo. (1995). Monitoring the training of the sprinter. *New Studies in Athletics, 10*(3), 39-44.

SOURCES FOR TABLES

4.1. Control Tests for Soviet Sprinters: Brunner & Tabachnik, 133

4.2. Control Tests for Sergey Bubka: Brunner & Tabachnik, 132

4.3. Long-Term Training Loads for Sergey Bubka: Brunner & Tabachnik, 132

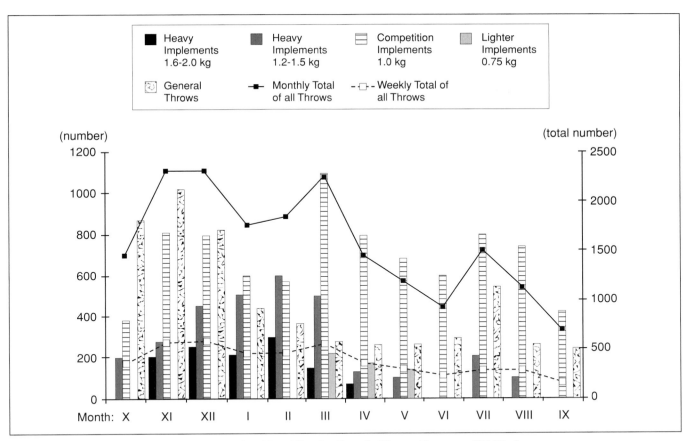

Figure 4.11. One Year Plan for Female Discus Throwers (67-71m)

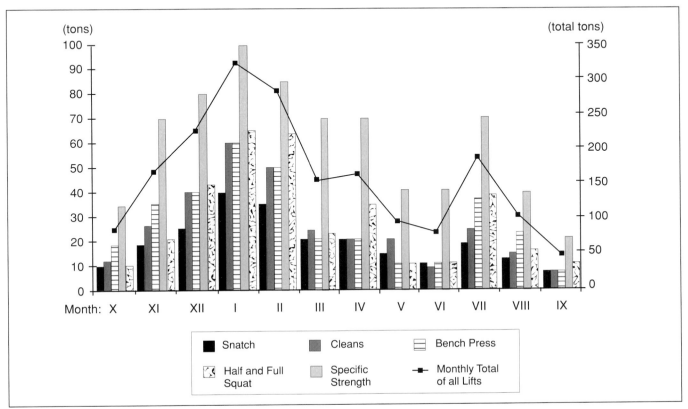

Figure 4.12. Volume of Weight Training in One Year

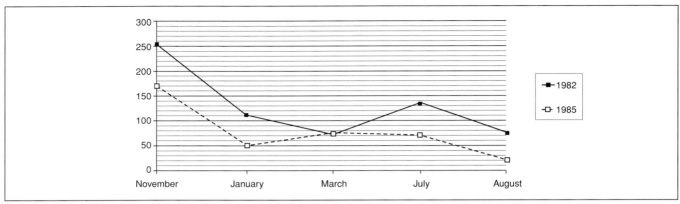

Figure 4.13. General Throws, 1982 vs. 1986

TRAINING LESSON PLAN NO. 148

DATE: June 14th   PLACE: York Stadium   OBJECTIVES: Perfect the start; specific endurance; power training   EQUIPMENT: Starting block; barbells.

PART	EXERCISE	DOSAGE	FORMATIONS	NOTES
I	- describe the lesson's objectives and how to achieve them. - what the athletes are expected to stress during training.	3 min.		John: Pay attention to arm work
II	- warm up - jogging - callisthenics - arm rotations - upper body rotations - hips flexibility - ankle flexibility - bounding exercises - wind sprints	20 min. 1200m (meters) 8 x (8 times) 12 x 8-10 x 8-20 x 4 x 20 m. 4 x 40-60 m.		Rita: have two warmup suits Stress hip flexibility Stress the weak leg
III	- starts - specific endurance - power training	12 x 30m Rest (1) = 2 min. 16 x 120m 3/4 (14 sec) 60kg 4 sets 8-10 reps		Stress arm work Maintain a constant velocity throughout all repetitions In between exercises relax arms and legs
IV	- jogging - massage	800m. 5 min.		Light and relaxing Work with a partner

Figure 4.14. A Training Lesson Plan for Sprinters

Day: Date: Morning pulse:
Sleep: From   To: Total hrs.
Naps:
Food:

Weather: Temp   Hum   %   Wind spd.   Direc.
Notes:

Training location & conditions:

Workout:

Fatigue levels: Before   Mid   After
Any problems?

Body weight: Before wo-   After wo-
Total miles: Daily total: Weekly total:

Figure 4.15 Training Diary Form

SOURCES FOR FIGURES

4.1. Hypothetical Annual Training Plan: Bompa (1st ed., 1983), p. 172

4.2. Hypothetical Plan for a High Jumper: Bompa (1983), p. 174

4.3. Annual Training Plan: Litovchenko, 55

4.4. Comparative Training Loads: Litovchenko, 55

4.5. Yearly Training Buildup of Wodars: Neuhof, 74

4.6. Annual Pattern of Concentrated Strength and Speed-Strength: Polunin, 97

4.7. Control Tests and Parameters for Sprinters: Vittori, 43

4.8. Control Test Record Form: Vittori, 43

4.9. Variations of Three Load Volumes: Jianrong, 3789

4.10. Proportional Changes of Three Patterns of Javelin Throw Volumes: Jianrong, 3790

4.11. One Year Plan for Female Discus Throwers (67-71m): Rachmanliev & Harnes, 72

4.12. Volume of Weight Training in One Year: Rachmanliev & Harnes, 73

4.13. General Throws, 1982 vs. 1986: Rachmanliev & Harnes, 91

4.14. A Training Lesson Plan for Sprinters: Bompa (1983), p. 111

4.15. Training Diary Form: Dellinger & Freeman, pp. 65-70

CHAPTER 5:
The Big Picture—Planning From Setting Long-Term Goals To The Annual Plan

An athlete uses periodization in training so he or she can:

1. *Peak at the ideal moment.* Every athlete has a single competition that is the year's most important event. Ideally, the athlete's best performance of the year should occur at that meet.

2. *Achieve the optimal training effect from each phase of training.* If an athlete gets the most from each phase of the training cycle, the ultimate performance will be far greater than with other training plans. At the same time, the athlete will not have to spend unnecessary training time.

3. *Make training a more objective process.* Training should be quantifiable. That is, the coach and athlete should be able to measure and record the quantity and quality of training for each performance characteristic, as well as control tests and trials to assess the athlete's progress toward achieving his or her goals in each training component. This allows the training plan to be modified along the way, rather than waiting until the end of the year to learn whether the training plan worked.

Also, because the training plan produces objective records of training and progress, the coach

and athlete have a comparison for future training. They can objectively measure how much more training is being done in the new year, what changes are made in the types of training, and the amount of improvement in the performance characteristics along the way. They will also have more objective standards for how improvement in the performance characteristics or control tests translates into actual event success.

THE PROCESS OF PERIODIZATION IN TRAINING

Periodization divides the training time into periods or cycles of time (Fig. 2.1). We will examine how training is planned from the top down, beginning with a period of several years and continuing until we are down to the components of a single training session.

Experienced and elite athletes should plan their training from the multiple-year perspective. Younger athletes and those at lower levels of performance should plan their training for only one year at a time. This is because younger or less-experienced athletes have less predictable improvement curves. A young athlete may suddenly mature physically, with an unusually sharp rise in performance over a very short period of time. The same is true for athletes in a new event. The early learning and performance curve is sharp. Sudden improvements are rare for more experienced, older athletes. Their training needs can be planned farther ahead.

This recommendation (planning only one year at a time) for younger or less-experienced athletes is not the ideal situation. The Eastern European system planned the long-term development of athletes from youth through their peak as international athletes. However, that system cannot be adapted to the United States with any degree of ease because of the difference between the functional structures of the systems. The nations using such long-term youth programs are nations that organize all of their sports through the state.

Centralized planning and sport opportunities allow a more highly organized program of youth sports. Standards can be set in place for every age group, and the young athletes can be tested against those norms each year. Those who meet the highest standards are placed on a track designed for the long-term development of elite athletes. The system is much like the "track" system (sometimes seen in American schools) for dividing students into groups according to their presumed learning capacity.

LONG-TERM PLANNING: THE OLYMPIAD AND BEYOND

Planning for more than one year at a time is easiest for more experienced, accomplished athletes, as they are a known quantity to the coach. Their strengths and weaknesses are well-known. Their competitive needs (performance characteristics and level) are also well-known. For this reason, planning the long-term training of an elite athlete is far simpler than planning for a less experienced athlete. A long-term training plan must consider four factors:

- Number of years of organized training needed to achieve a high performance level
- Average age when high performance is achieved
- Amount or degree of the athlete's natural ability
- Age that the athlete began specialized training.

Just as with the annual training plans, there is a preparation phase and a specialization phase.

Long-term training plans change the proportions of general (multilateral) training and specialized training (divided into the foundation for specialized training and the specialized training itself).

Some factors to consider in developing the long-term plan are listed in Table 5.1, along with the aspects of each factor that the coach and athlete must list in the plan (exactly what the training will include).

An effective long-term plan will include these objective criteria:

1. Relate the performance objectives to factors specific to the sport. The objectives should reflect the requirements of both national and world success in the event.

2. Increase these measures each training year, assuming that the athlete improves:

    a. Number of training lessons

Table 5.1. Components of the Athlete's Long-Term Plan

Component to Define	Aspect to List
1. Strong and weak qualities	Training Tests Standards
2. The scope and objectives of the long-term plan	
3. Performance predictions	
4. Calendar of competitions and phases	
5. General training guidelines for each year	Priority for each Specific proportion for each
6. Physical preparation and improvement	Main physical deficiencies Objectives to improve each deficiency Means of improving each deficiency
7. Technical preparation and improvement	Main technical deficiencies Objectives to improve each deficiency Means of improving each deficiency
8. Tactical preparation and improvement	Main tactical deficiencies Objectives to improve each deficiency Means of improving each deficiency
9. Psychological preparation and improvement	Psychological trait Means of improvement
10. Periodization model for each phase	Number of competitions Number of competition days Number of training hours Number of days of rest
11. Tests and standards	List of tests Standards (by test) for each year
12. Medical control	Type of control Frequency of control

b. Number of training hours
c. Number of competitions
d. Frequency of competitions.

At the highest stages of development, the number of major competitions should level off; it may even decrease.

3. Forecast the annual increase of volume and intensity of training according to the event's dominant component (Table 5.2) and the athlete's needs. For Groups Number 1 and 3, the training intensity should increase toward the end of the training year. While this is also true for Groups Number 2 and 7, they should also stress an increase in volume as a dominant component of the training.

4. Change the emphasized training exercises yearly, especially for the best athletes. The training year will begin with a wide variety of exercises, but by the end of the year only a small number of very event-specific activities should be used.

5. Specify the control tests and standards to be met. The selection criteria for the tests include their being:

a. Limited in number
b. Very specific to the event or sport
c. Used over a long period of time for consistency
d. Used with higher performance standards each year
e. Accompanied by medical controls in the assessment.

6. Specifically cover all of the needs of the event, including:

a. The number, grade, and variety of technical elements
b. The number, grade of difficulty, and variety of tactical maneuvers
c. The degree of general and specific physical preparation
d. Test standards reflect physical requirements of good technique
e. Performance predictions.

7. Show the progression of the number of training lessons and hours per year. Typical figures range from 200-250 lessons per year, with about 400 hours of training, for less experienced athletes, ranging up to 500-650 lessons and 1000-1200 hours of training for world-class athletes.

The process of long-term training requires much careful thought. Good training records must be kept for each athlete, with measurable control tests spread carefully across the training year for comparative purposes. Well-planned training is quantifiable, so you can make tables, charts, or graphs of the training progress. You should be able to show how much of the training load (time and percentage) was devoted to the development of each specific performance component.

A record sheet can list the objectives for each year in a four-year (Olympiad) plan. The coach and athlete should work together to develop the long-term plan, though the coach's part will be far greater than the athlete's part with younger athletes (because of their lack of practical experience).

Table 5.2. Classification of Event Skills

Group Number	Training Goal	Examples	Skill's Structure	Dominant Intensity	Bimotor Ability	Functional Demand
1	Perfect the coordination and form of a skill	Pole Vault	Acyclic*	Alternative	Complex blending of coordination, strength, and speed	CNS,** neuro-muscular
2	Attain a superior speed in cyclic sports	Running	Cyclic	All intensities from maximum to low. Alternative	Speed, Endurance	CNS, neuro-muscular, cardio-respiratory
3	Perfect the strength and speed of a skill	Throwing, Jumping	Acyclic, Acyclic Combined	Alternative	Strength, Speed	Neuro-musclar CNS
7	Combined sports	Decathlon Heptathlon	Cyclic, Acyclic, Acyclic Combined	Specific to each event	Complex blending of most abilities	CNS, locomotor, and cardio-respiratory

* Acyclic: Integral functions performed in one action: Shot, Discus
  Acyclic Combined: Cyclic movement, followed by acyclic movement: Jumps, Hurdles, Javelin, Hammer
  Cyclic: Motor skills are repetitive cyclic acts: Running Events

** Central nervous system

The basic steps in developing the long-term plan are to:

- Set performance goals (the athlete's time, distance, or height) for each year.
- Set the objectives of each type of preparation (physical, technical, tactical, and psychological) for each year.
- Select the control tests that will be used to evaluate the athlete's progress, along with the standards that will show if the athlete is making satisfactory progress.
- Graph the athlete's training factors (training volume, training intensity, and progress toward peaking) across the bottom of the plan. This gives a condensed version of each year's training plan.

For younger athletes, the former East German sports leaders had "developmental norms" that allowed them to compare whether young athletes were progressing normally toward elite performances as adults. That list of standards is shown in Table 5.3.

An example of a hypothetical four-year plan for an 800-meter runner (Fig. 5.1) shows how an effective four-year plan is constructed. It gives the objectives that are planned for each year, with the performance goals, the tests and standards, and the rough graph of the training progress and periods of training over the four-year period.

MULTI-YEAR TRAINING EMPHASES

At least three approaches are taken to planning the multi-year training emphases:

1. Steady overall performance improvement
2. Varying stress loads, with a light year before the peak Olympic year
3. Varying performance component emphases for each year.

The steady overall performance improvement is the most common approach to training in the United States. With that approach, the athlete's goal is to reach a higher performance level every year. The training load for each year is increased over the load of the previous training year, with the expectation of a commensurate performance improvement.

The varying stress loads approach, with a light year before the peak Olympic year, is often seen with Eastern European athletes, particularly with

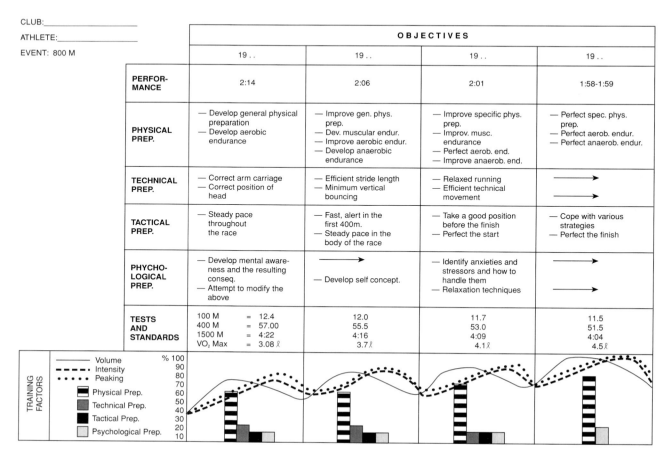

Figure 5.1. Hypothetical Four-Year Training Plan for 800 Meters

46

Table 5.3. Developmental Norms for Young Athletes

Event	Buildup training			Connecting training		
	13 years	14 years	15 years	16 years	17 years	18 years
Male						
60 meters [sec]	7.80	7.50	7.35	-	-	-
100 meters [sec]	12.20	11.75	11.45	10.95	10.75	10.60
200 meters [sec]	-	24.10	23.50	22.35	21.55	21.00
400 meters [sec]	52.50	51.00	49.50	47.50	46.80	46.00
110m hurdles [sec]	-	-	14.80	14.80	14.20	14.00
400m hurdles [sec]	-	-		-	53.00	51.50
Female						
60 meters [sec]	8.10	7.90	7.75	-	-	-
100 meters [sec]	13.00	12.50	12.20	12.05	11.85	11.60
200 meters [sec]	-	26.00	25.30	24.50	24.20	23.50
400 meters [sec]	59.00	58.50	57.00	56.00	54.00	53.00
100m hurdles [sec]	-	14.80	14.20	14.00	13.60	13.35
400m hurdles [sec]	-	-	-	-	58.50	57.00
Male						
400 meters [sec]	56.05	54.04	52.05	-	-	-
800 meters [min]	2:09.00	2:04.00	1:58.00	1:54.50	1:52.00	1:50.00
1500 meters [min]	4:28.00	4:18.00	4:05.00	3:56.00	3:51.00	3:47.50
3000 meters [min]	9:45.00	9:25.00	9:05.00	8:40.00	8:26.00	8:15.00
5000 meters [min]	-	-	-	15:05.00	14:18.00	
Female						
400 meters [sec]	60.06	58.05	57.05	-	-	-
800 meters [min]	2:20.00	2:15.00	2:12.00	2:08.00	2:06.00	2:04.00
1500 meters [min]	4:45.00	4:42.00	4:35.00	4:26.00	4:22.00	4:16.00
3000 meters [min]	10:40.00	10:15.00	9:50.00	9:38.00	9:25.00	9:18.00
Male						
high jump [m]	1.70	1.80	1.92	1.98	2.05	2.12
pole vault [m]	3.00	3.70	4.20	4.50	4.80	5.00
long jump [m]	5.80	6.30	6.70	6.90	7.20	7.50
triple jump [m]	-	13.00	13.50	14.20	14.90	15.60
decathlon [points]	4800	5250	5900	6400	6650	7000
Female						
high jump [m]	1.60	1.66	1.72	1.76m	1.80m	1.84
long jump [m]	5.30	5.55	5.75	5.90m	6.10m	6.35
pentathlon [points]	4150	4550	4850	5150	5350	5550
Male						
shot put [m]	13.00	14.00	15.00	16.00	17.00	18.00
discus [m]	40.00	42.00	48.00	50.00	54.00	57.00
hammer [m]	50.00	55.00	58.00	60.00	64.00	68.00
javelin [m]	45.00	53.00	57.00	61.DO	6S.00	69.00
Female						
shot put [m]	11.75	13.00	14.00	15.00	15.00	16.00
discus [m]	31.00	37.00	43.00	47.00	51.00	55.00
javelin [m]	36.00	39.00	45.00	49.00	53.00	57.001

the older, more experienced athletes. No athlete can perform at the highest levels for a decade without having off days, sometimes at the most major meets.

For example, Yuriy Syedikh (Soviet Union) took 1987 as an "off" year, skipping the World Championships to try to peak at the Seoul Olympics in 1988. Syedikh, world record holder in the hammer (284'7"/86.74m) and two-time Olympic champion, first won the Olympic gold in 1976. In 1987 he trained and competed at a less intense level, so that he would then feel more ready (physically and psychologically) to make a major training effort to prepare for Seoul. His best mark for 1987 (263'7") still placed him 13th in the world, but it required much less intensity and stress for the training year. This approach is best for athletes at the highest world levels, with years of international experience. However, it can be applied usefully to the plan for any athlete accustomed to competing in a large number of high-level competitions.

Istvan Balyi describes one approach to long-term planning, dividing an athlete's career into three 4-year blocks, each with a different emphasis:

- Training to train
- Training to compete
- Training to win.

The first block covers the developmental training of the young athlete, with basic conditioning and a grounding in event-specific training, along with a slowly rising number of competitions. The second block is the development of complete control over the training and peaking process, with the athlete usually rising to the national level by the end of this time.

The final block of time focuses on competition at the high performance or elite level, the pinnacle of the sporting career. This is similar to the approach used with great success in Eastern Europe in the past, when young athletes were brought along slowly, with a focus on thorough training and development through carefully selected competitions, rather than quick success.

PLANNING THE COMPETITIONS

You can design a rough pattern for the year by fixing the date (or dates) when the athlete needs to peak, then developing a curve similar to one of the annual training curves shown in the next chapter.

The entire year's training is simply a process of preparing for competition. The process is a cycle of training, competition, and regeneration (recovery). Meets should be classified into two groups, the main competitions and the preparatory meets.

If concern about won-loss records is a factor in the process, no meet that is important in those terms should be scheduled for the last two or three weeks before the season's main competition, as the effort affects the season's final preparation. Preparatory meets are used as tests to assess the athlete's progress. Coaches should include meets that create the same meet conditions (time schedules, level of competition) and meets at the same facility (track) or course (cross country, road racing). At those meets, the primary goal is to adjust to the environment for the sake of future success, rather than to win at that specific competition.

The decisions on meet selection should be a joint coach/athlete venture, if choices are available. For younger athletes, the schedule may be completely set by a league, with little choice available even for the coach. For the college level and higher, the choices are much more open. Usually only conference and national meets (and regional meets in cross country) are fixed on the schedule. This allows far more schedule planning.

For the elite American athlete, the USATF Championships are the only fixed event, as it is used to select members of all national teams except for the Olympic Games. An athlete who competes in Europe, hoping to peak for a World Championships in September, will have to place well at the USATF meet in June, as there is no automatic team selection in the United States. A truly elite athlete may have only one or two preparatory meets, then open his or her season at the USATF Championships, and travel soon afterward to Europe for the start of the international racing season. This approach is possible only if the athlete is virtually assured of making the national team without being in peak condition.

Qualifying for the Olympic Trials is made simpler by the international custom (because of differing summer seasons in the two hemispheres) of allowing a full year to meet the qualifying mark. Thus, in the United States you could begin to qualify for the 2004 Trials late in the 2003 season. Qualifying a year early removes the risk of peaking too soon while trying to qualify. The training process can then be planned with no peak before the Trials. For the 2000 men's marathon Olympic Trials, the qualifying period ran for about one year, from early in 1999 to about a month before the 2000 Trials.

Two approaches to scheduling meets are the *grouping* and the *cyclic* approaches. In the grouping approach, the athlete goes through alternating phases of training with bunched meets (several in a few days) and training without meets. The cyclic approach (more common in track and field) involves meets on a repeating cycle, such as once a week, or every two weeks. It may close with a training phase or two, each ending with a single major meet.

The number of competitions is critical, as both coach and athlete want the athlete to peak at the proper time, rather than competing too many times and losing fitness. Table 5.4 suggests the number of meets per year for athletes at different levels. Figure 5.2 illustrates a multi-cycle annual plan for swimmers.

These factors should be considered in planning the athlete's meet schedule:

- The most important meet of the year is the only one that determines the athlete's ranking. All other meets are steps to prepare the athlete for that one competition.
- If the meets are planned properly, the athlete will peak at the most important meet of the year.
- Having too many meets interferes with a proper balance of competition and training. This lessens both the athlete's physical and psychological potential.
- The athlete should compete only when capable of meeting that meet's objectives for each training factor (physical, technical,

Table 5.4. Suggested Number of Meets Per Year

Event	Beginning Athletes Winter	Summer	Elite Athletes Winter	Summer
Sprints, Hurdles, Jumps, and Throws				
Primary Event	3-4	12-16	3-5	16-20
Secondary Event	2-3	4-6	1-3	3-5
Middle Distances				
800-1500	—	4-8	2-3	10-16
Shorter Distances	2-3	8-10	2-4	8-10
Marathon	—	1	—	2-3
50 km Walk	—	6-8	—	8-10
Combined Events				
Decathlon	—	1-2	—	2-3
Heptathlon	—	2	—	2-4
Individual Events	2-4	10-12	3-5	12-16

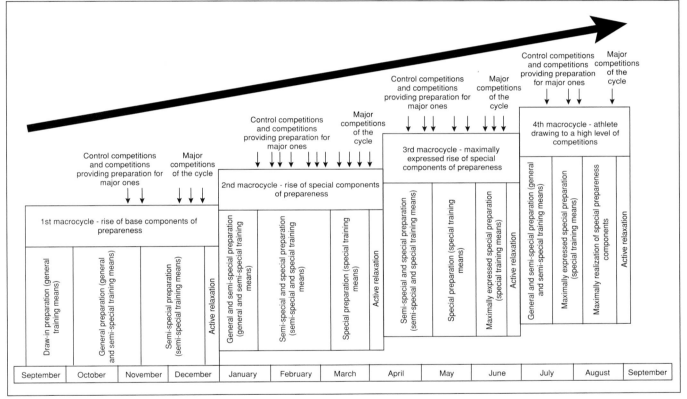

Figure 5.2. Multi-Cycle Annual Training Plan For Swimmers

Notes: (1) change "mcarocycle" to "mesocycle" in 4 sections
(2) words in arrow are "Increase of loading requirements"

tactical, and psychological).
- Each meet should be a more difficult competition for the athlete than the previous meet.
- A meet with too little competition provides no motivation.
- Superior opponents should not be avoided.

BLOCKING OUT THE TRAINING YEAR

After the coach assesses the athlete's training progress, considers the athlete's strengths and weaknesses, and makes plans for improving the training and performance, the focus must be set for the year's competitions. When does the athlete need to peak?

49

A major reason for using periodization in training is to help the athlete to achieve his or her best performance of the year at the most important meet of the year.

While he does not use many of the traditional terms of periodization, Yuri Verhoshansky provides a detailed discussion of the process of designing the training program structure for a year. That discussion is too detailed to summarize here, but he focuses on the importance of developing a training strategy that is based on a knowledge of physiology and of the biology of the athlete's body.

The training year is divided into one or more macrocycles, with one macrocycle for each peak. Most elite athletes will peak either once or twice a year. Few sporting activities permit more than two peaks in a calendar year. Each macrocycle has three major periods: preparation, competition, and transition.

When a training year includes more than one macrocycle, a transition period is included between them. If an athlete peaks for both indoor and outdoor track, there should be several weeks of low-key transitional activities following the major indoor competition. The athlete's fitness level will drop during this period, but that drop enables the athlete to undertake more effective training later, resulting in improved performances during the outdoor competitions. If the transition period is not included, the athlete will "hit the wall" at some point, ending further progress and effectively ending the season.

Examples of problems and solutions in planning for the American training year are given in Chapter 8. The next chapter shows how to progress from having a racing schedule and annual plan to planning the training periods, phases, microcycles, and individual training sessions.

REFERENCES

1. Frank W. Dick. (1978). *Training Theory* (pp. 56-81). London: British Amateur Athletic Board.

2. Norman N. Shneidman. (1978). The Soviet system of athletic training. In *The Soviet Road to Olympus: Theory and Practice of Soviet Physical Culture and Sport* (pp. 101-125). Champaign, IL: Human Kinetics.

3. N.G. Ozolin. (1971). Athlete's training system for competition. In Dietrich Harre, ed. (1982). *Principles of Sports Training: Introduction to the Theory and Methods of Training* (2nd ed., p. 210). Berlin: Sportverlag.

4. Tudor O. Bompa. (1983). *Theory and Methodology of Training: The Key to Athletic Performance* (pp. 131-205). Dubuque, IA: Kendall/Hunt.

5. Ekkart Arbeit. (1998). Principles of the multi-year training process. *New Studies in Athletics, 13*(4), 21-28.

6. Istvan Balyi. (1995). Long-term athlete development model. In *Australian Strength and Conditioning Association 1995 National Conference and Trade Show Proceedings* (pp. 17-35). Gold Coast, Australia: Australian Strength and Conditioning Association.

7. Istvan Balyi. (1998, December). Long-term planning of athlete development. Part 2: The training to compete phase. *Faster Higher Stronger, No. 2*, 8-11.

8. Istvan Balyi & Anne Hamilton. (1999). Long-term planning of athlete development. Part 3: The training to win phase. *Faster Higher Stronger, No. 3*, 7-9.

9. Istvan Balyi & Anne Hamilton. (1999). Long-term planning of athlete development. Part 4: Multiple periodization, modelling and normative data. *Faster Higher Stronger, No. 4*, 7-9.

10. V. N. Platonov. (1996). Formation of athletes' preparation within [the] year. *Athletic Asia, 21*(1), 37-74.

11. Tudor O. Bompa. (1987). Peaking for the extended athletics calendar. *New Studies in Athletics, 2*(4), 29-43.

12. Harre, pp. 78-87.

13. Juri Verchoshanskij (Verhoshansky) (1999). The skills of programming the training process. *New Studies in Athletics, 14*(4), 45-54.

SOURCES FOR TABLES

5.1. Components of the Long-Term Plan: Bompa, pp. 191-195

5.2. Classification of Event Skills: Bompa, pp. 4-9

5.3. Developmental Norms for Young Athletes: Arbeit, p. 20

5.4. Suggested Number of Meets Per Year: Bompa, p. 210

SOURCES FOR FIGURES

5.1. Hypothetical Four-Year Training Plan: Bompa, p. 198

5.2. Multi-Cycle Annual Training Plan for Swimmers: Adapted from Platonov, p. 53

CHAPTER 6:
Planning The Details—
From The Annual Plan To
The Daily Workout

PLANNING THE MACROCYCLES

A macrocycle is the largest cycle of time within the training year. Its three different training periods (preparation, competition, and transition) are planned to result in a peak performance at a major meet. Explosive events (such as sprints, jumps, and throws) may allow up to three major peaks (therefore, three macrocycles in a year), but for other events only one or two peaks are possible. The greater the part that the influence of endurance (aerobic component) plays in the performance, the fewer peaks that are possible in a year. For the highest possible performance level, a marathoner should plan only one major peak in a year.

The schedule of macrocycles is largely a function of the meet schedule that you develop. After you choose your most important meets of the year, you will know when your macrocycles will occur. Each major meet (1-3 in a year) will require a macrocycle. The macrocycle will end after the transition period that follows the major meet (1-4 weeks after the major meet. At that point, the next macrocycle will begin.

PLANNING THE TRAINING PERIODS

Each of the three types of training periods (preparation, competition, and transition) should have specific training objectives consistent with the annual plan. Once again, those objectives must be consistent with the performance requirements of the event. The objectives should be listed in the order of their importance to performance, so you can assess the relative training time that is applied to their development.

The preparation period develops the basic conditioning and technique that is needed for competition. The length of this period depends on the athlete's fitness level. A more fit, more highly skilled athlete needs much less preparation time than a young, inexperienced athlete or an older athlete who is not fit at the start of the macrocycle.

The competition period tests the athlete in steps along the way toward the season's major meet. After each meet, the athlete's progress is evaluated, refinements are made in the next microcycle's training, and the athlete trains to improve again. The goal of the entire macrocycle lies in the major meet at the end of the competition period.

The transition period involves recovery from the competition season, while providing a low-key transition to the start of the next macrocycle. If the year includes more than one macrocycle and peak, the mid-year transition periods may be as brief as a week or so. The transition period at the end of the training year should last for at least one month.

When the objectives of the periods are decided, you must select the best training means to meet each objective. Alternative training methods should also be decided. If any outside factors (weather, facilities, or such) might interfere with the plan's success, alternative plans should tell what you will do if those situations occur.

The athlete's success or progress in meeting the goals or objectives should be evaluated and recorded at the end of each period.

Yuri Verhoshansky has argued that some of these terms (such as preparation and competition) are outdated, preferring a focus on the main adaptation cycle (MAC). However, that opinion has been vigorously attacked by other experts, who argue that the earlier terms are based on scientific research, the MAC approach has not been heavily researched, and that it is as old a concept as the traditional ones.

PLANNING THE PHASES

The macrocycle below the period level is divided into six subdivisions called *phases* (Table 6.1). A phase lasts for 3-6 weeks. Table 6.2 shows the primary objectives of each phase.

Table 6.3 suggests approximate ratios of the different types of training to use during each of the phases of a macrocycle. These suggestions are for less experienced athletes. The suggested ratios for experienced athletes are given in the chapters on the individual events.

For periodized training programs that stress a repeated cycle based on the biological model, a phase is divided into three parts, each lasting for one to four microcycles:

- Preparation: General conditioning for the phase goal
- Adaptation: Specific conditioning for the phase goal
- Application: Control testing, simulations, or competition.

This pattern repeats from the individual training session or level up to the macrocycle, and it can be applied to multi-year training plans, with a year devoted to each part.

Phase 1: General Preparation

This is the first of two phases in the preparation period. Its function is to improve the base fitness and technique levels of the athlete, "training to train," requiring up to one-third of the macrocycle. While it prepares the athlete for more advanced training in Phase 2, it has **three primary tasks.**

First, any problems from the previous season must be defined. Is the athlete completely free of injury? If not, the injury must be treated and cured completely. Did the athlete have technical flaws in the meets? Were there tactical errors? Were there fitness problems? All of these questions must be answered, and for each problem a solution must be planned. Rest

Table 6.1. Periods, Phases, and Time Spans

Period	Phase	Phase Type	Length
Preparation	1	General preparation	3-6 weeks
	2	Specific preparation	3-6 weeks
Competitive	3	Pre-competition	3-6 weeks
	4	General competition	3-6 weeks
	5	Special competition	2 weeks
Transition	6	Transition or recovery	1-4 weeks

Table 6.2. Objectives of the Phases

Period	Phase	Objectives
Preparation	1 General prep.	1. Diagnose problems from competition 2. Develop endurance, strength, mobility 3. Fine-tuning of technical model 4. Preparation for Phase 2
	2 Specific prep.	1. Develop event-specific fitness 2. Develop the advanced technical model 3. Preparation for Phase 3
Competition	3 Pre-comp.	1. Progressive intensity of meets 2. Improve meet performances 3. Technical evaluation in meet setting
	(If appropriate) (If appropriate)	4. Expansion of meet experiences 5. Qualifying for advanced meets
	4 General comp.	1. Refine the advanced technical model 2. Prepare for the peak performance
	5 Special comp.	1. Achieve peak performance at major meet
Transition	6 Transition	1. Active recovery from season 2. Preparation for Phase 1

Table 6.3. Suggested Training Ratios for Phases

	Ages 10-14			Ages 15-17			Ages 18-19			Novice Seniors		
Phase	General	Special	Specific	General	Special	Specific	General	Special	Specific	General	Special	Specific
1	70	10	20	60	20	20	50	25	25	50	25	25
2	60	20	20	50	25	25	40	25	35	40	25	35
3	50	20	30	50	20	30	25	25	50	25	25	50
4	60	20	20	50	25	25	45	30	25	45	30	25
5	50	20	30	50	20	30	15	25	60	25	25	50
6	80	10	10	70	20	10	75	15	10	75	15	10

Percent distribution of:
- General Training (mostly compensatory strength and mobility work)
- Special Training (includes aerobic endurance)
- Competition Specific Training

Note: These are only rough suggestions, to be used as a starting point.

or rehabilitation must be prescribed for any injuries. Specific training objectives and methods must be planned to strengthen the athlete in the areas of weak performance.

Second, the athlete's general fitness level must be raised. This is the "training to train" aspect of the phase. The endurance must be improved, the strength level raised, and the mobility (flexibility and resilience) improved. These goals involve general training at high loads, but with low intensity. It is quantity with limited quality.

Third, the technical model that is used to judge the athlete's performance in competition must be refined or fine-tuned. Regardless of the event, the coach and athlete will develop an objective model of the characteristics of the highest level of performance in that event. Those characteristics must be objective, so that their achievement will not be simply a matter of opinion. The task of studying and fine-tuning the model is critical, because the training plan is designed to prepare the athlete to conform to that model.

Phase 2: Specific Preparation

This is the second phase in the preparation period. While its basic goal is to prepare the athlete for the third phase, it does so through **two major tasks.**

First, the fitness needed for the athlete's specific event must be developed. During the first phase, the primary emphasis was on general fitness, which is largely the same regardless of the athlete's event. Different events require different types or degrees of fitness. Those types must be defined, and the training must be planned to develop those specific aspects of fitness.

Second, the advanced technical model must be reproduced in the athlete. Technical training will emphasize correcting any faults noted during the

previous competition phase. The athlete will train to conform to the refined technical model that was defined in Phase 1.

Phase 2 requires only a limited increase in the training load, but it calls for a rising intensity in the training. Dick notes that this phase is perhaps the most difficult one for coach and athlete, as it occurs during the early winter. As the training intensity rises, combined with the effects of training in bad weather conditions, the tendency toward catching colds and flu rises sharply. A fatigued athlete is very susceptible to illness, so the training load and the athlete's reaction to it must be observed very carefully.

Phase 3: Pre-Competition

This is the first of three phases in the competition period. It represents the majority of the competitive season. It involves **three primary tasks,** with **an additional two tasks** that may or may not be needed.

First, the athlete competes in a series of meets that increase in intensity or in the skill of the competitors. The athlete will gradually improve his or her performance level, while meeting more skilled opponents as his or her meet fitness improves. The performance level of the meets should become more and more challenging, but the challenge should never become insurmountable.

Second, the athlete works to improve performances in meets. As the athlete gains meet experience and the quality of the opponents rises, the athlete's performance level should rise also. The goal is to peak toward the end of the season. If the athlete reaches a high level of performance very quickly, it may be difficult to maintain that level until the end of the season. Further improvement may be impossible at the critical end-of-season meets.

With younger athletes, this avoidance of an

early peak may be very difficult, simply because predicting the final peak level of a growing or inexperienced athlete is largely guesswork. These athletes tend to improve by leaps and bounds, often in a rather abrupt, stop-and-go fashion. You can avoid a premature peak by decreasing the training load or having fewer sessions of hard training (while making sure that the athlete is not sneaking away for extra training on his or her own).

Third, the athlete's technique is evaluated in the meet setting. Good technique is more easily demonstrated in practice than in competition. All coaches have known athletes who were great in practice, but who could not reach their best in a meet or away from home. The whole point of training is to achieve excellence in the major meet. The athlete's technical performance in the meets is a critical indicator of progress. The advent of relatively inexpensive videotaping tools has helped immensely in this area, as coaches can more easily tape the performances, then evaluate them at their leisure. This point is critical, as the coach may have a wrong on-the-spot impression of some point of the athlete's technique.

Fourth, the athlete's meet experiences may need to be expanded. This is true primarily with younger or less-experienced athletes. The athlete needs to participate in meets with more competitors, meets away from home, meets where he or she cannot have the coach beside them, meets against more skilled opponents, and meets on the sites of the upcoming major competitions. An experienced competitor may already be very familiar with all of those situations.

Fifth, the athlete may have to qualify for advanced meets. For less-skilled or younger athletes, this task may not be needed, as thez.may not yet have the skills to go to higher-level meets. Some more advanced athletes may not be required to qualify, or they may have qualified through their previous year's performance. However, most athletes face the task of either qualifying for a major meet (state meet, national meet, Olympic Trials) or making a national team by their performance in a single meet (USATF or U.S. Olympic Trials). Many nations will require athletes to "demonstrate their competitive fitness" at one or more of a series of "selection" meets. Without successful completion of this qualifying procedure, the athlete will not even have the opportunity to compete in the major meet of the season (the goal of the training).

Phase 4: General Competition

This is the second phase in the competition period. It has two tasks, refining the advanced technical model and preparing for the peak performance. For elite athletes, it may include a mid-season re-

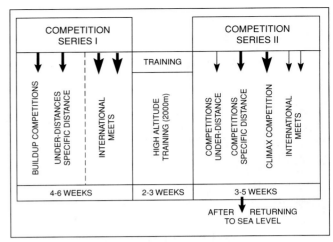

Figure 6.1. Mid-Season Preparation Phase for Elite Athletes

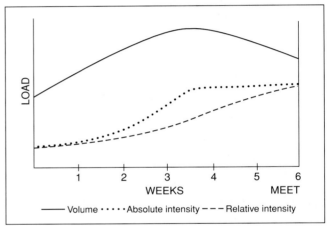

Figure 6.2. Varying Load Demand During a Phase

turn to basic training, often at altitude, for two to six weeks (Fig. 6.1). It is used as a "breather" from competition, a time to concentrate on the final adjustments in the technique and fitness levels. The training will reach its peak intensity (quality) at this time, but the loading (quantity) will be falling sharply (Fig. 6.2).

Phase 5: Special Competition

This is the last phase in the competition period. It is the peak of the season and includes the most important meet of the year. The training load will be very light, allowing the athlete to be rested and fresh, so the highest level of performance is possible. It may include one or more final "tune-up" meets before the major meet. This phase will usually last for only one or two weeks.

Some athletes may perform even better in low-key meets just after the peak meet. This is usually because the psychological pressure to perform is ended. At the same time, with the low level of train-

400m Sprinter Alvin Harrison

(rebuilding) phase. It involves active recovery from the season, with other physical activities in low-key, relaxing situations. It includes recovering from any injuries. The activity level is high enough that the athlete will be physically ready to begin general training with Phase 1 after Phase 6 is ended, but the activity level is low enough that the athlete will be psychologically rested and recovered enough to be enthusiastic about the coming of Phase 1 and the return to more structured training.

It is critical that the athlete truly use this time for regeneration, rather than continue specific training at a lower level. Ideally, activity should be non-specific; that is, do recreational activity in other sports and pastimes. Failure to limit specific training will generally result in less progress during the next sport season or year.

PLANNING THE MICROCYCLES

Characteristics of Microcycles

Each phase is divided into a series of microcycles. A typical microcycle is one week long, though it may vary in length from three to 21 days. Microcycles have four features:

1. The structure (the relative volume to the intensity) of the load demand changes during the cycle.
2. The load degree differs from one training session to the next, alternating between lower and higher loads according to the athlete's load tolerance and ability to recover.
3. The training sessions have differing main tasks that use either special or general training exercises.
4. The training load rises for as long as is necessary to meet the objectives of the training phase.

Each training session is followed by a recovery period long enough to remove the fatigue that prevents the athlete from meeting the required standard of performance in the next training session. Sessions with general exercises are useful as active recovery, which makes the recovery process shorter than passive rest does.

Depending on the activity, an athlete may not need a full recovery before the next training session. This is possible if the coach plans sessions with varying tasks, methods, and loads, so the stress on a given bodily system is not consistently high. As an example, strength training may concentrate on the upper body on one day, allowing the lower body to recover from its hard training session on the previous day.

ing, the athlete is very refreshed and able to devote very high energy levels to performance. For some athletes, it is their last chance to prove themselves if they performed poorly in the major meet.

Other athletes will perform poorly after the major meet. In some cases, they will feel no need to make a major effort. The new Olympic or World Champion feels that he or she has nothing left to prove. He did it when it counted, and gold medals and championships will not be taken away. An example is the aftermath of Ben Johnson's sensational world 100m record at the 1987 World Championships, as his post-Championships record that year was mediocre. On the other hand, some athletes succumb to the stress of the major meet and are psychologically drained, regardless of their physical state.

Phase 6: Transition

This is the primary phase of the transition period. It is also called the recovery or regeneration

The coach may plan some training sessions that focus on a single task, rather than trying to mix conflicting systems during the same session (such as speed and endurance).

The cycle should be planned so that sessions with special demands on speed, speed strength, and high-level technique are before sessions emphasizing endurance. Generally, more than 24 hours recovery is needed after very hard training. Meets should occur during the overcompensation phase that follows such recovery (usually two or three days after the optimum load training session). However, no pattern of training microcycles has proven to be infallible.

The "optimum succession" (best order of training activities) for a microcycle is:

1. Learn and perfect technique with medium intensity.
2. Perfect technique at submaximal and maximal intensity.
3. Develop speed of short duration (up to personal limit).
4. Develop anaerobic endurance.
5. Improve strength with a load of 90-100% of personal maximum.
6. Develop muscular endurance with medium and low loads.
7. Develop muscular endurance with high and maximal intensity.
8. Develop cardio-respiratory endurance with maximal intensity.
9. Develop cardio-respiratory endurance with moderate intensity.

This succession of training is very similar to Korobov's recommended progression for the single training session, which is to develop:

1. Technique and/or tactical training
2. Speed and/or coordination
3. Strength
4. General endurance.

Use these factors to plan the content of a microcycle:

1. Set the objectives, particularly the dominant training factors.
2. Decide the type of microcycle:
   a. Development microcycle: Improves fitness
   b. Tuning microcycle: Maintains fitness
   c. Unloading microcycle: Peaking cycle.
3. Set the absolute level of work:
   a. Number of training sessions
   b. Volume of training
   c. Intensity of training
   d. Complexity of training.
4. Set the relative level of effort (how many peak sessions, alternating with less intensive training sessions).

5. Decide on the character of training (training methods and means for each training session).
6. Set control testing or meet days.
7. Begin with low to medium intensity sessions, progressing to more intensive sessions later.
8. Before an important meet, use a microcycle with only one training peak, occurring 3-5 days before the meet.

Microcycle Patterns

A normal one-week microcycle will have two peak sessions. Training lessons should be repeated 2-3 times per microcycle for each different objective. Learning technical skills requires much repetition. The frequency of repetition varies, depending on the type of training:

- Daily training:
    General endurance
    Flexibility
    Strength in small muscle groups
- Every other day:
    Strength for large muscle groups
- Three sessions per week:
    Specific endurance (submaximal intensity)
- Two sessions per week:
    Specific endurance (maximal intensity)
    Maintenance of strength
    Maintenance of flexibility
    Maintenance of speed
- Two to three sessions per week:
    Bounding drills and speed exercises under strenuous conditions (sand or snow).

Microcycles can be classified according to the number and pattern of training sessions in a given week. The most common microcycle involves six days of training, followed by a day (Sunday) of rest or regeneration. Types of training sessions include the regular training session, supplementary training, and weight training. Four intensities of training session are possible, ranging from high, downward through medium, low, and rest. Figure 6.3 shows a microcycle with two peaks and one day of rest.

A week with a single peak should have the peak occur at mid-week, while a two-peak week should have the peaks toward opposite ends of the microcycle, allowing some recovery between the peaks. Peaks or hard days usually will be together only when the microcycle is modeling or simulating a later meet that has competition on successive days, as in the combined events or a heats-and-finals competition.

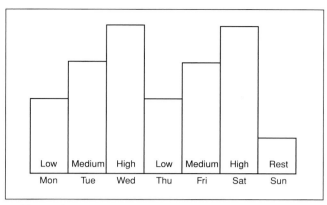

Figure 6.3. Intensity Levels in a Two-Peak Microcycle

A simple microcycle pattern is six afternoon sessions, with a day of rest on Sunday. An athlete with additional weekend time might have eight sessions in a week, one each afternoon from Monday through Saturday, with additional morning sessions on Saturday and Sunday. This allows 24 hours of recovery from Sunday afternoon to Monday afternoon.

Many athletes train twice a day. Tudor Bompa suggests patterns of 3+1 5+1, and 5+1+1 as examples for such training.

In the 3+1 pattern, the athlete has three training sessions, then rests instead of having a fourth session. The result is three sessions every two days, with every other morning (or afternoon) off. This permits nine training sessions in a week, with three half-day recoveries, and Sunday as an additional recovery day.

In the 5+1 pattern, the athlete has five training sessions, then rests instead of having the sixth session. This results in a morning or afternoon off on every third day, or 10 sessions a week, with two half-days and Sunday as rest and recovery times. A variation of the 5+1 pattern is the 5+1+1 pattern. The only difference is that one training session is included on Sunday, resulting in 11 training sessions and three half-day recoveries in a week.

The intensity of the training sessions should vary according to a preset pattern. If the sessions are primarily high in intensity, the athlete will self-destruct. Regeneration is needed during the training process for both physiological and psychological reasons. The coach may write the intended intensity for each training session on the written training plan itself.

During the competitive period, the microcycles should include some modeling of the conditions of the most important meet of the year. If the athlete must compete for two days in a row, this practice should be simulated every second or third week. In some cases an athlete qualifies in the morning, then competes in the finals in the afternoon.

In meets such as the Olympic Games, some events will take place over a series of days and times. For this reason, the Olympic schedule (including dates, times, starting heights and sequences, with lists of approved implements and equipment) are published a full year before the event takes place. This permits coaches and athletes to be fully prepared for the actual meet conditions.

For example, East German athletes practiced going through their warmup, then sitting quietly for up to half an hour before competing or performing in a high-intensity training session. This procedure simulates the conditions of the Olympic Games, where competitors have access to the track (or field) for only a very few minutes before the event.

In another example requiring special preparation, 800m candidates for the 1972 U.S. Olympic Team had to compete in four races in three days. During the first day, heats were held in the morning, followed by quarter-finals that afternoon. Semifinals were held on the next afternoon, then the finals were on the third afternoon. While this may seem to constitute cruel and unusual punishment, it was an exact copy of the procedure for that year's Olympic Games, won by Dave Wottle of the U.S.A.

In a final example, at one U.S. Olympic Trials, the high jump qualifying was held at 10:00 am on a chilly, breezy morning, with the crossbar set at 7'3". Each competitor had three jumps to clear the bar and advance to the finals. While preliminary jumps were allowed at lower heights, the contest was at the final height. As long as 12 people cleared 7'3", no lower height was useful. Again, harsh though it was, it was an exact copy of the Olympic Games that year. Athletes must be prepared to succeed *in the meet conditions*, not simply if the conditions are ideal.

We should look at some graphic figures of planning for phases and microcycles. Figure 6.4 gives a one-month phase of four microcycles, showing the

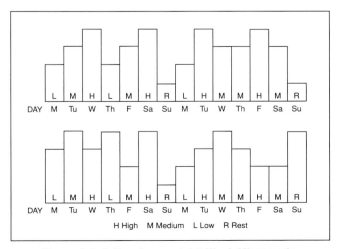

Figure 6.4. A Developmental 4-Week Microcycle

57

relative workload of each day's training during that time. This phase averages two peaks per week, but the loading reaches a peak during the second week, then unloads or "tunes" during the fourth week, peaking for a competition or test effort on the fourth Saturday.

Figure 6.5 shows a hypothetical example of the training plan for a javelin microcycle during the competition phase. It includes a 5-point intensity code for each training session (upper right-hand corner), ranging from 1 to 5 for light to very intense training.

PLANNING THE PEAKING MICROCYCLE

Ben Johnson's schedule for the 1985 World Cup is an example of planning a peak for the year's major meet (Figure 6.8). Peaking is as much a psychological state as a physical one, "with an intense emotional arousal. . . an important attribute of peaking seems to be the athlete's capacity to tolerate various degrees of frustration which occur before, during and after competition."

While peaking is a very complex process, the primary factors that facilitate it are the athlete's:
- High working potential
- Quick rate of recovery
- Near-perfect neuromuscular coordination (technical skill)
- Overcompensation
- Unloading
- Recovery

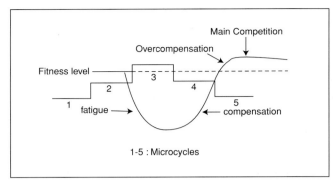

Figure 6.6. Unloading Cycle Before the Main Competition

- Psychological factors (motivation, arousal, and psychological relaxation)
- Nervous cell working capacity (increased only for the last 7-10 days before the main meet).

The peaking process involves a final use of overcompensation in the training schedule. Overcompensation raises the athlete's performance to a higher level as a result of adaptations made during the recovery period after a hard workload is ended (discussed in Chapter 3). Overcompensation usually occurs from 24-36 hours after an optimal training session.

During the competition season, the training plan may alternate maximal- and low-intensity stimuli, resulting in a wave-like pattern of fitness. This approach helps to avoid exhaustion from overtraining while competing.

The correct unloading (tapering) procedure is

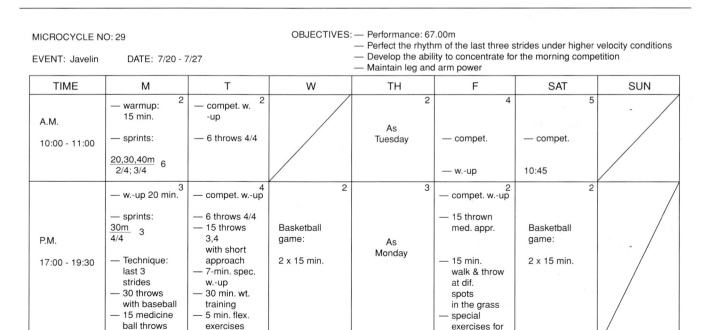

Figure 6.5. A Microcycle with Intensity Coding

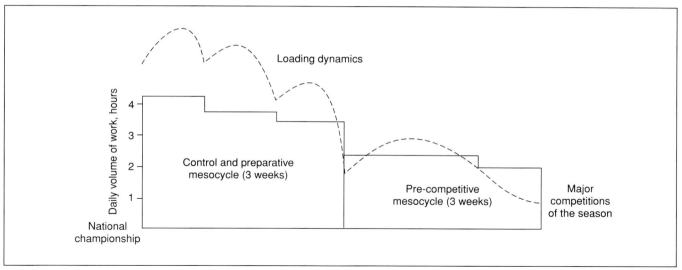

Figure 6.7. Peaking Cycle for an Elite Athlete

critical to performance in the major meet. The training load during the last five microcycles (Fig. 6.6) before the main meet shows the increase of the training load from low to medium to high (causing fatigue), with a drop back to medium and then low loads that results first in compensation, then in overcompensation for the main meet. Figure 6.7 shows another version of the peaking process used by Vladimir Platonov for elite athletes.

Recovery and regeneration are extremely important during the competitive season. Massage and sauna are useful, and proper diet is also a critical factor in the energy level.

The psychological aspects of training are also critical at this time. While the athlete is motivated to perform, reasonable goals and expectations should

be set. Otherwise, unnecessary frustration will become a post-meet factor. The athlete should not be overmotivated or too aroused, as his or her psychological state will already be "on edge." At this time the coach is more useful in the role of relaxing the athlete than in "pumping him up."

We cannot objectively determine when an athlete physically peaks, other than through competition. Soviet research has been based on the relation of the athlete's performance to the marks of the previous year, with a mark within 2% of the athlete's best indicating "high athletic condition" (Zone One), and therefore ready to peak. Of course, this is not very useful with less experienced or younger athletes, who may improve dramatically over their previous year's marks.

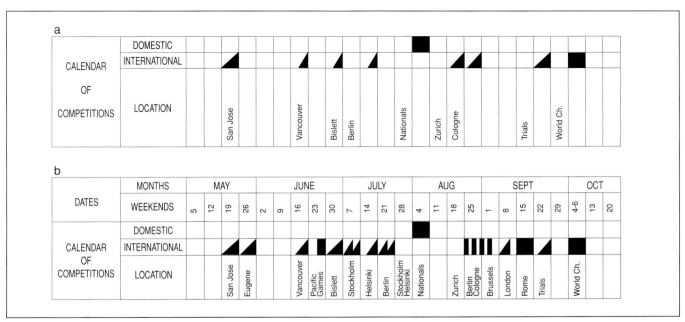

Figure 6.8. Competition Plan for Ben Johnson, 1985

While numerous physiological tests have been used (blood chemistry, for example), perhaps the resting heart rate upon awakening is the most useful for the non-scientist coach. Many subjective measures can be noted, such as the athlete's alertness, optimism, appetite, quality of sleep, enthusiasm for training and competing, and ease of performance.

The length of time that a peak can be maintained depends upon the length and quality of the underlying preparation period, as well as other factors that are very individualistic. The Zone One level (performance within 2% of one's best) may be as long as two or three months, with 3-5 peaks during that time, if the preparation period was long enough and the training process during the competition period is handled properly. The peaking process itself is about 7-10 days in length, after which the performance level falls off.

Maintaining that performance level requires a short phase of regeneration after each peak for a major meet, followed by more training. If those conditions are not met, the peak period will be shortened considerably. The number of competitions is also a factor, as too many competitions will cause a performance plateau, instead of ever-higher marks.

To avoid the onset of fatigue during the competitive season, the training plan should follow this constant pattern:
- Competition
- Regeneration
- Training
- Unloading
- Next competition.

An athlete usually needs 4-6 microcycles to rise from the pre-competition phase to Zone One performance level. Extending the Zone One performances beyond the eighth microcycle of competition (two months) requires careful planning and monitoring of the athlete's training.

Coaches have observed that the appearance of an IAAF "racing circuit" in Europe is very confusing for athletes and their coaches, as it offers too many "important" competitions for the world-class athlete. Coaches and athletes face the question of how many meets they can attend without damaging their chances of an Olympic or World title. The racing plan of Ben Johnson (100 meters) of Canada for 1985 (Fig. 6.8) shows how he and his coach planned his races, compared to the actual races that he ran.

For the question of how many meets an athlete can compete in during a season, the events fall into four groups: the throws, the short sprints and jumps, the long sprints and middle distances, and the long distances and combined events. The stress of competition rises from the first group to the fourth. Recommendations on the number of meets, as well

Table 6.4. Recommended Competitions by Event Groups

Event Group	Time to Overcompensation	Meets per Year
Short sprints	3-5 days	16-20
Long sprints	6-7 days	16-20
Middle distance	6-7 days	10-15
Long distance	2 weeks or more	6-10
Marathon	More than 2 weeks	3-5
50 km walk	More than 2 weeks	3-5
Jumps	3-5 days	16-20
Throws	2-3 days	16-20
Combined events	2 weeks or more	3-5

as the recovery time needed, are in Table 6.4 (see also Table 5.4).

PLANNING THE TRAINING SESSIONS

The training session has three or four primary parts. A three-part session includes the:
- Preparation (usually the warmup)
- Body (content) of the session
- Conclusion (usually the warmdown).

A four-part session adds an introduction before the preparation. The three-part session is used by more advanced athletes. It is the dominant form during the competition period. The four-part version is best for beginners and group sessions, as it allows the goals of the lesson to be explained.

Earlier we outlined Korobov's 4-step progression for the body of the training session, from learning or perfecting technique and/or tactics, to developing speed and/or coordination, then strength work, and finally training for general and specific endurance.

Technique and tactics are practiced first because they require a rested body. If other types of training are performed first, then fatigue will interfere with the learning rate. When perfecting technique that is fatiguing or heavy in its workload (such as in the throwing events or weight lifting), the speed and coordination exercises should be performed before the technique development exercises. When developing maximum speed, the speed training should be performed first, immediately after the warmup.

In learning or perfecting technique, the sequence of learning should be to:
1. Consolidate the skills learned in the last session.
2. Perfect the skills that are most important to the event.
3. Apply the skills under simulated competitive conditions.

The complete training session should not last more than two hours. Younger athletes may improve more rapidly with shorter training sessions.

This time includes the warmup and warmdown, leaving 90 minutes or less for the body of the training session. With less-skilled athletes, the concluding part of the training session may include supplementary conditioning exercises, especially if the entire session is not too demanding and the athletes are not exhausted.

The conclusion or warmdown is often neglected by coaches. It is critical in enhancing the body's recovery. Light running, jogging, and walking help to clear the lactic acid from the muscles, so they will be less tight or sore at the start of the next training session. Light stretching aids the body's recovery from weight training sessions. Every athlete should learn a relaxing warmdown procedure and follow it after every training session. It is even more critical following intensive competition. Even 10 minutes of cooldown activities will be very helpful to the athlete's recovery.

Now that we have examined the basics of periodized training, we will look at how periodization is applied to training in the different individual events.

REFERENCES

1. Yuri Verhoshansky. (1998). Organization of the training process. *New Studies in Athletics* 13(3), 21-32.
2. Vladimir N. Platonov. (1999). The concept of "periodisation of training" and the development of a training theory [abridged translation]. *Leistungssport, 29*(1).
3. Peter Tschiene. (1999). Discussion of "periodisation" comments [abridged translation]. *Leistungssport, 29*(1).
4. Andrew McInnis. (1981). A research review of systematized approaches to planned performance peaking with relation to the sport of track and field. *Track and Field Quarterly Review, 81*(2), 7-12.
5. Manuel Bueno. (1998). Altitude training problems. *Modern Athlete and Coach, 36*(3), 10-14.
6. Anatoliy Bondarchuk. (Summer 1997). The transition period [abstract]. *Track Coach, 140,* 4480.
7. Dietrich Harre, ed. (1982). *Principles of Sports Training: Introduction to the Theory and Methods of Training* (2nd ed., pp. 80-87). Berlin: Sportverlag.
8. N. G. Ozolin. (1971). Athlete's training system for competition. In Dietrich Harre, ed. (1982). *Principles of Sports Training: Introduction to the Theory and Methods of Training* (2nd ed., p. 210). Berlin: Sportverlag.
9. Korobov. In Tudor O. Bompa. (1983). *Theory and Methodology of Training: The Key to Athletic Performance* (pp. 105). Dubuque, IA: Kendall/Hunt.
10. Bompa, pp. 112-131.
11. Tudor O. Bompa. (1987). Peaking for the extended athletics calendar. *New Studies in Athletics, 2*(4), 29-43.
12. V. N. Platonov. (1996). Formation of athletes' preparation within [the] year. *Athletic Asia, 21*(1), 37-74.

OTHER SOURCES

Balyi, Istvan. (1995). Planning, periodisation, integration and implementation of annual training programs. In *Australian Strength and Conditioning Association 1995 National Conference and Trade Show Proceedings* (pp. 40-66). Gold Coast, Australia: Australian Strength and Conditioning Association.

Bartonietz, Klaus, & Bill Larsen. (1997). General and event-specific considerations in peaking for the main competition. *New Studies in Athletics, 12*(2-3), 75-86.

Docherty, David, & Ben Sporer. (2000). A proposed model for examining the interference phenomenon between concurrent aerobic and strength training. *Sports Medicine, 30*(6), 385-394.

Gould, Daniel, et al. (Fall 2000). Positive and negative factors influencing U.S. Olympic athletes and coaches: Nagano Games assessment. *Track Coach, 153,* 4889- 4893.

Lehnert, Alfons. (1997). Short-term preparation for major competitions. In Jess Jarver, ed., *Middle Distances: Contemporary Theory, Technique and Training* (4th ed., pp. 20-24). Mountain View, CA: Tafnews.

Naughton, Geraldine, Nathalie J. Farpour-Lambert, John Carlson, Michelle Bradley & Emmanual Van Praegh. (2000). Physiological issues surrounding the performance of adolescent athletes. *Sports Medicine, 30*(5), 309-325.

Olivier, Norbert, & Marc-Oliver Dillinger. (Summer 1998). Is technical training under fatigued conditions harmful? [abstract]. *Track Coach, 144,* 4611-4612.

Pahlke, Ulrich, & Hans Peters. (1995). Recovery after training loads. In Jess Jarver, ed., *Long Distances: Contemporary Theory, Technique and Training* (3rd ed., pp. 29- 33). Mountain View, CA: Tafnews.

Schexnayder, Irving. (1998). Applied kinesiological concerns for athletes. *Track Coach, 145,* 4621-4626.

Steinhofer, Dieter. (1997). Terminology and differentiation of training methods. Trans. Peter Tschiene. In Jess Jarver, ed., *Middle Distances: Contemporary Theory, Technique and Training* (4th ed., pp. 10-16). Mountain View, CA: Tafnews.

Ungerleider, Steven. (1996). *Mental Training for Peak Performance.* Emmaus, PA: Rodale.

Verhoshansky, Yuri. (1995). Principles of the organization of training for high performance athletes. Trans. Kuulo Kutsar. In Jess Jarver, ed., *Long Distances: Contemporary Theory, Technique and Training* (3rd ed., pp. 11-14). Mountain View, CA: Tafnews.

Verhoshansky, Yuri V. (1996). Speed training for high level athletes. *New Studies in Athletics, 11*(2-3), 39-49.

Vernacchia, Ralph A. (Winter 1997). Psychological perspectives on overtraining. *Track Coach, 138,* 4393-4399, 4420.

Viru, Atko. (1995). Peak performance. In Jess Jarver, ed., *Long Distances: Contemporary Theory, Technique and Training* (3rd ed., pp. 43-46). Mountain View, CA: Tafnews.

Wann, Daniel L., & Brian Church. (Summer 1998). A method for enhancing the psychological skills of track and field athletes. *Track Coach, 144,* 4597-4605.

SOURCES FOR TABLES

6.1 Author
6.2. Objectives of the Phases: Frank W. Dick (1978). *Training Theory* (pp. 60-61). London: British Amateur Athletic Board.
6.3. Suggested Training Ratios for Phases: Dick, p. 62
6.4. Recommended Competitions by Event Groups: Bompa, p. 41

SOURCES FOR FIGURES

6.1. Mid-Season Preparation Phase: Bueno, p. 13
6.2. Varying Load Demand During a Phase: Harre, p. 86
6.3. Intensity Levels in a 2-Peak Microcycle: Bompa (1983), p. 117
6.4. A Developmental 4-Week Microcycle: Bompa (1983), p. 128
6.5. A Microcycle with Intensity Coding: Bompa (1983), p. 120
6.6. Unloading Cycle Before Main Meet: Bompa (1983), p. 34
6.7. Peaking Cycle for an Elite Athlete: Platonov, p. 71.
6.8. Competition Plan for Ben Johnson, 1985: Bompa (1987), p. 40

CHAPTER 7:
Periodized Strength Training

Strength training in the training program includes general strength, related power, and event-specific power. Strength training follows the General Adaptation Syndrome (Fig. 7.1), with three phases of adaptation:

- Alarm: Initial response to stimulus, declining performance
- Resistance: Attempts to adapt to new conditions
- Exhaustion: Unable to adapt further.

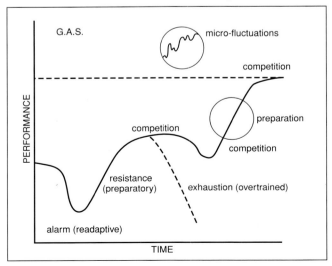

Figure 7.1. General Adaptation Syndrome

The micro-fluctuations represent the changes from workout to workout, or from one microcycle to the next, as is normal in training.

Training effects are very specific. "Speed-strength, strength-endurance and speed-endurance are not derivatives of strength, speed and endurance but are totally independent qualities which should be placed with the latter in a group, [and] which require, adequate and specific to them, means and methods of development." In other words, doing speed training and then endurance training separately will not necessarily improve the speed-endurance component. A specific component requires specific training.

Strength development is more effective when you use a combination of speeds—slow, moderate, and fast. This avoids full adaptation (which leads to a plateau), and you can adjust the speed of movement more closely to the needs of the event.

The coach must consider three factors in planning the strength training program:

- The dominant energy system for the event
- The limiting factors for performance (in strength training terms)
- The objectives of strength training.

As Bompa notes, "The terms 'limiting factors for performance' should mean that if one fails to develop them at the highest level possible, the desired performance will not be achieved."

Rest is a factor in three areas of strength training, with varying needs for rest:

- Intra-training rest: between sets of the same exercise
- Inter-training rest: between exercise sessions
- Pre-performance rest: between the last training session and a maximal test of strength in competition.

The intra-training rest requires 3-4 minutes between multiple sets of five or fewer repetitions. The inter-training need for rest is still unclear, as no definite physiological markers are identified.

For pre-performance rest, an athlete's strength level will remain constant for up to five days, and may peak four days (96 hrs.) after the last training session. In a peaking situation, the athlete would not do any heavy lifting during this period, but doing a small volume of tempo work 24 hours. before competition seems to maintain an optimal level of muscle tone. Keep in mind that recent research suggests that the strength peak is more likely to be 7-10 days after the last strength session, so you need to experiment to determine the most effective approach to peaking for competitions.

Merv Kemp suggests these applications of strength training during the phases of training:

- Phase 1: Buildup: Conditioning and preparation for specific training
- Phase 2: Development of maximum strength
- Phase 3: Explosive power or conversion of strength to specific needs

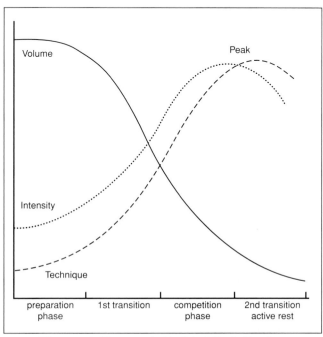

Figure 7.2. Matveyev's Model of Periodization

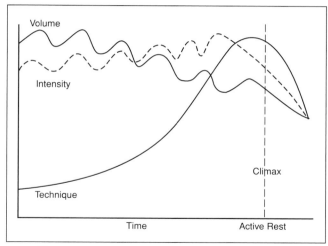

Figure 7.3. Periodization for Advanced Athletes

- Phase 4: Maintenance of strength gains
- Phase 5 (final week): Light, fast rhythm training.

In a peaking situation, the athlete would not do any heavy lifting during this period, but doing a small volume of tempo work 24 hours before competition seems to maintain an optimal level of muscle tone.

Matveyev's model of periodization (Fig. 7.2) represents the theoretical relationship between training volume, training intensity, and the development of technique (and performance) during a macrocycle. It forms the underlying structure for periodized training theory.

However, advanced athletes need a more complex model to produce improvements above an already elite model (Fig. 7.3). Current training theory has moved toward a wave-like model of training volume and intensity, with both at a relatively high level until late in the competition phase. Table 7.1 is an example of a program of strength training for this model.

Although specific results require specific training, at the same time complex training means can act in a "piggy-back" manner to give an improved result when combined. Verhoshansky shows how a

Table 7.1. Periodized Strength Training Model

| | Training Period | | | |
	Phase 1	Phase 2	Phases 3-4	Phases 4-5
Sets	3-5	3-5	3-5	1-3
Repetitions	8-20	2-6	2-3	1-3
Days/Week	3-4	3-5	4-6	1-5
Times/Day	1-3	1-3	1-2	1
Cycle Intensity	2-3:1*	2-4:1	2-3:1	—
Intensity	low	high	high	very high
Volume high	moderate to high		low	very low

* Ratio of heavy training weeks to light training weeks

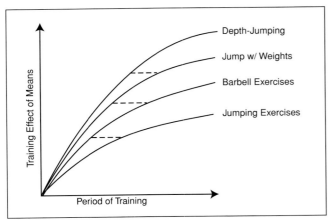

Figure 7.4. Combined Effects Training

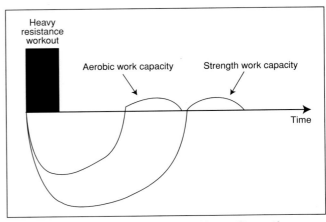

Figure 7.6. Recovery from a Heavy Strength Training Session

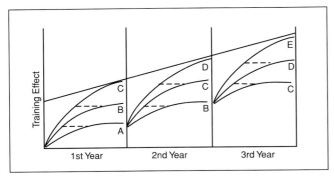

Figure 7.5. Multi-Year Effects

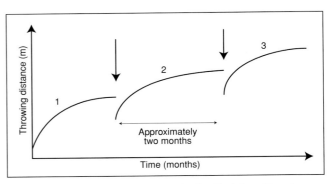

Figure 7.7. Effect of Changes in the Training Structure

Table 7.2. Parameters of Strength

Term	Area of Reference/Testing Means
Absolute Strength	Entire contractile muscle potential: Electro-stimulation / Muscle cross-section
Maximum Strength: Eccentric Isometric Concentric	Personal best within yielding muscle work Personal best within sustaining muscle work Personal best within overcoming muscle work
Strength Deficit	%-difference between eccentric and isometric maximum strength
Voluntary Activation Capacity	Threshold value of mobilization
Speed Strength	$\dfrac{\text{Strength maximum}}{\text{Time required}} \quad \dfrac{\text{(F max)}}{\text{(T max)}}$
Explosive Strength	Maximum rate of strength increase per time
Starting Strength	Strength figure achieved 30m after start
Relative Dynamic Strength Maximum	Peak of strength attained with varying size of load related to isometric strength
Reactive Strength Capacity	Ability to switch from eccentric to concentric contraction per time

Table 7.3. Synopsis of Strength Training Methods

Target	Criterion or Selection	Method	Type or Action
Cross-Section	Slight strength deficit (5-10%)	Bodybuilding methods (modified)/truncated pyramid/Load: 70-85%	Concentric Isokinetic
Neuronal Activation	Large strength deficit	Maximum use of strength/ Load: 90-100%	Concentric Eccentric
Reactive Strength Capacity	Long duration of support/ slight difference active: reactive/EMG-assessment	Plyometry/ Beat method/ "Multi-jumps"	Combined
Explosive Strength Starting Strength	Slight strength gradient with high max. strength	Maximum use of strength/ Against high loads (>90%) Against medium loads (30-60%) with time check!	Concentric Eccentric Explosive-Ballistic
Intermuscular Coordination	Technique deficits/ slight special strength	Special Strength Training (Analytical/Synthetic/Variable)	Congruent with target discipline

sequence of exercises, properly arranged, will yield a higher combined training effect than a single type of exercise, both during a single period of training (Fig. 7.4) and over a period of years (Fig. 7.5).

A heavy strength-training session requires less recovery for the aerobic work capacity than for the strength work capacity (Fig. 7.6). A change in the basic complex of exercises, such as from one training phase to another, will cause an initial drop in performance, but it will lead to higher performance

Table 7.4. Power Development Training Proportions

Phase	Emphasis	Strength	Velocity	Skill
Preparation I	General	100%	10%	5%
Pre-Competition I	Related	50%	50%	50%
Competition I	Specific	25%	75%	75%
Pre-Competition II	Related	50%	50%	50%
Competition II	Specific	25%	75%	75%

Note: As Figure 6.8 shows, the training emphases will overlap during different phases of the year.

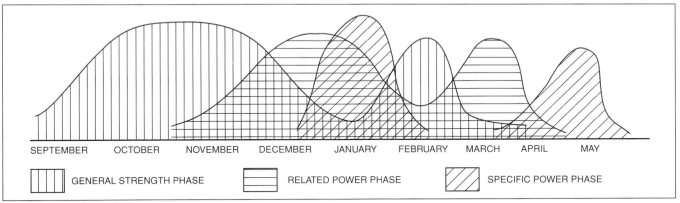

SEPTEMBER OCTOBER NOVEMBER DECEMBER JANUARY FEBRUARY MARCH APRIL MAY

| | GENERAL STRENGTH PHASE | | RELATED POWER PHASE | | SPECIFIC POWER PHASE |

Figure 7.8. Double-Periodized Power Program

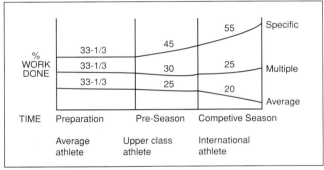

Figure 7.9. Power Training Proportions

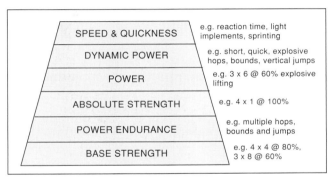

Figure 7.10. Pyramid of Power Training

levels as the athlete progresses (Fig. 7.7). Table 7.2 defines the different types or aspects of strength that the coach may consider in planning the training program, while Table 7.3 is a synopsis of strength training methods, both by Günter Tidow.

An example of a program of power development for a double-periodized year is shown in Figure 7.8. One suggestion for the training proportions is shown in Table 7.4 for a double-periodized training year, compared to Figure 7.9's plan for athletes at different competitive levels.

Power training is illustrated by the "pyramid of power training" (Fig. 7.10). Training should progress from developing the traits at the bottom of the pyramid, rising upward toward the top as training progresses. The relative volume and intensity follow the curves shown in earlier periodization figures, with volume peaking in the middle of the

Table 7.5. Modified Zatsiorsky Table

Repetitions	Average Effort Level	Elite Effort Level
1	100%	100%
2-3	95%	97%
4	90%	95%
5	85%	90%
6	80%	85%
7	75%	80%
8	70%	77%
9	65%	75%
10	60%	70%

preparation period, then falling to a low level during the competition period, while the intensity of training rises until almost the end of the competition period. Figure 7.11 shows another plan for training emphases during a strength training macrocycle.

The intensity of the effort is a major concern in planning strength training. Table 7.5 shows the relationship between the number of repetitions of a resistance exercise and the intensity of the effort for different percentages of the athlete's 1RM (one rep maximum). George Dunn's revision is designed for the more advanced athlete. Tables 7.6 through 7.8 show examples of maximal, submaximal, and mixed strength training methods.

For success at the highest levels, the coach and athlete must understand the complexities of strength and power and how they are developed. Excellent recent books on strength training include major works by Vladimir Zatsiorsky and Tudor Bompa. Coaches might note Zatsiorsky's comment

	PREPARATION PERIOD			COMPETITION PERIOD	ACTIVE REST
	PHASE I	PHASE II	PHASE III		
General Conditioning Strength Endurance	XXX	XX	X	X	X
Absolute Strength	XX	XXX	X	X	
Power	X	XX	XXX	XX	
Speed/Quickness	X	XX	XXX	XXX	
Maintenance				XXX	XX
Lifting Technique	XXX	XX	XX	XXX	
XXX High Emphasis XX Medium Emphasis X Low Emphasis					

Figure 7.11. Emphases in Strength Training Macrocycle

Table 7.6. Maximal Strength Training Methods

	Near-Maximal Contractions	Maximal Concentric Contractions	Maximal Isometric Contractions	Maximal Eccentric Contractions	Concentric-Eccentric Maximal
Form of work: Concentric	X	X			X
Isometric			X		
Eccentric				X	X
Force development Explosive	X	X	X	X	X
Continuous					
Intensity Load	90 95 97 100%	100%	100%	ca. 150%	70-90%
Repetitions	3 1 1 1+1	1	2	5	6-8
Sets	1 2 3 4+5	5	5	3	3-5
Length of contraction			5-6 sec.		
Rest Interval	3-5 min.	3-5 min.	3 min.	3 min.	5 min.

When maximal strength is sought, optimal increases in strength occur with loads permitting no more than 8 repetitions.

Table 7.7. Submaximal Strength Training Methods

	Standard Method I (constant load)	Standard Method II (progressively increasing load)	Bodybuilding Method I (extensive)	Bodybuilding Method II (intensive)	Isokinetic Method	Isometric Method
Form of work: Concentric Isometric Eccentric	X	X	X	X	X X	 X
Force development Explosive Continuous	X	X	X	X	X	X
Intensity Load	80%	70 80 85 90%	60-70%	80-95%	e.g. 70%	100%
Repetitions	8-10	12 10 7 5	15-20	8-5	15	10
Sets	3-5	1. 2. 3. 4.	3-5	3-5	3	3-5
Length of contraction						10-12s
Rest Interval	3-5 min.	5 min.	2-3 min.	3-5 min.	3 min.	3 min.

At loads of 50-70% of the maximal strength, calling for 11-30 R.M., the resulting fatigue levels cause supercompensation of glycogen stores to occur, producing increases in strength endurance. If the loads are heavier (75-80%), neo-synthesis of the contractile proteins structures occurs, therefore increasing the muscle's cross-section, maximal strength, creatine phosphate content. For optimal cross-section increases, one must work at both intensity zones, in different microcycles.

Table 7.8. Mixed Strength Training Methods

	Speed-strength Method	Pyramid Method
Form of work: Concentric Isometric Eccentric	X	X
Force development: Explosive Continuous	X	X
Intensity of Load	30-50%	80 85 90 95 100 95 85
Repetitions	7	7 5 3 2 1 3 7
Sets	5	1. 2. 3. 4. 5. 6. 7.
Length of contraction		
Rest Interval	3-5 min.	3-5 min.

Pyramid training, by its unique variability quality, can be adapted to the needs and objectives of all (circumstantial) varieties of strength training.

on the use of exercise machines: "The important limitation of many strength training machines is that they are designed to *train muscles*, not movement. Because of this, they are not the most important training tool for athletes."

REFERENCES

1. Yuri I. Verhoshansky. (1986). *Fundamentals of Special Strength-Training in Sport* [1977 ed.]. Trans. Andrew Charniga, Jr. Livonia, MI: Sportivny Press.
2. Michael Yessis. (1995). The speed principle in weight training. *Track Coach, 131,* 4194.
3. Tudor O. Bompa. (1993). *Periodization of Strength: The New Wave in Strength Training* (p. 105). Toronto: Veritas.
4. Lawrence W. Weiss. (1993). Contribution of rest to strength development. *Track Technique, 122,* 3904.
5. Merv Kemp. (1993). Periodization of strength training. *Track Technique, 123,* 3936-3937.
6. Schlumberger, Andreas, & Dietmar Schmidtbleicher. (Fall 2000). Temporally delayed effects of strength training [abstract]. *Track Coach, 153,* 4899.
7. Mike Woicik. (1982). Power development: Throwers. *Track and Field Quarterly Review, 82*(1), 48-49.
8. Toni Tenisci & Ralf Ubel. (1985). A Soviet approach to weight training. In Jess Jarver (Ed.), *The Throws* (3rd ed., pp. 32-37). Mountain View, CA: Tafnews.
9. Bob Myers. (1981). A year-round training program for javelin throwers. *Track and Field Quarterly Review, 81*(1), 36-36.
10. Vladimir M. Zatsiorsky. (1995). *Science and Practice of Strength Training* (p. 80). Champaign, IL: Human Kinetics.

OTHER SOURCES OF PERIODIZED STRENGTH TRAINING

Bondarchuk, Anatoliy. (1988). Constructing a training system, Parts 1 and 2. *Track Technique, 102,* 3254-3259, 3268; *103,* 3286-3288.
Bosco, Carmelo, Marco Cardinale, Olga Tsarpela & Elio Locatelli. (1999). New trends in training science: The use of vibrations for enhancing performance. *New Studies in Athletics, 14*(4), 55-62.
Brown, C. Harmon. (Fall 1996). Strength training for women:

Some hormonal considerations. *Track Coach, 137*, 4367-4368, 4370.

Chu, Donald A. (1996). *Explosive Power and Strength: Complex Training for Maximum Results.* Champaign, IL: Human Kinetics.

Donati, Alessandro. (1996). The association between the development of strength and speed. *New Studies in Athletics, 11*(2-3), 51-58.

Dunn, George D., Jr., & Kevin McGill. (1994). Training for throwers. In *The Throws Manual* (2nd ed., pp. 133-154). Mountain View, CA: Tafnews.

Fleck, Steven J., & William J. Kraemer. (1997). *Designing Resistance Training Programs* (2nd ed.). Champaign, IL: Human Kinetics.

Fleck, Steven J. (1999). Periodized strength training: A critical review. *Journal of Strength and Conditioning Research, 13*(1), 82-89.

Fleck, Steven J., & William J. Kraemer. (1996). *Periodization Breakthrough!* New York: Advanced Research Press.

Giroux, Jim. (2000). Weight training: Simplifying yearly cycles and exercises for track and field. *Track and Field Coaches Review, 73*(1), 24-26.

Herrick, Andrew B., & William J. Stone. (1996). The effects of periodization versus progressive resistance exercise on upper and lower body strength in women. *Journal of Strength and Conditioning Research, 10*(2), 72-76.

Kraemer, William J. (1997). A series of studies—The physiological basis for strength training in American football: Fact over philosophy. *Journal of Strength and Conditioning Research, 11*(3), 131-142.

O'Shea, Patrick. (1996). *Quantum Strength and Power Training: Gaining the Winning Edge: Textbook of Applied Athletic Strength Training and Conditioning for Peak Performance, ages 16-80.* Corvallis, OR: Patrick's Books.

Paish, Wilf. (1992). The development of strength and power. *New Studies in Athletics, 7*(2), 45-54.

Poletaev, Petr, & Vincente Ortiz Cervera. (1995). The Russian approach to planning a weightlifting program. *Strength and Conditioning, 17*(1), 20-26.

Siff, Mel, & Yuri V. Verhoshansky. (1999). *Supertraining.* (4th ed.). Denver, CO: Supertraining International.

Stone, M. H., H. S. O'Bryant, B. K. Schilling, R. L. Johnson, K. C. Pierce, G. Greg Haff, A. J. Koch, & Meg Stone. (1999). Periodization: Effects of manipulating volume and intensity, Part I. *Strength and Conditioning Journal, 21*(2), 56-62; Part II. *SCJ, 21*(3), 54-60.

Tan, Benedict. (1999). Manipulating resistance training program variables to optimize strength in men: A review. *Journal of Strength and Conditioning Research, 13*(3), 289-304.

Tidow, Günter. (1995). Optimization of strength training [abstract]. *New Studies in Athletics, 10*(2), 98-100.

Verhoshansky, Yuri. (Spring 1998). Concentrated blocks in strength development [abstract]. *Track Coach, 143*, 4577-4578.

Young, Warren. (1995). Laboratory strength assessment of athletes. *New Studies in Athletics, 10*(1), 89-96.

SOURCES FOR TABLES

7.1. Periodized Strength Training Model: Stone, p. 29
7.2. Parameters of Strength: Tidow, 96
7.3. Synopsis of Strength Training Methods: Tidow, 106
7.4. Power Development Training Proportions: Woicik, 49
7.5. Modified Zatsiorsky Table: Dunn & McGill, 140
7.6. Maximal Strength Training Methods: Dietmar Schmidtbleicher. (1987). Applying the theory of strength development. *Track and Field Quarterly Review, 87*(3), 40.
7.7. Submaximal Strength Training Methods: Schmidtbleicher, 40
7.8. Mixed Strength Training Methods: Schmidtbleicher, 41

CHAI VON DER LAAGE/THE SPORTING IMAGE

Shot Putter Adam Nelson

SOURCES FOR FIGURES

7.1. General Adaptation Syndrome: Stone, p. 25
7.2. Matveyev's Model of Periodization: Stone, p. 25
7.3. Periodization for Advanced Athletes: Stone, p. 25
7.4. Combined Effects Training: Verhoshansky, p. 195
7.5. Multi-Year Effects of Training: Verhoshansky, p. 195
7.6. Recovery from a Heavy Strength Training Session: Zatsiorsky, p. 112
7.7. Effect of Changes in the Training Structure: Zatsiorsky, p. 130
7.8. Double Periodized Power Program: Woicik, 49
7.9. Power Training Proportions: Tenesci & Ubel, p. 35
7.10. Pyramid of Power Training: Myers, 36
7.11. Emphases in Strength Macrocycle:

PART 2:
Periodization And The American Sport Seasons

Now we will look at how periodization can be applied in the American track community. The next chapter will discuss the general aspects of a periodized American system, then a chapter will examine training younger athletes, then the later chapters will discuss specific groups of events.

Tisha Waller

CHAPTER 8:
Applying Periodization To The American Program

A major problem in planning training for American athletes is the indoor track season, which crowds into the outdoor season in many areas of the country. Planning a long indoor season, with a peak during that time, often makes a quality preparation for the outdoor season difficult to achieve. Regardless of the year's plan, the athlete must get enough rest and recovery from training and competition.

We will examine the periodized year according to the number of peaks planned for the year. Most American athletes are in either a traditional school year (ending in late May or early June) or the more recent early semester schedule (ending in mid-

to late April). Figures illustrate the rough changes in volume and intensity for each peaking pattern, while tables give the order of the periods and phases for each year. The coach or athlete can easily modify the appropriate plan to fit their own athletic calendar. Table 8.1 gives an example of the peaking dates for most American athletes.

OUTDOOR TRACK PEAK ONLY

For many athletes, both in high school and in colleges in warmer states, only one annual season exists: outdoor track. This allows a well-designed

Table 8.1. Dates for Peaking Cycles

Level	Age	Meet	Cross Country	Track and Field Indoors	Outdoors
Middle School	12-15	City	Oct.	—	April-May
High School	14-18	State	Nov.	March	Late May
College	18-22				
Early Semester		Conference	Nov.	Feb.	Mid-April
Quarter System		Conference	Nov.	Feb.	May
Elite		NCAA	Nov.	March	Early June
Open	20+				
Regional			Nov.	Feb.	May
National		USATF	Nov.	Feb.	Late June
International		World Meet	March	March	Sept.

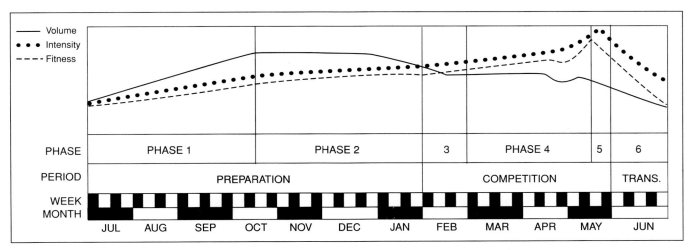

Figure 8.1. Phases for Regular School Year with Outdoor Peak

Table 8.2. Phases for Regular School Year with Outdoor Peak

Period	Phase	Phase Type	Length
Preparation	1	General preparation	15 weeks
	2	Specific preparation	15 weeks
Competition	3	Pre-competition	4 weeks
	4	General competition	11 weeks
	5	Special competition	2 weeks
Transition	6	Transition or recovery	5 weeks

program of a long, careful rise toward the year's goal. Ideally, a training program covers a calendar year. However, younger athletes are not put at a disadvantage if their program does not begin during the summer. They will still have from four to six months to prepare for competition.

Figure 8.1 shows an example of the varying emphases on training volume, intensity, and fitness (the athlete's performance level). This plan is for a school or college athlete on the traditional year, with a peak in late May (Table 8.2). A college athlete under the early-semester plan, with one peak (Fig. 8.2), will change the times of the periods and phases

to peak around mid-April (Table 8.3).

Ideally, the general preparation phase should take place during the summer, or it can be tele-

Table 8.3. Phases for Early School Year with Outdoor Peak

Period	Phase	Phase Type	Length
Preparation	1	General preparation	22 weeks
	2	Specific preparation	15 weeks
Competition	3	Pre-competition	4 weeks
	4	General competition	5 weeks
	5	Special competition	2 weeks
Transition	6	Transition or recovery	4 weeks

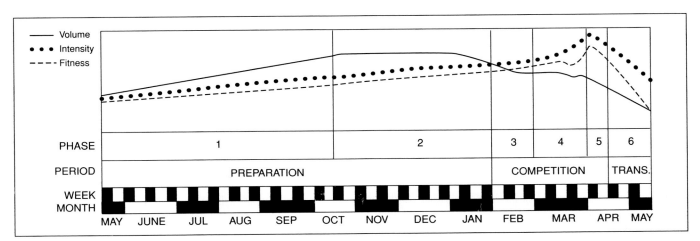

Figure 8.2. Phases for Early School Year with Outdoor Peak

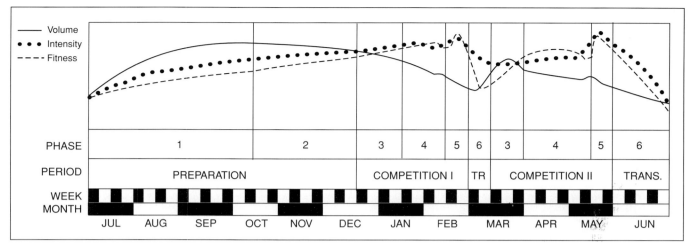

Figure 8.3. Phases for Regular School Year with Indoor/Outdoor Peaks

Table 8.4. Phases for Regular School Year with Indoor/Outdoor Peaks

Period	Phase	Phase Type	Length
Preparation	1	General preparation	15 weeks
	2	Specific preparation	9 weeks
Competitive (Indoors)	3	Pre-competition	4 weeks
	4	General competition	4 weeks
	5	Special competition	2 weeks
Transition	6	Transition or recovery	2 weeks
Competitive (Outdoors)	3	Pre-competition	3 weeks
	4	General competition	6 weeks
	5	Special competition	2 weeks
Transition	6	Transition or recovery	5 weeks

scoped into the first 6-8 weeks of the school year. It then blends into the special conditioning phase. Special conditioning includes the highest training loads of the year, as the training intensity gradually rises. For the peaking phase, the intensity will drop briefly, then rise sharply until just before the peak meet, when a complete unloading occurs. At that time, the athlete should be as rested and sharp as possible.

INDOOR AND OUTDOOR TRACK PEAKS

If possible, the athlete with two peaks in track should treat the season like the European elite season, as a split season with a break in the middle. In this case, the summer training becomes more critical. The longer that the preparation period lasts, the longer the competition period can last without the performances falling off.

Figure 8.3 shows the varying emphases for the traditional school year, with the outdoor peak in late May (Table 8.4). The month of March should be used as an unloading phase, with major decreases in both the volume and intensity of training. Imme-

diately after the peak indoor meet, the athlete should use at least a week for unstructured activities. This gives a mental break from the stresses of training and competition. The rest of the month should mix regular training with back-to-the-basics work, but the loading should be reduced and no testing should be included.

Figure 8.4 shows the emphases for athletes on the early semester plan, peaking in mid-April (Table 8.5). Summer and early fall training are even more important in this case, because a true recovery break between the seasons is almost impossible. Instead, the athlete should reduce the loading and structure of training for two weeks after the peak indoor meet. The training volume will rise during this phase, but only in comparison to the levels while unloading for the indoor peak. The volume will fall over the last three weeks of the outdoor season. The peaking methods are similar to those for the three-season distance runner.

DISTANCE RUNNING PEAKS

Two-Peak Year (Cross Country and Outdoor Track)

Table 8.5. Phases for Early School Year with Indoor/Outdoor Peaks

Period	Phase	Phase Type	Length
Preparation	1	General preparation	15 weeks
	2	Specific preparation	13 weeks
Competition (Indoors)	3	Pre-competition	5 weeks
	4	General competition	6 weeks
	5	Special competition	2 weeks
Competition (Outdoors)	3	Pre-competition	2 weeks
	4	General competition	3 weeks
	5	Special competition	2 weeks
Transition	6	Transition or recovery	4 weeks

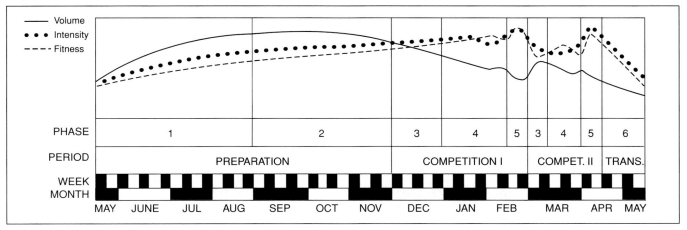

Figure 8.4. Phases for Early School Year with Indoor/Outdoor Peaks

The distance runner who peaks for cross country and outdoor track has an unusual year. Its structure allows two good peaks, but the track season allows a much better preparation for the peak (Fig. 8.5). The cross country peak comes after only 4-1/2 months, while the track peak follows by almost seven months (Table 8.6).

The early-semester athlete will have a more balanced training year (Fig. 8.6). In fact, the runner may be able to develop a better racing base during the winter than in preparation for cross country (Table 8.7).

Time is not the only factor in the preparation periods. Weather becomes a major factor. A large area of the United States has hot and/or humid weather throughout the summer. This creates very difficult training conditions for distance runners. While they can train at the dawn and dusk hours, high-mileage programs may be dangerous. During the winter, conditions in southern regions are more conducive to base training. However, the northern states must often confront harsh situations, such as extreme cold and poor footing, at that time.

Table 8.6. Phases for Regular School Year with Cross Country/Outdoor Peaks

Period	Phase	Phase Type	Length
Preparation	1	General preparation	6 weeks
	2	Specific preparation	4 weeks
Competition	3	Pre-competition	3 weeks
	4	General competition	4 weeks
	5	Special competition	2 weeks
Transition	6	Transition or recovery	2 weeks
Preparation	1	General preparation	5 weeks
	2	Specific preparation	8 weeks
Competition	3	Pre-competition	3 weeks
(Outdoors)	4	General competition	8 weeks
	5	Special competition	2 weeks
Transition	6	Transition or recovery	5 weeks

The weather limitations that arise from the large size of the United States may have some unexpected solutions. Many health clubs have appeared with air-conditioned training areas. Distance runners may be able to do more training on treadmills, which allows temperature and humidity controls, as well as heart-rate monitoring for more precise

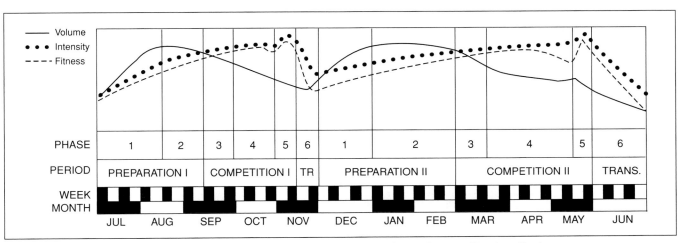

Figure 8.5. Phases for Regular School Year with Cross Country/Outdoor Peaks

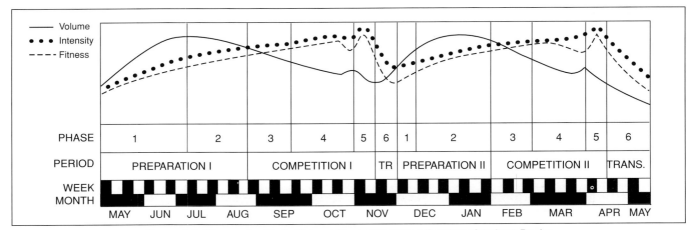

Figure 8.6. Phases for Early School Year with Cross Country/Outdoor Peaks

Table 8.7. Phases for Early School Year with Cross Country/Outdoor Peaks

Period	Phase	Phase Type	Length
Preparation	1	General preparation	8 weeks
	2	Specific preparation	6 weeks
Competition	3	Pre-competition	4 weeks
	4	General competition	6 weeks
	5	Special competition	2 weeks
Transition	6	Transition or recovery	2 weeks
Preparation	1	General preparation	2 weeks
	2	Specific preparation	7 weeks
Competition	3	Pre-competition	4 weeks
(Outdoors)	4	General competition	5 weeks
	5	Special competition	2 weeks
Transition	6	Transition or recovery	4 weeks

training efforts. Also, running with flotation jackets in swimming pools (not touching the bottom) provides another training variation, useful also in some cases of leg stress. If these options are used during racing seasons, some intense workouts should be performed outdoors under the conditions of racing weather for acclimation.

THREE-PEAK YEAR

The three-peak year creates the greatest problem for American athletes because distance events ideally need more preparation than is possible in a three-peak year. Most of the school year is spent in racing and recovering from races, rather than training. The summer training program becomes even more important, because at least 60% of the year's base training must occur then. Summer training should begin no more than six weeks after the peak outdoor track meet.

The traditional school year (Fig. 8.7) allows two recovery phases (Table 8.8). A major recovery is possible after cross country, eased by the Thanksgiving season. Athletes should enjoy alternate activities, mixed with light, recreational running, from the peak cross country meet until after Thanksgiving.

The month of December can be used as a short return to base training, with care that the volume is not increased too rapidly. The month of March serves the same function between the indoor and outdoor

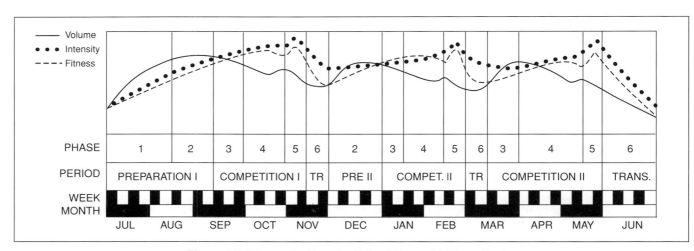

Figure 8.7. Phases for Regular School Year with Three Peaks

Table 8.8. Phases for Regular School Year with Three Peaks

Period	Phase	Phase Type	Length
Preparation	1	General preparation	6 weeks
	2	Specific preparation	4 weeks
Competition	3	Pre-competition	3 weeks
	4	General competition	4 weeks
	5	Special competition	2 weeks
Transition	6	Transition or recovery	2 weeks
	2	Specific preparation	5 weeks
Competition (Indoors)	3	Pre-competition	2 weeks
	4	General competition	4 weeks
	5	Special competition	2 weeks
Transition	6	Transition or recovery	2 weeks
Competition (Outdoors)	3	Pre-competition	3 weeks
	4	General competition	6 weeks
	5	Special competition	2 weeks
Transition	6	Transition or recovery	5 weeks

Table 8.9. Phases for Early School Year with Three Peaks

Period	Phase	Phase Type	Length
Preparation	1	General preparation	8 weeks
	2	Specific preparation	6 weeks
Competition	3	Pre-competition	4 weeks
	4	General competition	6 weeks
	5	Special competition	2 weeks
Transition	6	Transition or recovery	2 weeks
	2	Specific preparation	2 weeks
Competition (Indoors)	3	Pre-competition	3 weeks
	4	General competition	6 weeks
	5	Special competition	2 weeks
Competition (Outdoors)	3	Pre-competition	2 weeks
	4	General competition	3 weeks
	5	Special competition	2 weeks
Transition	6	Transition or recovery	4 weeks

periods.

For the athlete in an early-semester program, the summer training period is an absolute must (Fig. 8.8). It should begin about one month after the outdoor track peak meet (Table 8.9). It is most critical because of the lack of a break between indoor and outdoor track. Unless the runner has a strong summer and early fall base, the school year offers almost no chance to develop one, unless a racing season is skipped.

The athlete should unload as completely as possible after the peak cross country meet, then return to base preparation immediately after Thanksgiving. The training volume should not begin to fall until three weeks before the peak indoor meet. The most valuable approach is to use indoor track only as a "mini-peak," dropping the volume of training only for the last week or so before the peak meet, then returning to the earlier level within two weeks after the indoor peak. This brief unloading allows a minor peak performance, but it is only a brief inter-ruption to the training progress toward the more important outdoor track peak.

THE INTERNATIONAL PEAK

The peaking pattern for the international competitor allows an almost ideal two-peak year, as the major world meets are about six months apart (Fig. 8.9). A long distance runner can peak for the international cross country race in mid-March, while the other athletes will aim for the National or World Indoor Championship Meet at the same time. The major world outdoor meet of each year is usually in late August or early to mid-September. Planning a periodized schedule to meet these demands presents few problems.

The major difficulty for planned training was eased when the United States stopped using the USTAF Championships in November to select its cross country team for the World Meet in March. For international-level track athletes, the Outdoor USATF in June may be used as an early-season meet, then they will go to the European circuit. The most

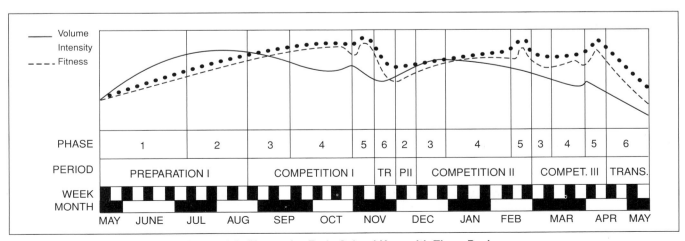

Figure 8.8. Phases for Early School Year with Three Peaks

75

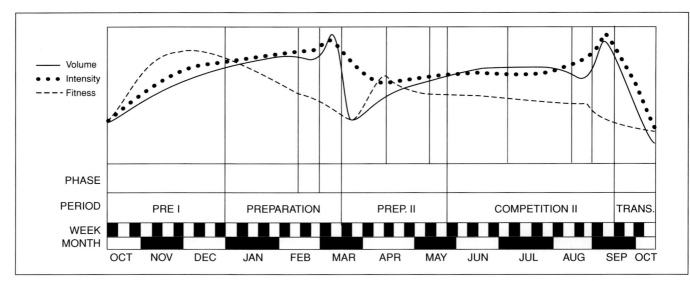

Figure 8.9. Peaking Pattern for the International Competitor

common competition pattern is a split season, with 3-4 weeks of meets, an intermediate recovery and training phase of up to a month, then a final 3-5 weeks of meets, leading to the year's peak performance.

A major problem for American Olympians is the time between peaking for the U.S. Olympic Trials and the ultimate peak for the Olympic Games. In many nations the team is pre-selected without a Trials meet, so the athlete can concentrate on building toward an Olympic peak. In other nations several different meets are used as "Selection Meets," with the athletes required to demonstrate their level of fitness. This allows them more than one opportunity to catch the selectors' eyes.

The catch for American athletes is that the United States is a huge nation with many potential Olympic-level athletes in many events. In a small nation, only a few athletes will be legitimate Olympic-level athletes, making the selectors' task far simpler. In 1987 the slowest of the four regional 4x400 relay teams at the U.S. Olympic Festival ran 3:00.92. Only six national teams ran faster than that #4 American team, whose members raced together only once. No selection system can deal fairly with that number of legitimate Olympic candidates.

Thus, we have the U.S. Olympic Trials every four years: one shot for all the marbles. Even with its inherent flaws, it is still the fairest system for our country. No athlete can afford to coast through the meet, assuming that making the team is a given. Every Olympic Trials has numerous surprise upsets.

The best way to deal with the Olympic Trials is to attain a true peak, then go to Phase 6 for 1-2 weeks afterward. Then a buildup should begin with two weeks of pre-competition, followed by Phases 4

and 5 leading to the Games. The athlete must remember that if you do not make the team, that higher, later peak is largely unattainable.

Perhaps the next greatest problem, after the closeness of the two peaks, is over-competing during the interim. While tune-up meets during that time may be useful for athletes who began competing late in the year, most Olympians have already competed in several dozen indoor and outdoor meets by the time of the Olympic Trials. Such meets should be optional, with the only limiting factor being a restriction on the number of meets permitted.

CHANGING APPROACHES TO PERIODIZATION

Periodization is not an inflexible approach to training. More advanced training patterns use more frequent variations in the volume and intensity of training, while keeping the overall training level relatively high until unloading for the peak meet (Fig. 8.10). This pattern is more useful for elite competitors than for average athletes, as it addresses the need for more intensified challenges if a high-level athlete wants to continue to improve.

We will look at more specific training and peaking cycles in later chapters. However, even though the Russians have experimented with this type of training for 25 years, they have warned their own coaches against applying the research in too rigid a manner. It is safer to accept a slightly slower progression in performance than to try to force the athlete to progress too quickly.

A physical breakdown from overtraining can cost the athlete a season, and it may even result in one or more years of lost progress. For younger athletes (into their early 20s) mononucleosis some-

76

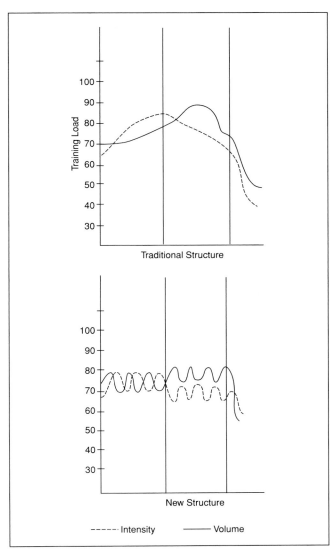

100
90
80
70
60
50
40
30

Training Load

Traditional Structure

100
90
80
70
60
50
40
30

New Structure

----- Intensity   —— Volume

Figure 8.10. Training During a Macrocycle

times occurs during times of over-stress (too much training, combined with too many other activities or needs). It most often appears in the first two years of college, as young athletes make the transition to harder training, along with their new academic demands, increased personal responsibilities, and wider social opportunities. More rest must be built into the system for younger athletes.

ADAPTING TRAINING FOR YOUNG ATHLETES

One way to explain how to adapt the training process to the needs of different athletes is by examining the factors in planning periodized training in this all-too-flexible world of sport.

1. *Every person is an individual.* This means that no two people react in the same manner or degree to a given stimulus. Because people react differently, we must plan different training patterns for differ-

ent athletes. For example, one athlete may be able to recover from a hard workout in 24 hours, while another athlete may need 48 or more hours to recover from the same workout. As a result, each athlete must follow a different training program.

2. *Young athletes progress at irregular, unpredictable rates.* This is due as much to maturation factors as it is to training factors. As an example, less experienced athletes may make unanticipated progress. A 15-year-old may cut 20 seconds from his 1500m PR in only a month. This does not happen with older athletes, because they have developed closer to their performance potential.

We must remember that the human body is not a machine. It will not improve at a constant rate. It must be monitored on a regular basis, or we will not be able to determine the best course of training.

3. *Detailed plans should be based on the athlete's present fitness.* Many athletes have highly variable levels of health and fitness during the training year. Because of changes in those levels, the coach must be flexible in applying the training plan.

4. *The athlete's internal training factors may change.* An injury (physical or psychological) may require modification of the training plan to permit the athlete to recover and return to training and racing. The coach may have to get the athlete through the difficult times without causing injury. While some coaches may try to skip past unperformed training (moving on to the next level of training), this practice is ultimately risky. Each step of the training process builds on the foundation of the previous training steps. By assuming that the athlete must improve at a steady rate regardless of his or her current fitness, the coach creates the risk of future failure or injury.

This factor is a critical one. Too many athletes and coaches do not pay sufficient attention to the athlete's internal state on a daily basis. The coach and athlete must monitor those factors daily, as they are the early warning indicators of future injuries.

5. *External training factors may interfere with the training plan.* The coach may encounter a long cycle of bad weather that interferes with training and forces changes in the plan. For example, in very windy weather I will change from an interval workout on the track to fartlek workouts elsewhere. While my athletes will lose the pacing skills aspect of the session, pacing cannot be learned under very windy conditions. Thus I will deal with other necessary aspects of the training process instead.

6. *We have less control over the outside lives of athletes in a free world.* The original applications of periodization took place in nations where the athletes had severely limited personal freedom. We coaches cannot control all training factors. There are many external and internal factors in an athlete's

life, many of which were cited by the Finns in predicting the potential adult performance of junior middle distance runners (see P. Luhtanen, et al.).

7. *The school year pattern may not conform to the traditional patterns of sports seasons.* This matter becomes critical when the primary route for young athletes is through school teams. It can also affect young adult athletes, such as those in the U.S.A. Many American universities follow an early semester plan, with classes completed by late April. As a result, the athlete's primary training is under poor weather conditions, followed by a short racing season of about six weeks in unstable weather. The conference meet may be between 6 weeks and 2 months before the national championships. In most of these cases, there is no school support for the athletes after May 1st. This is a serious handicap to athletes of national potential, as they may lose many training and racing opportunities that they need to rise to higher levels of performance.

8. *The training plan has ethical implications.* We should not overlook the fact that any training program exists in a philosophical context. Each society and each individual has some belief about what behavior is proper. This value structure is extended to include the sport setting. All people set some limits on proper sport training behaviors.

Another concern about training is how to deal with a high school season with many meets in a short period of time: What do you do when you have several meets each week? The first concern is to see that your athletes are well-rested. The three cornerstones of training (with another added element that is critical to success as an athlete in any sport:) are:

1. Moderation
2. Consistency
3. Rest
4. Focus.

We often overlook the importance of focus. Young athletes must be taught how to train toward a long-term goal. They must learn how to put their other activities into perspective, so that all of life's other events and options do not prevent them from meeting their serious goals—athletic, academic, whatever they may be.

This is where teaching the use of a training diary can be valuable. This is when young athletes learn the importance of quality training, the need for intensity and specificity of training, rather than low-quality, high-quantity training.

Coaches must focus on the positive with young athletes. This does not mean that criticism is a no-no. It means that the most-used feedback should be positive. With positive feedback, young athletes develop confidence and the belief that success is attainable.

An athlete should have a competition or training goal for every meet. However, this does not mean a goal of setting a PR, or having their best performance of the season. Those extra meets in a week can be great opportunities for young athletes to learn. The goal may be to try a different racing tactic— or to experiment with a variation in technique— or to try a different event, to assess potential, to give specific supplementary training (speed or endurance), or simply as a psychological break for the athlete.

It is too easy to overwork young athletes, because they will overdo their efforts out of enthusiasm. All meets or events are not equally important. Every athlete needs breaks or "down" meets in a heavy competition schedule. Athletes who compete too often, and who are constantly running multiple events in each meet, are less likely to develop to their highest potential in their specialty event. Instead, they learn to hold back in the early events, so they can still do well in the later events—but they are tired when they get to those events.

Young athletes learn focus in part by having the opportunity to focus. They need meets where they are competing only in their primary event. They can learn to succeed in the major meets by first simulating those conditions in minor meets. The use of simulation drills will help young athletes to lose any fear of competition. They will not fear the unknown, because there will not be an unknown.

Other general recommendations for planning the training program and the peak for young athletes include these four brief recommendations, to be applied in this order:

1. Plan all tests and competitions for the entire season.
2. Plan the broad outline of the season's training.
3. Plan the major training aspects for each phase.
4. Develop highly detailed plans only for the current phase.

The reason for doing detailed planning only for the current phase is that young athletes can change so rapidly in terms of their fitness and level of talent that they may move far beyond the level at which their training was designed. Other young athletes may progress more slowly, usually due to the ups and downs of the physical maturation process.

Now, with that in mind, I want to add these points:

1. Train for the meet conditions.
2. Elevate the training intensity to a peak.
3. Taper carefully and thoroughly.
4. Ensure proper diet and rest.
5. Develop a positive mental outlook.
6. Remember that the best athletes are "hungry" to compete.

When do you want to peak? Aim at the most important meet at which the athlete is *assured* of competing. Unless your state has automatic state qualifying marks (as a few states do), plan for a district or regional or even the conference meet.

For some athletes the conference meet is the highest level to which they are guaranteed entry. Further meets depend on their performance at that meet, so they should try to peak there.

World-ranked American athletes have found themselves watching the Olympic Games on TV because they assumed they would be there, and forgot that the U.S. Olympic Trials is the highest-level meet guaranteed for them. They planned to train through the Trials, but ended their season there. When did they achieve the marks they were saving for the Olympics? Many of them didn't—they were all dressed up, and had nowhere to go.

To peak when it counts, using the basic principles of periodization, you want to remember these major points:

1. Model the meet conditions.
2. Vary the training load for the last five weeks, moving from easy to medium to high to medium to easy.
3. The critical elements include:
   a. Recovery and regeneration
   b. Proper diet
   c. The psychological elements.
4. The final peaking process lasts 7-10 days.

These suggestions are not as simple as they may initially appear to be. Sport training programs are by their nature complex. They are more complex beneath the surface, for there are many different routes to reach the same training goal. The coach is trying to deal with both physical and psychological strengths and weaknesses in the athlete—and, I might add, in the coach also.

The training process is to develop a pattern, test the pattern with athletes, and refine it constantly. Each season the pattern will be more effective.

REFERENCES

1. Lothar Kipke. (1987). The importance of recovery after training and competitive efforts. *Track Technique, 98,* 3128-3135.
2. Adam Zajac & Gregory Prus. (1988). Training for middle distance. *Track Technique, 102,* 3250-3253.
3. Anatoliy Bondarchuk. (1988). Constructing a training system, Parts 1 and 2. *Track Technique, 102,* 3254-3259, 3268; *103,* 3286-3288.
4. Yevgeniy Kashkalov. (1971). Varying work loads in middle distance training. *Track Technique, 43,* 1375-1378.
5. William H. Freeman. (1985). Principles of middle distance training for junior athletes (ages 15-19). Presented at the First International Young Runners Clinic, Helsinki, Finland, September 13, 1985.
6. William H. Freeman. (1994). Factors in planning periodized training in a flexible world. Presented at the 10th Commonwealth and International Scientific Congress, University of Victoria, BC, Canada, 11 August 1994.
7. P. Luhtanen, H. Rusko, S. Puuronen, M. Mäkelä, J.-P. Santanen, & J. Haverinen. (1992, March). Validation of an expert system for talent searching in long distance running. Paper presented at the First International Congress on Computer Science and New Technologies in Sport, Torremolinos, Spain.
8. William J. Bowerman & William H. Freeman. (1991). *High-Performance Training for Track and Field* (p. 3). Champaign, IL: Human Kinetics.
9. William H. Freeman. (1995). Peaking when it counts. Presented at the Massachusetts Track Coaches Clinic, Mansfield, March 25, 1995.

OTHER SOURCES

Bar-Or, Oded. (Ed.). (1996). *The Child and Adolescent Athlete.* Oxford: Blackwell Scientific.

Brunner, Rick, & Ben Tabachnik. (1990). *Soviet Training and Recovery Methods* (pp. 122-150). Pleasant Hill, CA: Sport Focus.

Fairall, Dennis. (1994). Matveyev periodization of training adapted to high school programs. *Track and Field Quarterly Review, 94*(2), 16.

Gould, Daniel, et al. (Fall 2000). Positive and negative factors influencing U.S. Olympic athletes and coaches: Nagano Games assessment. *Track Coach, 153,* 4889- 4893.

Martens, Rainer. (1997). *Successful Coaching* (2nd ed.). Champaign, IL: Human Kinetics.

Naughton, Geraldine, Nathalie J. Farpour-Lambert, John Carlson, Michelle Bradley & Emmanual Van Praegh. (2000). Physiological issues surrounding the performance of adolescent athletes. *Sports Medicine, 30*(5), 309-325.

Thompson, Peter J.L. (1991). *Introduction to Coaching Theory.* London: International Amateur Athletic Federation.

SOURCES FOR TABLES

All Tables are by the author.

SOURCES FOR FIGURES

8.10. Training During a Macrocycle: Zajac & Prus, 3250.
All other figures are by the author.

CHAPTER 9:
Challenges For The American Coach

American coaches face a number of problems or challenges that are peculiar to our nation. Those challenges affect our ability to provide quality coaching, including the development of periodized training programs. We need to examine several of those challenges and their possible solutions.

CHALLENGE # 1: THE AMERICAN COMPETITIVE SEASONS

The United States stands alone among advanced nations in having virtually no summer racing season. Our outdoor season is designed to fit into the school year, which severely limits the length of training year and the racing season. This decreases the preparation time for athletes, then penalizes them further by causing a short outdoor season with poor weather conditions in many parts of the country.

American athletes face a wide range of dates when they must peak, depending on their age, experience, and performance level. Most athletes have two or three possible peaks as goals: cross country (for middle and long distance runners), indoor track, and outdoor track. The result often is an inability to achieve a genuine peak.

Younger athletes (middle and high school levels, ages 12-18) and open athletes who have not

reached the national level (non-USATF qualifiers) generally have their highest-level meets for those seasons in November, February, and May respectively.

Some college athletes suffer the unfortunate reality (from a performance standpoint) of the early semester college system that has appeared over the last few decades. Its disadvantage is that while the cross country and indoor seasons are unchanged, the conference outdoor meet must be held in mid-April, with graduation and leaving school by early May at the latest. The outdoor season is reduced to a month or so, particularly in the northern states where true spring may not arrive until the athletes have gone home. For those athletes and their coaches, the indoor season often receives the greatest emphasis. Training can be difficult for the elite athlete, as school has ended 4-6 weeks before the national outdoor championship meets begin.

For most college and university athletes, the year's potential peaks are in November (cross country), February, and May for the conference meets. For the elite university athlete (NCAA qualifier), the year is extended a bit, with the peaks at the NCAA Meets in late November, mid-March, and early June. If the NCAA athlete goes on to the open championship (USATF), he faces the disadvantage of having one month less time between the indoor and outdoor peaks, plus having a second outdoor national championship only one or two weeks after the first one. The Olympic year adds a third peak for the Olympic Trials, with a fourth peak if the athlete qualifies for the Games.

The elite open athlete has two sets of possible peaks, depending upon his or her competitive level. The national-class athlete has peaks at the ends of November (for cross country) and February, then mid-to late-June. The international competitor may prefer to look at the world meets, with both cross country and indoor track in mid-March and outdoor track in September. This is an ideal pattern for elite athletes, as the potential peaks are six months apart, which is far more appropriate for two peaks per year. At the same time, it shows that the idea of an indoor peak for runners who race farther than a mile is foolish (*unless* they are international class). That is, it works against their achieving the highest levels of performance.

Runners who race farther than a mile generally should avoid trying for an indoor peak. Attempting three peaks in a nine-month school year makes achieving the highest levels of performance very difficult, as it severely limits the preparation and recovery periods. In the long run, most athletes will not realize their full potential because of the overemphasis on competition. Elite success comes from long periods of careful preparation, not from competing for six to seven months of a nine-month school calendar.

CHALLENGE # 2: THE HANDICAP OF COLLEGE ATHLETICS

At first, the idea of competing on a college team seems like a great opportunity, which it is for many athletes. However, it has some genuine disadvantages for the athlete. One disadvantage is the extreme range of peaking dates, mentioned earlier. An excellent example is in the northeast, where indoor track is the dominant season, with major outdoor meets largely limited to the Penn Relays and IC4A Championships.

In contrast, an elite 400m runner at a southern California school will begin competing in outdoor meets by early February, continuing through the NCAA Meet in early June. The top athletes will continue into the European season in August and September. In an Olympic year like 2004, he will try to be at peaks in June (NCAA), July (Olympic Trials), and August (for the Olympics). The result is an outdoor season that lasts for seven or eight months. This is a problem only for the elite athlete, but it requires the coach's willingness to delay the start of the athlete's competition season, while also limiting the number of lower-level meets.

A second disadvantage, true for many prep or collegiate athletes at all levels of skill, is the heavy emphasis on frequent competition, often in multiple events or races, for much of the year. This common practice works against good training practices and long-term progress. Athletes too often find themselves burned out from competing in meaningless events for a few additional team points.

The solution requires a change in the coach's focus. The focus should be shifted from short-term success to long-term growth. The result of limiting the number of events for each athlete in a meet is that each athlete can put more energy into reaching a higher performance level in that event. Allowing longer to develop means longer preparation periods and more years of development without great pressure to reach the top levels too soon. This greater patience lessens the risk of injury and should ultimately yield higher-level performances.

The practice of over-competing is one that discourages foreign athletes from going to American colleges. Lasse Viren tried to run for an American university for one year, but the heavy competitive schedule left him injured for much of the year. He returned to Finland, then won two Olympic gold medals (5 and 10 km) two years later. His story is far from a rare one. It is to some degree a result of the next challenge.

CHALLENGE # 3: THE PRESSURE TO WIN IMMEDIATELY

Unfortunately, the quest for quick results seems to be the American way of life, and the solution is not simple. We have a society that has come to expect immediate gratification; we want it all, and we want it *now*. The result is extreme pressure from schools and athletic departments for success as quickly as possible. While track does not suffer as severely as the big-money American sports (football and basketball), the carry-over is evident.

The coach is expected to prove his or her skill immediately, if not to protect a job, then to protect the budget. In some cases, the existence of the team itself is at stake, as schools must decide which sports survive when the money is tight. When the pressure is placed on the coach, it travels downward to the athletes.

As we said, there are no easy answers for this one. The primary answers are the coach's philosophy of sport and his or her sales job for that philosophy and the team. The coach needs to believe strongly that a more long-term outlook will result in greater success, then sell that viewpoint to the athletic director, the school board, the booster clubs, the president or principal, or the trustees. The kind of sales job that the coach does for the team will affect how the school and community view that team. Public relations and the public perception of your team may be more important than the actual accomplishments of the team. It requires salesmanship at all times.

CHALLENGE # 4: TOO MANY ATHLETES TO COACH

Most coaches read with amazement about the European systems, with coaches who train athletes only in a single event, and train only half-a-dozen to a dozen athletes in all. Most American coaches coach a team, which means from 30-100 or more athletes, perhaps both men and women, and covering the full range of events. The specialist usually coaches a block of events, such as all four throws or jumps, or the sprints, hurdles and relays. In addition, the abilities of the athletes are widely divergent. The male 800m runners on a high school team may have times ranging from 1:55 to 2:25. This range of abilities and numbers of athletes creates tremendous difficulties for the coach.

The first part of the solution is to work on the organization of the team, so that minimal time is lost in dealing with different groups during the training session. Find good methods for teaching skills, assigning and recording training, and working personally with athletes in large numbers. One method of assigning workouts to a large number of athletes is by using standard workout schedule sheets. You can use the workout sheets in combination with a rotation schedule showing when each group of athletes will receive personal attention, if the number of coaches is limited. Sample rotation and workout schedules follow.

At the same time, during the summer the coach or coaches should begin to developed periodized

Table 9.1. Coaching Assignments

Week of February 8-14		
Day	**Coach**	**Event**
Monday	Jones	Shot, Discus
	Sanchez	Sprints, Relays
	Smith	Long Jump, Triple Jump
Tuesday	Jones	Distance Runners, Javelin
	Sanchez	Hurdles, Walkers
	Smith	High Jump, Pole Vault
Wednesday	Jones	Shot, Discus
	Sanchez	Sprints, Relays
	Smith	Long Jump, Triple Jump
Thursday	Jones	Distance Runners
	Sanchez	Hurdles
	Smith	High Jump, Pole Vault
Friday	Jones	Javelin
	Sanchez	Relays, Walkers
	Smith	Pole Vault

training programs for each event, based on general training and performance goals. This approach, which would be an important advance for American coaches, is discussed with the next challenge.

CHALLENGE # 5: NO NATIONAL MODEL TRAINING PLAN

Unlike nations such as the Soviet Union and East Germany, the United States has no model national training plan. Ideally, USA Track & Field (USATF) should develop a national training plan in broad outline form to cover the development of athletes in every Olympic event from about ages 12-26, providing an Olympiad plan for the elite athlete who has Olympic hopes after leaving college. Such a plan would include objectives, goals, and control tests with norms for each year, period, and phase for the athlete of elite potential. It would be similar to the plans discussed in previous chapters.

Because of the American school system and its varying programs and demands, I recommended planning only one year at a time. However, any coach or teacher who deals with several age or grade levels ideally should plan a long-term program for the range of ages and sexes that he or she coaches. For example, a middle school teacher should plan a periodized training pattern of goals and targets for each event or event group for the 7th, 8th, and 9th grades (about ages 12-14). The goals or targets should be different for each grade. This is expected in a good physical education program, where the same sports or activities may be used every year, but the students learn more advanced skills and tactics each succeeding year.

The same process should be followed by the high school coach, planning for the 3-4 years of high school competition (9th or 10th through 12th grades, ages 14 or 15 through 18). Ideally, the high school coaches should work with the local junior high school coaches, producing a model general plan with the basic skills to be taught, fitness levels to be developed and target performance levels for each event for boys and girls in the 7th through 12th grades.

College and university coaches should plan similar programs for the four years of undergraduate study (about ages 18-22). Their planning would include performance targets for each academic year, freshman through senior. Since the coaches of every major college program in the United States gather at the NCAA Championship meets two or three times each year, they could make a major contribution to the long-term future of American track and field by collaborating on the preparation of such programs and performance targets.

Since making these recommendations, I have read of the German Athletics Federation's Frame-

1. A. Jog 1 to 3 miles
   B. Weights & jog
2. Fartlek   A. Varied   (1) 30 min.   (2) 60 min.
   B. Steady   (1) 2-4 mi.   (2) 4-6 mi.   (3) 7-10 mi.
   (4)
3. Weights and jog
4. High knee and power run
5. Intervals
   A. 110   (1) 18-16-14   (2) 17-15-13
   B. 165   (1) 25   (2)
   C. 220   (1) 35   (2) 28   (3) 25-26
   D. 330   (1) 52   (2) 48   (3) 45   (4)
   E. 440   (1) 70-73   (2) 60
   F. 660   (1) 1:45   (2)
   G. 880   (1) 70   (2)
   H. 3/4   (1) 70   (2)
   I. Mile   (1) 72   (2) 68-70   (3) 64-67   (4)
   J.
   K.
   L.
6. Sets   A. 660-440-330-220-110
   (1) 1:45-68-49-32-15   (2)
   B. 440-660-440-220   (1) 63   (2)
   C. 550-165-165   (1) 55 pace   (2)
   D. 220-440-220
7. Squad meeting
8. Special   A. Sauna   B. Swim   C.
9. Drills   A. Sprint-float-sprint (165)
   B. 1-step acceleration (165)
   C. 40-30 drill   (1) 4 laps   (2)
   D. 70-90 drill   (1) 1-1   (2) 2-1
   (3) 3-1   (4)
   E. Cut-downs   (1) 110   (2) 165   (3) 220
   (4) 330   (5) 440   (6) 880   (7)
   F. Simulate race drills   (1) 1st 220-last 220
   (2) 2½-1½   (3) 10 miles-3/4 drill   (4)
   G. 2-4 miles at   (1) 80   (2) 75   (3)
10. A. Test   B. Trial   C. Compete
    (1) 3/4 date pace   (2) Over   (3) Under
11. Hill interval   A. 110   B. 220   C.
12. With coach   (A) Bill B.   (B) Bill D.   (C)
14. A. Wind sprint   B. Hurdle drill
    C. Spring and bound   D.
15. Finish work
16. Acrobatics or apparatus
17. 3/4 effort
18.
19.
20. Secondary event
21. A. Pictures   B. Film

Day		Workout
M	Jog	4x 2x 1A-5E(2)-5C(2)-6A(1)
T	2x 5A(1)	1A-4-3-8A
W	Jog	2A
T		2x 4x 2x 2x 10A(Mile)-5B-5D-5B-2A-5A(1)
F	5x 5A(1)	2A(1)-3r8A
S		2x 10A(500 or 1,000)-2A-5A(1)
S		2B(3)
M	Jog	3x 4x 1B-5C(1)-2A(1)-55y.
T	2x 5A(1)	2x 4x 1A-6D-6A(1)-2A(2)-5A (grass)
W	Jog	1B-8A
T	2x 5A(1)	1A-6C-9A (880)-2A(1)
F		2x Light jog-5B(7/8 effort)
S		10A(1,000 or 500)-2A
S		2B(3)
M	Jog	2x 1A-5B(9/10 effort)-2A
T	2x 5A(1)	2x 2x 2x 1A-5C(3)-6C-6B-6A(1)-5A(1)
W	Jog	3x 3x 1A-5A(1)-2B(2)-5A(1)-8A
T	Jog	3x 2A-5A(1)
F	2x 5A(1)	2x 2x 1A-9A-9A(220)
S		2A(2)
S		Country jog
M	Jog	3-6x 2A(2)-5A(1)
T	2x 5A(1)	2x 3x 1A-6C-2B(2)-5A(1)
W	Jog	3x 1A-5B(9/10 effort)-2A(1)-5A(1)
T	2x 5A(1)	1A-3-8A
F		1A
S		10A (600y.)
S		Run-choice

Figure 9.1. 800m Training Schedule

work Training Plans (FTPs), designed to assist coaches with useful training and modeling information. These FTPs are in seven volumes, with the first aimed at basic training for youngsters aged 10-12. The other volumes are described as buildup training for ages 15-19, and are arranged into basic training principles and five event groups (sprints, runs, jumps, throws, and combined events).

Their plans include aptitude characteristics, performance and training goals by phases and training years, data on the performance structure for different levels of performance, technique models, training models, methods of increasing the training load over a period of years, methods of structuring the annual training load, and materials for planning and evaluation.

This would be a good approach for every country to follow, as such plans need to fit into the social structure of the athletes' culture. USA Track & Field should be developing such plans in cooperation with coaches at all levels (from youth through college) and sport scientists. No reason exists why we can't produce an outstanding model for such teaching and training guidelines.

CHALLENGE # 6: MAKE OUR NATIONAL MEETS A TRAINING GROUND

Rising young athletes need the experience of national-level competition as they develop. This goal could be met by a more open approach to entry standards at the national meets, particularly the Senior USATF Meet. Qualification standards for USATF should be similar to the Olympic Trials, with both a set qualifying mark and a set number of heats and athletes for each event. If the desired number of entries is not met, the field should be filled with the next highest ranked non-qualifiers.

Early rounds should not cut out the majority of the competitors. We have forgotten that the national meets are not run solely for the benefit of a few elite professional athletes who want to avoid unnecessary free races. It is an unconscionable affront to the development of young athletes to run a national meet in which only one or two athletes may advance from a section in the first round. This makes athlete development as much a matter of luck as of skill or potential. We want to encourage our young talent, not discourage it.

The Junior and Intermediate USATF Meets should be held before the Senior Meet, and at least the top two finishers in each event in those meets should be advanced to the Senior Meet regardless of their qualifying marks. They should be advanced purely for the experience. We now show interest in helping athletes only after they have risen almost to the top. We need to start much earlier.

CHALLENGE # 7: THE INFORMATION CIRCUIT IS CLOSED

Coaches need more *applied* information on coaching methods and practices. They need guidelines, testing norms, and sample periodized training schedules that are appropriate for their local athletes. At the same time, the system is largely closed to the coaches out in the field.

USATF and the USOC need to plan a program to get usable, applied coaching information distributed to every track coach in the United States. Two fine publications for track coaching methods are *Track Coach* (the official USATF organ) and *Track and Field Coaches Review* (by the NCAA coaches). However, the number of coaches who read either magazine is very limited (probably 10-15%). At the international level, the IAAF produces *New Studies in Athletics*, with the aim of higher-level technical articles. *American Track & Field*, a private enterprise, is provided to many schools, but it is more promotional and provides limited coaching information. Indeed, we are failing to ensure a future generation of trained coaches. A USATF coaching periodical should go to *every* school in the nation on a *regular* basis.

At the same time, participation in producing the coaching information should become an open system, rather than the traditional buddy system. USATF and the USOC should announce publication plans well in advance, advertising a call for papers on the subject. Each paper should be judged by several coaches and athletes. We should open the doors. The Olympic team is not selected by invitation to a closed-doors session; neither should our coaching information be produced this way.

On a positive note, the development of the USATF Level I, Level II and Level III Coach Education courses has been an important step forward in the improvement of coaching and the dissemination of up-to-date information through the coaching network.

Coaches need to let the USATF and the USOC know what kind of information or other help would be most useful. Many people have worked for years for both groups to try to advance America's sports programs. They need help and encouragement from outside. They cannot help coaches and athletes effectively unless those coaches and athletes communicate their needs and offer their help. Let's work together to move America's track and field training back to its old status of being the world's model.

REFERENCES

1. William J. Bowerman & William H. Freeman. (1991). *High-Performance Training for Track and Field* (2nd ed.). Champaign, IL: Human Kinetics.
2. Herbert Czingon. (1993). Framework Training Plans in the German Athletics Federation [abstract]. *New Studies in Athletics, 8*(3), 100-102.
3. Michael Robins. (1991). Training of NCAA Division II men's track coaches. *Track Technique, 114*, 3637-3638.

SOURCES TO THE FIGURES

9.1. 800m Training, February: Bowerman & Freeman, 1974, p. 51

PART 3:
Periodization For The Individual Events

This part of the book will help you to apply the principles of training and periodization to the different track and field events. Each chapter briefly discusses the training needs of a single event group and includes a list of articles with more information on periodization for that event, a specific athlete's periodized training program, or control tests that can be used for that event.

The figures and tables in these chapters give general recommendations for event training emphases during the different phases of the training year, some adapted from Soviet research. These include the general, special, and competition specific types of training that affect performance in each event, as well as what percent of the total training time during each phase should be devoted to those general, special, and competition-specific training areas. Chapter 8 showed when the different phases occur in the typical American track year, with examples for every combination of racing seasons.

For example, if you want to develop a general plan for the pre-competition part of the outdoor season (Phase 3) in the high jump, first you can check for the fitness characteristics of the high jump, given in Table 12.1. Next, check for the recommended training proportions for that phase in Table 12.3.

For Phase 3, it suggests that 10% of the high jump training should develop the general factors from Table 12.1, 40% of the training should develop the special factors from that table, and 50% of the training should develop the competition-specific factors from the table.

Those guidelines are only a starting point. As you work with periodization, you will be able to make your training plan more precise. As a further guide, other tables give recommendations for the proportion of time to spend on each one of a set of training factors during the first four phases of the macrocycle (Phases 5 and 6 are the brief peak phase and the transition). Those suggestions will give you another perspective for planning, while other tables give some sample event training plans.

Training is still as much art as science, even when using periodization. That is the challenge of coaching, and much of the pleasure of it. There are no guarantees. Almost any reasonable training plan that has the athlete's confidence will result in good performances. This book is a "how to" book for using periodization, but not for detailed training for the individual events. The real-life application is the task of the coach and athlete.

CHAPTER 10:
Periodized Training For Runners

BASIC COMPONENTS OF DISTANCE PERFORMANCE

Training in middle and long distance running requires developing a broad aerobic base, then adding strength endurance, speed endurance, and speed training to it (Fig. 10.1). This basic training progression from the general to the specific is the heart of training for distance runners.

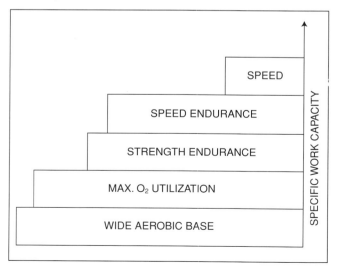

Figure 10.1. Structure of Middle Distance Training

SPEED

SPEED ENDURANCE

STRENGTH ENDURANCE

MAX. O$_2$ UTILIZATION

WIDE AEROBIC BASE

SPECIFIC WORK CAPACITY

Sample basic training emphases for the phases of distance training are shown in Tables 10.1 to 10.4. No two runners have the same needs or talents. The necessary balance of emphasis between aerobic and anaerobic training depends on the athlete's racing distance. Table 10.4 shows the aerobic and anaerobic contributions to performance at different racing distances. The distance events fall into three rough groups: the middle distances (800 to 3,000 meters), long middle distance (5 km), and long distances (10 km and longer).

Table 10.5 shows a more detailed breakdown of the energy components of each racing distance, giving better guidance for structuring high-level training. However, keep in mind that sport scientists are changing their views on these proportions. Current thinking argues that more than 50% of the contribution to 800m is aerobic, rather than the old 33%. In reality, any distance race calls on different aspects of the human system at different stages of the race, beginning aerobically and becoming increasingly anaerobic as fatigue grows from the effort. Even elite specialists disagree on the correct proportions.

In recent years, the aerobic and anaerobic thresholds in distance runners have been emphasized in the testing of European athletes. These

Table 10.1. Fitness Characteristics of Distance Events

Event	General	Special	Competition-Specific
Middle Distances	Aerobic endurance Strength endurance Mobility Maximum strength	Speed endurance Speed Elastic strength Special endurance Event distance	Sprint technique Time trials Tactical trials
Steeplechase	Aerobic endurance Strength endurance Mobility Maximum strength	Speed endurance Speed Elastic strength Special mobility Special endurance	Hurdles technique Water jump technique Time trials Tactical trials
Long Distance	Aerobic endurance Strength endurance Mobility	Speed endurance Speed Elastic strength Special endurance Event distance	Sprint technique Time trials Tactical trials

Table 10.2. Phase Training Ratios for the Distances

Middle Distances			
Phase	General	Special	Specific
1	20	75	5
2	20	70	10
3	10	70	20
4	10	85	5
5	10	80	10
6	55	40	5

Long Distances and Road Races			
Phase	General	Special	Specific
1	10	85	5
2	10	85	5
3	5	90	5
4	10	85	5
5	5	90	5
6	45	50	5

Percent distribution of:
• General Training (mostly compensatory strength and mobility work)
• Special Training (includes aerobic endurance)
• Competition-Specific Training

Table 10.3. Phases 1-4 Training for Middle and Long Distances

PHASE 1: Increase of General Endurance
40% Sustained runs (6-10 miles, varied terrain, easy pace)
20% Tempo-endurance (4-8 x 1-2 km., medium effort, 3-5 min. recovery)
20% Conditioning; running exercises, circuit training and total training
10% Interval training (10-30 x 100-200m, medium pace, 1-2 min. recovery)
10% Fartlek (1 hour slow, with faster parts on hills and flat)

PHASE 2: Increase of Speed Endurance
30% Sustained running (a bit faster, but not as far)
30% Speed endurance (3-6 x 300-500m, demanding pace, 6-8 min. recovery)
20% Interval training (slightly faster than in Basic period)
10% Fartlek (open terrain or beach)
10% Hills (2-4 x 5 x 100m, not very steep, 3 min. recovery)

PHASES 3-4: Improve Speed and Gain Peak Form
40% Competition pace (2-4 x shorter than racing distance, at race pace, 10-20 min. recovery)
30% Cross country running, Farlek, or easy runs
20% Interval training (fewer repetitions, faster, but not full effort)
10% Sprints (6-8 x 100-150m, very fast, 5 min. or more recovery)
Also Competition (1 time a week, sometimes at other distances)

thresholds indicate the level of an athlete's specific fitness for endurance racing. Most coaches and runners are familiar with the effect of the VO_2max as a measure of distance running endurance. The thresholds are related to the VO_2max as a measure, while they are pinpointed through the level of lactic acid in the blood during a running test. They can be estimated as percentages of the athlete's highest pulse or heart rate (HRmax).

An athlete's HRmax is about 220 beats per minute (BPM), minus his or her age. That is, a 20-year-old's HRmax is probably about 220 minus 20, or 200 BPM. Estimating the HRmax is more difficult for well-trained people, who are able to achieve higher figures.

The aerobic threshold equals the athlete's resting HR (HRmin), plus 70% of the difference between the HRmax and the HRmin. That is, if the athlete's HRmax is 200 BPM and the HRmin is 50 BPM, the difference is 150, 70% of 150 is 105, and the aerobic threshold is 50 + 105, or 155 BPM. To improve their endurance, athletes must train at a level that raises their HR above their aerobic threshold.

Table 10.4. Aerobic and Anaerobic Effects

Race	Factor Percentage Anaerobic	Aerobic
800	67%	33%
1 km	55%	45%
1500	49%	51%
Mile	48%	52%
3k	44%	56%
5k	20%	80%
10k	10%	90%
Marathon	5%	95%

Table 10.5. Contribution of Energy Systems to Performance

Race	Speed/Strength (ATP-CP)	Anaerobic Power/ Endurance (ATP-CP + LA)	Aerobic Endurance (O$_2$ System)
800	30%	65%	5%
1500	20%	55%	25%
3k	20%	40%	40%
5k	10%	20%	70%
10k	5%	15%	80%
Marathon	0%	5%	95%

The anaerobic threshold is a higher level of effort, where breathing becomes labored. If the pace is continued for much longer, the athlete will be forced to stop running. The simplest test of it is the "Talk Test." If you cannot carry on a conversation while running, then you are above your anaerobic threshold. The threshold varies from 50% of the VO$_2$max in untrained persons to 80% of the VO$_2$max in the best endurance athletes.

The aerobic training zone lies between the two thresholds, while above the anaerobic threshold is the anaerobic training zone. Longer races involve more emphasis on training in the aerobic training zone, while shorter races (which involve rapid increases in lactic acid) require a higher proportion of anaerobic training.

Two estimates of the training paces for different types of training are shown in Tables 10.6 and 10.7. The first table is based on physiological measures, while the second table is based on best time at 10 km. Table 10.8 is an example of the intensities of the endurance training zones based on heart rates.

We can also look at training in terms of training loads and load characteristics, as shown in Tables 10.9 and 10.10.

Mature distance runners need about 60 miles of training per week to reach their highest VO$_2$max. Middle distance runners do not need as much mileage, because their mileage is more intense, and because the anaerobic component is as important as the aerobic component in their events. Marathoners will need more mileage (80-120 miles per week) to improve their fat metabolism and glycogen-sparing. However, research suggests little need for over

Table 10.6. Performance References

	% Best Mile	%AT HR	%VO$_2$ Max	%Max HR	mM/L (Theor.) Lactate
Long Steady Runs (1.5-2 hrs.)	70	87	70	79	1
Medium Runs (45-60 min.)	75	91	82	83	2
Tempo Runs (30-60 min.)	80	97	87	89	3
AT Intervals (3-8 min.)	85	100	90	91	4
Intensive Intervals (2-5 min.)	92	100.03	100	94	5

Table 10.7. Optimal Training Speeds Based on 10 km Time

10,000m time (min)	VO$_2$ Max tempo (min/km)	Anaerobic threshold speed (min/km)	Aerobic threshold speed (min/km)
27:00	2:34	2:55	3:37
28:00	2:39	3:01	3:46
29:00	2:45	3:08	3:53
30:00	2:50	3:14	4:00
31:00	2:55	3:20	4:09
32:00	3:00	3:26	4:16
33:00	3:05	3:32	4:23
34:00	3:11	3:38	4:32
35:00	3:16	3;44	4:39
36:00	3:21	3:51	4:46
37:00	3:27	3:57	4:54
38:00	3:32	4:03	5:01
39:00	3:37	4:09	5:09
40:00	3:43	4:15	5:16

Table 10.8. Intensities of Endurance Training Zones

Zone	Description	% of HRmax
6	Maximal aerobic	Above 90%
5	Anaerobic threshold	85-90%
4	Intensive endurance	80-85%
3	Extensive endurance	75-80%
2	Aerobic	65-75%
1	Recovery	Below 65%

80-90 miles per training week.

Mileage can become a trap for the overzealous runner. Many runners fail to reach their racing potential because of overtraining. They lack the confidence in their fitness that lets them recover properly between hard training sessions, and they lack the courage to taper their training or rest enough before their races. Long, hard runs should be followed by a day of only 30-40 minutes of easy jogging, even for marathoners. Runners should avoid excessively long warmups and cooldowns. Many racing failures result from too much worship at the altar of mileage.

TYPES OF DISTANCE TRAINING

There is very little that is new under the distance training sun. Every training method used today has been used in some form since the last century. Distance training is categorized in many ways, but all of the methods are either *continuous* or *interrupted running*, which should be mixed in training. Figure 10.2 shows one model of the structure of distance training, while Figure 10.3 shows a popular British model. Figure 10.4 shows a model of the types of training.

Continuous Running

Continuous running includes steady and uneven paced runs, as well as competition and race simulations. *Steady paced running* is aerobic training, either medium-paced runs (2-6 miles, run at the anaerobic threshold) or long slow runs (from 30 minutes to several hours long, run in the aerobic training zone).

Mixed pace running increases the stress of continuous runs by varying the pace or using more difficult terrain. Fartlek (varied pace running over varied terrain) is the most common method of mixed pace training, though its method can range from a loose "go as you feel" to structured fartlek, with the route, intensity, and components of the training ses-

Table 10.9. Load Characteristics in Endurance Events

ESTIMATED LOAD LEVEL	LOAD CHARACTERISTICS	TASK
Small	12-20% of the load volume that leads to a drop in the work capacity	To speed up restoration
Intermediate	40-60% of the load volume that leads to a drop in the work capacity	To maintain the performance level
Heavy	60-75% of the load volume that leads to a drop in the work capacity	To improve performance
Large	The work is performed in the compensated fatigue phase	To improve performance

Table 10.10. Training Loads for Endurance Training

TASK	LOAD	CONTROL CRITERION
Basic endurance	60 to 70% of the best performance over the distance	Lactate < 3 mmol/l Heart rate 130 to 150/min. (60 to 70% of max. O_2 uptake)
Development range 1	70 to 85% of the best performance over the distance	Lactate 3 to 4 mmol/l Heart rate 140 to 160/min. (70 to 80% of max. O_2 uptake)
Development range 2	85 to 95% of the best performance over the distance	Lactate 5 to 7 mmol/l Heart rate 160 to 180/min. (80 to 95% of max. O_2 uptake)
Border range (Competition range)	Over 95% of the best performance over the distance	Lactate over 7 mmol/l Heart rate over 180/min. (90 to 80% of max. O_2 uptake)

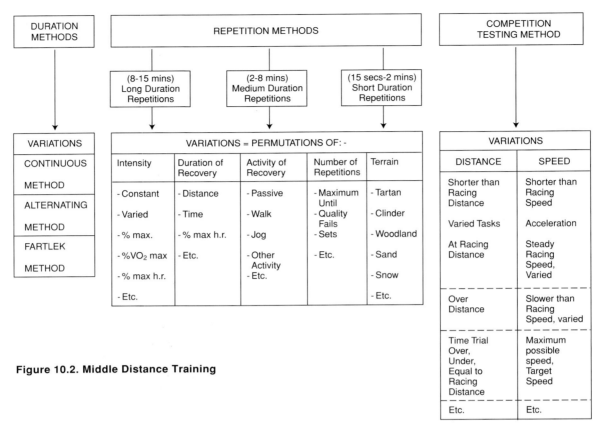

Figure 10.2. Middle Distance Training

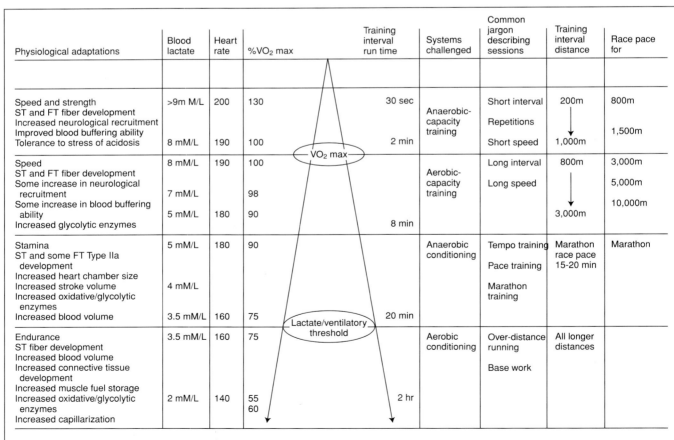

Figure 10.3. Primary Training Zones of Performance

sion planned carefully before starting the run. Fartlek is usually run on ordinary surfaces, such as forest paths or roads. Because it can be less structured, it is more pleasant, but it is harder to evaluate objectively. It is also harder for inexperienced athletes to use effectively without careful guidance, as they tend to interpret fartlek to mean "easy fun run."

Competition includes simulations and races, ideally run at high to maximum intensity over a set distance with some opponents (solo time trials are not as emotionally stressful as competing against other runners). Simulations can also be used to adapt the runner to the racing distance and pace by mixing the goal pace with slower portions of the distance.

Interrupted Running

Interrupted running is repeated runs with periods of rest or recovery between them. These repetition or interval systems are most often used on the track, though they may be done over any terrain. They involve variations in five elements:

1. Distance (length of interval)
2. Speed (time or intensity of effort)
3. Repetitions (number of intervals)
4. Recovery interval (time or distance)
5. Recovery method (complete rest, jog, stride, and such).

There are three types of interrupted running: interval training, speed-endurance training, and tempo training.

Interval training consists of repeated runs of 100-400m at about 75% effort (under 180 HR), with a recovery interval (usually jogging) of 2-3 times the fast interval time (jog until the HR is below 120 BPM). The HR is the key to the number of repetitions. The workout is ended if the athlete's HR is still over 120 BPM after two minutes. This type of training improves aerobic endurance. Table 10.11 shows a typical estimation of the running and recovery intervals for a training session.

Hill training (to develop muscular power) is a popular variation of interval training, largely as a result of its prominence in the Lydiard system of training, where it served as a bridge between base training and track training. An example of hill training (Fig. 10.5) is very close to Lydiard's practices, mixing hill running with jogging, striding, and short sprints at the top and bottom of the hill.

Speed-endurance training employs repeated runs of 150-500m at up to 90% effort, with 4-8 repetitions and recoveries of 5-6 minutes. This type of training prepares the athlete for intense efforts, improving the resistance to oxygen debt. It is not recommended for younger athletes.

Tempo training can be either tempo-endurance running or competitive pace running. *Tempo-endurance running* is running at about 75% of the race pace for distances longer than the race (for races under 5 km). The distance is repeated 4-8 times, with 3-6 minute recoveries. This training improves aerobic endurance.

Jack Daniels describes this type of training as

The types of training listed below are arranged by intensity, from easitest ot hardest (slowest to fastest).

	EASY (E)	LONG (L)	TEMPO (T)	CRUISE (C)	INTERVAL (I)	REPS ®
PURPOSE	Warmup Recovery Cooldown Easrly season build up	Skeletal and cardiac muscle adaptation	Improve endurance by raising lactate threshold		Improve VO₂ max	IImprove speed and running economy
INTENSITY	Conversational, 70% of VO₂ max		Comfortably hard 86% of VO₂ max 15 seconds per mile slower than 10K race pace		5K race pace or slightly slower 95%-100% of VO₂ max	5 seconds per 400m faster than interval pace or race pace, whichever is fastest
DURATION OF EACH WORK BOUT	23-60 minutes	60-120 minutes	20 minutes	3-10 minutes	1/2-5 minutes	30-90 seconds
RECOVERY TIME BETWEEN WORK BOUTS	Not applicable	Not applicable	Not applicable	1 minute	1 to 1 work/rest ratio	1 to 5 work/rest ratio
NUMBER OF WORK BOUTS IN ONE SESSION	Not applicable	Not applicable	Not applicable	Repeat work bouts until quality work totals 8% of 1 weekly mileage; not over 6 miles/session		5% of weekly mileage; not over 5 miles/session

Figure 10.4. Types of Training

Table 10.11. Estimated Recovery Times Between Running Intervals

Loading	Running Time (RT)	Recovery Time	Recovery Activity
Short Speed (all-out) (anaerobic capacity training)	10 sec.	3 x RT	Walking and/or stretching
	20 sec.	3 x RT	Jogging
	30 sec.		
Long speed (95-100% of maximal effort) (anaerobic capacity training)	30 sec.	3 x RT	Jogging
	60 sec.	2 x RT	Jogging
	80 sec.		
Speed + endurance (90-95% of maximal effort) (VO$_2$max to anaerobic capacity training)	80 sec.	2 x RT	Jogging
	2:40	1 x RT	Rest
	3 min.		
Endurance (80-90% of maximal effort) (anaerobic conditioning)	3 min.	1 x RT	Rest
	4 min.	1 x RT	Rest
	20 min.		

tempo-pace or *threshold training*, which he divides into two types. Steady threshold training is tempo running, usually for 20 minutes at a pace of 15-20 seconds per mile slower than 10k racing pace, not including the warmup or cooldown runs. These tempo runs are supposed to be at a set intensity, so they are done on flat terrain. More experienced runners may run this pace for up to an hour.

Daniels refers also to intermittent threshold training, which he calls "tempo intervals" or "cruise intervals." While the running intensity is similar to that of the steady runs, the athlete does a series of shorter runs of 3-8 minutes each, with 1-minute recoveries, to a total workout of 30-40 minutes.

Competitive pace running consists of 3-6 repetitions of a portion (usually 1/3, 1/2, or 2/3rds) of the racing distance, with 8-12-minute recoveries. This also improves aerobic endurance, but its aim is to develop the rhythm of the racing pace.

The difference between interval training and repetition training can be confusing. Basically, both use repeated fast intervals, so both are interval training. However, interval training uses incomplete recoveries, so that fatigue and oxygen debt become factors, while *repetition training* allows relatively complete recoveries, avoiding fatigue. The object of repetition training is to learn the pace or achieve the goal time, while with interval training the goal is adaptation to the stress.

Interval training involves either anaerobic or aerobic repetitions, depending upon the facet of en-

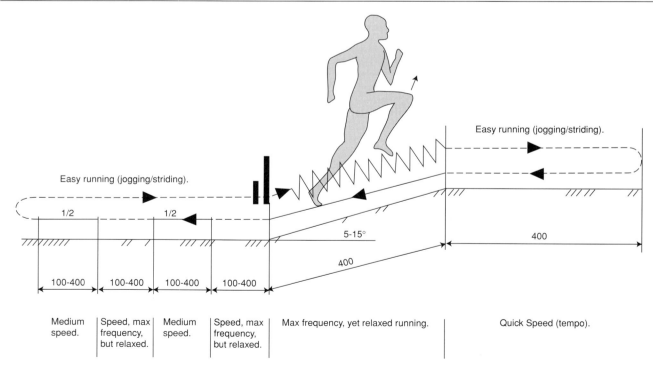

Figure 10.5. Hill Training (Lydiard System)

durance that it is designed to improve. *Anaerobic repetitions* are either short-term (to 200m), medium-term (200-400m), or long-term (400-800m). The types of anaerobic intervals are:

- Speed work
  Up to 60m at top speed
  60-150m extended fast runs
  Adequate recoveries
- Short duration, short recovery work
  200-400m, with an effort-to-recovery ratio of 1:1
  Maintain quality with rest or small sets
- Long duration, long recovery work
  400-1,000m, with up to 10 minutes between sets
  Pace is 85-90% of runner's best time.

Aerobic repetitions are also short-term (800m to 3000m), medium-term (3000- 10,000m), or long-term (10,000m and longer). Short-term aerobic training is usually interval training. The older method of Woldemar Gerschler used many repetitions of 100-400m, with short recoveries. Longer intervals (800m to 3 km) are run with relatively short recovery periods (about half of the running time). This extensive interval method trains the runner above the anaerobic threshold.

Many European coaches have commented on the overuse of interval training by American coaches and athletes. They prefer to use more steady and variable pace running, with only moderate use of interval and repetition running.

WOMEN'S DISTANCE TRAINING

While women's training is no longer very different from men's training, the differences need to be considered. Because of the trends in women's training in the United States, with the overemphasis on body weight, American women have given away the edge in strength to their foreign opponents. Generally speaking, American women have been only marginally competitive against their heavier, stronger European opponents. Much of this difference grew from the different attitudes toward weight training and muscular appearance in women. The lifting of large quantities of weights during winter training has been a feature of Eastern European training for more than two decades. That strength difference is a major factor in the quality of women's middle distance running in Europe.

Though women can do similar workouts, they do not require the same mileage loads as men. The training load should be based on the total running time per week, rather than on the number of miles run. If men and women run the same number of hours per week, the women will run about 15% fewer miles than the men. Thus, a roughly equal

training load to a man's 60 miles per week would be a woman's 50 miles per week.

An East German approach to women's middle distance training divides the year into four parts (basic conditioning, specific conditioning, pre-competition, and competition periods). The main components of training are:

- Endurance runs (three speeds, based on an endurance running test of either 3000 or 5000m)
- Tempo runs (three speeds, based on the new goal pace)
- Speed runs (to 80m at maximal or submaximal speed)
- Non-specific training (games, circuit training, gymnastics, stretching, and swimming)
- Jumping exercises (used to develop strength, with circuit training in the winter and hill training in the spring, using both bounding and vertical jumps).

The control measures for the runs are shown in Table 10.12. The training emphasis throughout the year is on the tempo running, to engrain the racing tempo in the athlete's system.

The Soviet approach to middle distance running emphasized the importance of making a model of the race (to learn the specific requirements for success). It stressed the overall development of the athlete over a 5-7-year period, strongly warning that attempts to speed up the training process usually led to the flash-in-the-pan junior runner who retires early, a victim of burn-out or injury.

The training loads fall into six intensity zones, ranging from recovery running at slow speeds (8 min./mile or slower) upward through faster runs, then interrupted runs, and finally to competitive runs of 1000 to 1500 meters at 96-100% of maximum, repetitions of 800 to 1,000 meters at 96-100%, and interval sprints of 50 to 150 meters at 91-100% (with a maximum total of 1500m of intervals in a training session at Zone Six levels).

Table 10.12. Endurance and Tempo Paces and Controls

Runner Type		Training Distances Speed	Endurance
Endurance Run *			
Level 1	Under 80%	6-8-10 km	8-12 km
Level 2	80-95%	8-12 km	10-15 km
Level 3	95%+	3-5 km	5-8-10 km
Tempo Run **			
Level 1	Under 85%	100m-200m-1,000m-2,000m	
Level 2	85-95%	400m-600m-1200m	
Level 3	95%+	3,000m-600m-1,000m	

* Based on endurance test at 3 km or 5 km
** Based on goal time for 800m or 1500m

800 METERS

An example of elite training at 800 meters is Joachim Cruz's training under Luiz de Oliveira, which resulted in Cruz winning an Olympic championship (1984) and just missing the world record. His training year had five periods:
- Readaptation (8-9 weeks)
- Basic preparation (13 weeks)
- Specific preparation (13 weeks)
- Competition (13 weeks)
- Transition (4-5 weeks).

The training alternates hard and light weeks. A hard week has a pattern of two hard days, followed by a light day, while an easy week has a pattern of two light days followed by a hard day. The last week of the basic and specific preparation periods are transition weeks, devoted to easy running of five miles a day.

The two-month *readaptation* period begins with easy jogging on grass and sawdust trails on four days a week, with two days devoted to volleyball and swimming. The workload rises to 40 miles a week of training, including longer runs on soft and hard surfaces, outdoor gymnastic activities, and the start of an outdoor circuit training program.

The three-month *basic preparation* period peaks at 65 miles a week of running, mixing long runs, circuit training, weight training, interval training and drills, hill training, mountain training, and speed drills.

The three-month *specific preparation* period varies from 40 to 65 miles of running per week. It includes long runs, hill training, fartlek, a second phase of circuit training, interval training and drills, and race practice drills.

The three-month *competition* period gradually drops the mileage from 50 to 28 miles a week. It includes shorter runs, fartlek under the coach's supervision, race-practice drills, interval training and drills, and speed training.

The one-month *transition* period avoids running, using alternative active rest activities instead. Swimming and biking are the primary activities mentioned, though the month is generally unstructured.

Cruz's training made excellent use of the local environment in Eugene, Oregon, adapting the local training setting into patterns that de Oliveira had used in Brazil. Cruz easily won dual NCAA championships, took the Olympic 800 gold, and was a favorite in the 1500 before becoming ill, completing the year with a phenomenal set of racing marks at 800 meters.

Another excellent 800-meter racer was Sebastian Coe, whose training is discussed under the 1500 meters.

Steve Ovett

1500 METERS AND ONE MILE

Two examples of training programs at this distance are those of Steve Ovett and Sebastian Coe, both of whom set world records and won Olympic championships in the 1980s.

Steve Ovett and Harry Wilson. Harry Wilson coached Steve Ovett from age 16, when Ovett was already showing signs of great talent. His broad training year falls into four periods of training: basic preparation, pre-competition, competition, and transition (though he does not use those terms to describe them).

The *basic preparation* (Autumn/Winter) period involves short (4-6 miles) steady state runs and low mileage (40 miles a week) for the first month. A second daily training session is added gradually, with the training load for an experienced athlete reaching about 80 miles a week in 12-14 training sessions by the end of December (after about 10 weeks of training). It includes shorter, faster runs of four miles and longer steady runs over 12 miles. Some long repetitions (1000-1500m) are added, along with a weekly session of sprint drills.

Wilson particularly emphasized regular training in sprinting techniques throughout the training year as critical to success at 800 and 1500 meters. Several low-key cross country races were included every three weeks.

Late during this period the mileage was increased to about 100 miles a week (for experienced runners only), with a session of hill running included in each week. The mileage was then decreased and shorter runs at a quicker pace were added, allowing a peak for the major cross country races. A very easy week of running was included at about five-week intervals throughout the period.

The *pre-competition* (Spring/Early Summer) period begins with several transitional weeks involving an increase in anaerobic work. By about six weeks before competition begins, the athlete is doing about 10 training sessions per week, including steady state runs, hill running, long and short interval work, and sprint drills. Wilson used a two-week pattern, emphasizing a different set of activities each week.

This period involves progression, increasing the number, length, or speed of intervals or decreasing the recovery periods. The type of progression differs for each runner. Late during this period several low-key races will be run, most often two races at 3 km, and one race each at 1500 and 800 meters. At least two weekends are spent training at the beach, including sand dune running. These sessions in Wales are apparently modeled on Percy Cerutty's training practices with Herb Elliott in Australia.

While the winter training was more relaxed, the pressure on the athlete begins to build during this period. Increased emphasis is placed on performing quality training sessions. An easy week was used for recovery in the middle of the period, with another easy week at the end of the period, just before the serious races begin.

The *competition* period can last for up to three months. The training program revolves around the racing schedule. The coach eases the pressure for quality training sessions, encouraging the athlete to try to perform with "relaxed quality." This means that the athlete learns to perform at close to capacity, but in a relaxed manner with a bit held back. Making an all-out effort to perform top-quality efforts in practice leaves little room for improvement in the races. An accurate reading of the athlete's energy level is important, so the athlete can rest enough to allow top-quality racing results.

The *transition* period is simply a two- to four-week period of rest, with no planned activities. When it concludes, the return to training is very gradual.

Sebastian Coe and Peter Coe. Sebastian Coe, who set records from 800 meters through the mile, was trained by his father, Peter Coe. The elder Coe, an engineer by training, only trained his son. Because of this, he studied training theory on his own,

Sebastian Coe

developing an independent program that he considers the most effective for the 800/1500 runner. Coe's gold medals at 1500m in Moscow and Los Angeles show the effectiveness of the system.

The *basic preparation* period (November through January) is 5000m training. It includes three types of training sessions:

- Runs of 6-8 miles at a fast tempo (5 days per week)
  Long run (10 miles, 1 day per week)
- Repetition runs of 100-1000m, with short jogs to recover (2-3 days per week).

Supplementary training includes:

- Weight training (2 days per week)
- 90-minute circuit training session (1 day per week)
- Flexibility exercises were not scheduled, but were a regular, necessary training feature.

As a test at the end of the period, the runner competes in two indoor races (without speed training), running a 3000m and an 800m in different meets. These serve as control tests.

The *special preparation* period (February through early June) involves three months of "multi-tier" training, followed by a month of pre-competition training. This period involves an increase in speed endurance work, completing the sharpening work during the last month of the period.

The multi-tier training involves sessions of intervals at paces for races from 400 to 5000m in length (the paces are not mixed in a single training session), with one long run (10-12 miles) per week. Sprint work begins with short intervals (indoors), with the intervals becoming longer when outdoor surfaces become available around April. Hill running is used for power training at this point. Some short, highly intense controlled fartlek is used, as are longer, less intense training sessions. These are a factor in both power and technique, as knee-lift is important in middle distance races.

Hard speed endurance training also begins about this time, leading into shorter, harder speed endurance intervals and sprint drills in May and early June. Weight training ends in May, with only weekly light maintenance sessions after that point.

The *competition* period (mid-June through mid-September) is highly individualized, so it is not planned ahead of time. Rest and recovery must be observed closely, so the runner can compete successfully and not become discouraged with poor results.

The *transition* period (mid-September through October) is a time for complete relaxation, with a little swimming and a bit of optional jogging, if the athlete wishes. When the runner does run, it should not be slow (5:40 per mile or 3:30 per km).

3000 METERS (WOMEN)

While this is not solely a women's race, it has been a national, world, and Olympic championship event only for women, though it has now been replaced by the 5000m race. The best detailed look at elite training for the women's 3000 meters is by Yuri Tiurin, discussing Svetlana Ulmasova, 1982 European champion and former world record holder. She was trained as a 1500-3000 specialist, with bests of 1:59.60, 3:58.3 and 8:26.78.

Her training year was a double-periodized plan with nine periods:

1. Transition (4 weeks): September-October
2. Introduction (3 weeks): October
3. First Basic (8-9 weeks): November-December
4. Winter Pre-Competitive (4 weeks): January. Includes 2-1/2 to 3 weeks at 5,250' altitude
5. Winter Competitive (4 weeks): February
6. Second Basic (7-8 weeks): March-April. Includes 2-1/2 to 3 weeks at 5,250' altitude in April
7. Summer Pre-Competitive (4-5 weeks): May-June. Includes 2-1/2 to 3 weeks at 5,250'

altitude; return from altitude 16 days before meet
8. First Competitive (6-7 weeks): June-July
9. Second Competitive (5-6 weeks): August-September. Main meet of the year as a conclusion.

Her training is an excellent example of a carefully-planned program designed to improve the athlete throughout the training year. Altitude training is used to improve the training capacity, allowing increased capabilities in practice sessions. It is not used for a racing effect, as that effect lasts for only a few days.

Interestingly enough, Ulmasova did not begin training until age 20, running 10:23.5 in her first year, then improving to 8:55.8 in her third year of training, as a 22-year-old. Too often we have emphasized overtraining and heavy racing schedules for girls (and boys), too many of whom peak and disappear from the running scene after high school. This Soviet success shows that the top rung of sport is not limited to the early developers.

One question is how many races should runners attempt in a season. Table 10.13 summarizes Russian research on the subject, based on elite performers.

5000 METERS

An example of training at this distance is John Andersen's training of David Moorcroft, who ran a world record 13:00.42 in 1982. One of the benefits of many non-American systems is the long-term cooperative effort of coach and athlete. Just as Steve Ovett was coached from age 16 by Harry Wilson, Moorcroft was coached from his very early development by Andersen.

Andersen sets long-term targets for his athletes (1-3 years for a mature athlete, up to 10 years for a younger runner). With Moorcroft he began

Table 10.13. Numbers of Annual Races by Women

3,000m Competitors	
#	Type of Race
3-4	Cross country or indoor meets
4-6	Under-distance races (800m to 1 mile)
1-2	Over-distance races (5 km, 10 km.)
2-3	Relays or road races
3-6	3,000m races

10,000m Competitors	
#	Type of Race
3-4	Cross country or indoor meets
3-4	Short under-distance races (800m to 1 mile)
3-4	Longer under-distance races (3 km, 5 km)
5-6	Relays or road races
2-4	3,000m races

with a five-year plan to promote speed and speed endurance without losing any aerobic capacity. Andersen was a strong believer in the importance of speed, including speed work in the training throughout the year, just as Harry Wilson did. As Andersen said, "The more the athlete learns to run fast as part of his development, the more he learns to *expect* to run fast and, as a consequence of expecting to run fast, he *does*."

His program has three components: the aerobic, the anaerobic, and the linking of those two components. He preferred to keep the recovery or rest component of training constant, while increasing the speed of the running.

His aerobic training uses five methods:

- Long, slow distance running. Run 1-2 times every two weeks, used as active rest (8-10 miles for younger athletes, up to 15-17 miles for mature, more experienced runners).
- Medium intensity running. Basic conditioning runs, done at steady pace close to 80% of maximum (6-8 miles for younger, 8-10 miles for older runners).
- Short, fast running. Extended runs as fast as possible for the full distance, thus not used often (1-3 miles for younger runners, 3-5 miles for older ones).
- Fartlek running. Used to link the three types of aerobic running. Traditional fartlek, never over 80% of maximum.
- Intensive fartlek (compared to traditional fartlek). Uses bursts of 100-600m at 80-100% maximum, with minimal recoveries between.

The anaerobic training also has five methods, focusing on developing speed and speed endurance:

- Short repetitions with short recoveries. Back-to-back sprints of 60 or 100 meters, usually four sets of four sprints, with either short or diminishing rests.
- Longer runs with longer recoveries. Usually sprints of 150m to 200m, such as 3 sets of 4-6 x 150m, or a ladder of 150m to 200m to 150m in increments of 10 meters.
- Technique running with acceleration running. Uses the types of speed intervals above.
- Longer maximum effort runs with longer recoveries. Run at top speed for 60-600 meters.
- Combinations of the other four methods.

The link or bridge between the aerobic and anaerobic elements is made with repetitions run at faster than race pace, with reasonable recoveries. Two workouts were chosen, though at his peak Moorcroft had to use a longer interval than the origi-

nal long choice. The choices were:

- 8 x 300m with 3 min. recovery
- 4 x 600m with 5 min. recovery
- 4-6 x 1000m with 6:30 recovery (replaced the 600s).

The kilometer interval was first used in 1981, five years after Moorcroft had first been an Olympic Games finalist.

The emphasis on keeping a steady load in terms of volume, with little difference from winter to summer (a drop of about 10 miles a week) makes estimating the intensity of training difficult. However, two points are noteworthy. First, during his peak in 1982 Moorcroft was racing only about every two weeks, allowing good recovery between his peak efforts (3:49.3 mile, 7:32.8 3 km, and 13:00.42). A common day was 5-7 miles in the morning and 5 miles in the evening, both steady runs. However, the pace is not mentioned, and Andersen believes in running faster as the athlete's fitness rises.

Second, speed work was only done about once a week. However, the quality of the sessions was uniformly high. One session, in windy conditions, included a kilometer in 2:23, followed by 8 x 300m in under 40 seconds each. Another session was 4 x 600m in 1:23 each. These indicate (as the race times did) a very high level of fitness. They also indicate that there is no single answer to the best way to train.

The Portuguese approach to training had many similarities, as it stresses the importance of intensity in training. As Pompilio Ferreira said, "It is better to do 100km [60 miles] a week training with a correct stimulus than 200km without the appropriate intensity." His runners used a mixture of steady runs at different heart rates with fartlek, hill, and interval training. They began the macrocycle with low-intensity running, gradually raising the intensity and volume until January, then decreasing the volume as the intensity continues to rise. The Lydiard influence on the pattern is noticeable, as it is in the training of Lasse Viren in Finland.

American programs that use a gradual buildup of the intensity of training, but with a steady volume until the peaking period, include the traditional Oregon System and the more intensive Oregon System of Bill Dellinger. Dellinger used a series of simulations at regular points throughout the training year to condition the athlete to the tempo and distance of the race. Those simulated races gradually increased the portion of the racing distance run at the runner's goal pace. The simulations were used about every three weeks, until the racing season began.

Saïd Aouita's training produced outstanding results across the full range of the middle distance races. Enrico Dionisi has described the core of

Aouita's preparation (Phases 1-3) as follows (Table 10.14, which does not agree completely with the provided training examples):

Table 10.14. Single Periodization (Morocco)

Periodization	Period of Time	Aim/Contents
I Transition	45 days (October) for detoxification	Genuine holidays Reestablishment of condition
II Preparation I	November - March	Development of muscular strength and cardio-respiratory capacity
III Preparation II	April - May	Increase in intensity and reduction of volume
IV Competition	June - September	Competitions

Phase 1: November to December
- 6-8 sessions per week for developing aerobic capacity
- 1 fartlek session per week (45 min.)
- Interval session to develop maximal aerobic capacity; intensity is rated as a percentage of athlete's basic speed
  2 x (5 x 1 km), 90 sec. between reps, 3 min. between sets, or
  25 x 400m, 40-60 sec. recovery
- Timed circuit training
- 10-20 x 150m uphill runs, 10-degree incline
- Weight training.

Phase 2: January to March
- Fartlek (track or cross country, up to 10 km)
- Interval training, total of 3-4 km per session; the intensity was not given, but the recovery intervals suggest high intensity; examples:
  10 x 400m, 80 sec. to 2 min. recovery, or
  6 x 500m, 1:40-2:30 recovery, or
  3 x 1000m, 3:30 to 5 min. recovery
- Speed training (Rhythm variations): 300m repetitions (100m medium, 100m varied, 100m maximum)—at least 100m at sprint tempo
- 1-2 hill running sessions per week
- Strength training, combined with relaxation practice.

Phase 3: April to May
- Development of maximum aerobic capacity, in 1 session (5-6 km total):
  3 x 500m, 75 sec. recovery
  5 x 300m, 45 sec. recovery

  4 x 400m, 60 sec. recovery
  2 x 500m, 65 sec. recovery
- Interval training:
  3 x 1 km, or
  5 x 600m, or
  5 x 300m
- Fartlek
- Changes of pace over distances from 1500 to 3,000m (recovery based on lactate accumulation)
- Easy competitions.

These program elements show the current trend in training toward lower total volume, with much higher intensity of training.

10,000 METERS AND ROAD RACES

Perhaps the classic 10,000-meter racer is Lasse Viren, who gained racing immortality with his back-to-back double victories at 5000 and 10,000 meters in the 1972 and 1976 Olympic Games. His coach, Rolf Haikkola, used a mixture of ideas from other coaches:

- Long aerobic runs (Arthur Lydiard)
- Tempo runs faster than marathon pace (Paavo Nurmi)
- Intensive surges, running 2000-5000m of alternately sprinting 50 meters and jogging 50 meters (Mihaly Igloi)
- Uphill running and occasional use of three training sessions per day (Percy Cerutty)
- Controlled fartlek, using fast repetitions of several minutes' duration thrown into the middle of a tempo run (Haikkola).

During the competitive season, most of Viren's training was slow (compared to his fitness level), low stress runs in the forest for 60-90 minutes. Some intervals were run, along with buildup races. He ran three test workouts of 20 x 200m (with 200 jogs) with the same rhythm for each test, with a fast last 200m, then took his heart rate. His HR would become lower as he became more fit.

Viren increased his annual mileage from 3400 km in 1968-69 to 3728 km in 1969-70, 5332 km in 1970-71, and then 7348 km (about 88 miles per week average) in 1971-72. While his Olympic year training was a 38% increase over the previous year, the physical recovery was watched closely. He trained on a 3-day pattern, with two easy days after each hard day.

While long periods of training time primarily involved distance runs at varying paces, repetitions within some distance runs increased the intensity of the training. For example, during the summer he inserted 3 x 600m into a 9-mile run, and in another session ran 3 miles (5k) of 50/50 drills (sprint 50m, jog 50m) during a 7-mile (12k) run. His depletion workout before Munich (five days before his first race) was 5k of 50/50 on the grass in spikes, designed to raise his HR to 200 BPM and push him to exhaustion (resulting in overcompensation for his race).

Perhaps his greatest strengths as a racer were in his highly efficient running form, which allowed maximal use of his capabilities, and his ability to become completely absorbed in his own race, so that no distractions interfered with his racing tactics. Few distance runners have made fuller use of their capabilities.

Another example of 10,000-meter training is that of Alberto Salazar (27:25.61) under Bill Dellinger. His training pattern was a complex mix of overdistance and tempo runs, fartlek, intervals, simulations, and drills. The mixture of types of training permitted Salazar to be in good racing condition throughout much of the training year, resulting in elite performances up to the marathon distance (2:08:13).

To further illustrate the trends in training loads, the coach of Arturo Barrios (27:08.23 in 1989) argues that it takes about 6,000 km of training in a year to prepare to run 10 km in 28:00. Barrios' periodization tables show loads of up to 90-100 miles a week (150-170 km) at times of heavy training, but drops to about 60 miles a week (100 km), including the races, during his competition cycles.

RECENT DISTANCE TRAINING PRACTICES

Figure 10.6 gives a good example of planning a school distance running program, along with a graph of the training load throughout the year. This is another way to plan and record an athlete's training. A coach should begin to experiment with a very simple form, then increase the form's (and the plan's) complexity as his or her experience increases. Effective training uses a complex mixture of training methods, but it does not have to be complicated to be effective.

Triple seasons for distance runners (cross country and indoor and outdoor track), along with the increased number of meets in a season, create many problems in planning an effective training program. Because of the lengthy racing calendar, the traditional macrocycle structure must be modified to yield elite performances throughout the year. Figure 8.10 in Chapter 8 shows an almost weekly flip-flop from high volume and low intensity to low volume and high intensity in training. The volume

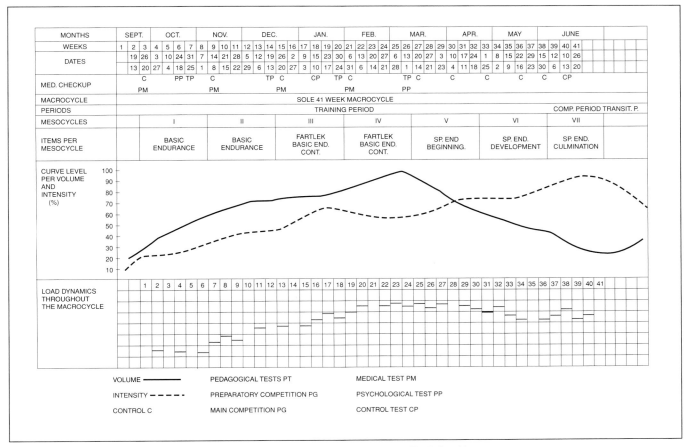

Figure 10.6. Graph of Middle Distance Training Year

and intensity will fluctuate until the final training period, rather than follow the traditional gradual buildup and tapering over time.

Three new terms have been suggested for the three periods (preparation, competition, and transition) of the macrocycle: accumulation, intensification, and transformation.

• *Accumulation* (transition) includes regeneration from previous races. It is used to accumulate energy for later, more intensive training. Training variety is important, as most of the training is low-intensity, high-volume activity.

• *Intensification* (preparation) includes improving the aerobic and anaerobic endurance and increasing the psychological resistance to stress.

• *Transformation* (competition) means converting the training into effective competitive performances.

As we can see, the terminology does not necessarily mean radical changes in the content of the training periods. These three progressive periods of training should occur within the phases and microcycles also, according to some coaches. The primary difference from the traditional periods is that the training load and intensity alter on a far shorter wave pattern, so that a large variation (or drop-off) in training loads does not occur except at the end of the macrocycle.

The final training time before racing is called the *direct competition preparation* (DCP). It is a 4-6-week phase with the accumulation, intensification, and transformation order in its microcycles. Table 10.15 shows a recommended order of training loads.

"The main goal of the DCP cycle is to direct the supercompensation phase of the athlete's body for the time of the major competition . . . The ability to prepare peak form at the desired time lies mainly in the proper distribution of volume and intensity in the macro-, meso-, and microcycles."

This approach shows continuing attempts of coaches and researchers to quantify training, so that it will become simply a matter of learning the right measures and proportions. However, we are not yet at that stage.

As a note on guiding athletes into the best

middle distance race, Soviet coaches evaluated 19-year-old male runners with control tests. According to the athlete's best marks at that time, they would be placed in one of these three groups:

• 400-800m: needs above-average speed
• 800-1500m: needs speed and specific endurance
• 1500-5,000m: needs high general endurance, but less speed.

The tables were based on event modeling by Soviet coaches and researchers.

The training and racing pattern has been strongly affected by the arrival of professional track and field. The competition year has grown longer and the competition more intense. The need to race more often and at a higher level (if one is to make a good living) has led to even more intensive training methods. Frank Dick describes the changes of the last three decades as a move from single periodization, with eight months of training, to double periodization to include a two-month indoor season. The current form of elite training is five months of preparation, followed by six months of money-driven competition. Dick expects sooner or later to see a year-round competition calendar—and he appears to be right. He predicts these changes in the design of training:

• Shorter duration mesocycles (3-6 weeks)
• Multiple objectives within the cycles
• A shift from large blocks of work to more specific training objectives
• Alternating "consolidation" priority years with "performance acceleration" priority years
• Training through competitions.

An example of the concept of training through competitions is one table that suggests how many competitions are needed for an athlete to peak (Table 10.16). It is based on a combination of races longer and shorter than the primary racing distance (for specific endurance and speed), combined with races at the racing distance.

This move toward more intensive training affects how we define the focal training concepts (Fig. 10.7). Günter Lange notes increased focus on training control: monitoring the training process with heart-rate monitors, lactate testing, and urea testing. In a discussion of training female Asian distance runners, he illustrates the training cycle (Fig. 10.8) in a pattern that represents the increased complexity of the cycles at the elite level.

Training loads are rising for elite athletes—in some cases to phenomenal levels (which also raises the question of whether drugs are used as enablers of the high loading). Altitude training is used increasingly by elite athletes, as is improved nutritional awareness as an aid to the recovery process.

Table 10.15. Direct Competition Mesocycle Load Pattern

Microcycles			
Day	Accumulation	Intensification	Transformation
Mon	Medium	Medium	Medium
Tues	High	Medium	Low
Wed	Medium	High	Medium
Thurs	High	High	Low
Fri	Medium	Medium	Medium
Sat	High	Medium	Low
Sun	Rest	Rest	Rest

Table 10.16. Races to Peak

Event	Primary Distance	Over-Distance	Under-Distance	Total Races
800	5-7	4	4	13-15
1500	5-7	4	4	13-15
3 km	4-6	3	3	10-12
5 km	4-6	3	3	10-12
10 km	2-4	2	2	6-8

At the same time that training is becoming more intense, there is greater emphasis on aggressive racing tactics and on pace-setting to ensure higher-quality races.

We still see prominent examples of attempts to maintain very high to extremely high training loads at a higher level of intensity. Look at the training programs of the Kenyan runners, in particular their junior runners, and the Chinese women who set a number of astounding records in the early 1990s. There are still many questions about the validity of Ma Junren's training methods, particularly after most of his training squad was disqualified from the 2000 Olympics after drug tests given by Chinese sports officials.

Currently popular systems of distance training in the United States are Jack Daniels' system, based on physiological building blocks; Tony Benson's *Run With The Best* system, based on the philosophies of Arthur Lydiard and Percy Cerutty; David Martin and Peter Coe's work based on physiological research; Bill Bowerman's Oregon System, a complex program based on fartlek, interval training, and speed development after a solid base; and Arthur Lydiard's system, still extremely influential after nearly half a century. Joe Vigil's approaches are also very influential.

NOTES ON THE MARATHON

Kenny Moore was perhaps the first American marathoner to show the value of track speed. Before Moore, America had produced only one truly fast marathoner—Buddy Edelen. Edelen made his breakthrough with high mileage training over a period of years while training in England. In contrast, Moore was a very successful racer for Bill Bowerman at Oregon, focusing on the steeplechase and the 3-mile, while moving down to the mile and up to six miles.

Moore, an Olympic team member in 1968 and 1972, continued to follow the Oregon system as a marathoner, following a schedule similar to a long middle distance runner, with two exceptions. He

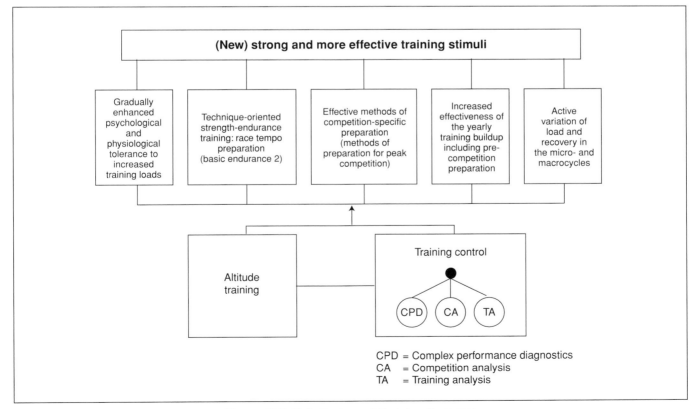

Figure 10.7. Main Factors of Training Concepts

101

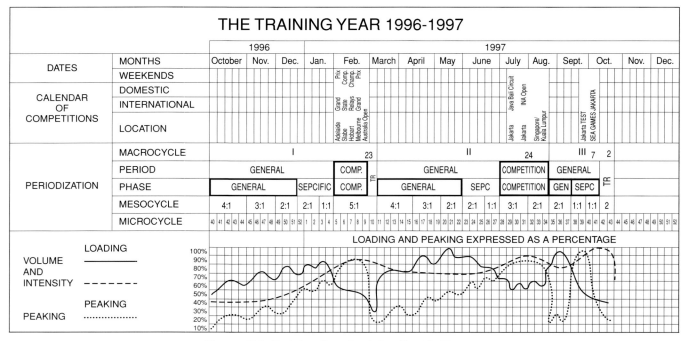

Figure 10.8. Training Year for Asian Female Runner

would do some repetition workouts at 1200m or one mile at 70 seconds per 400m, which was appropriate for 10 km training at that time (29:00 pace). He also ran Sunday runs of up to 30 miles, saying that because his technique was not very smooth, he needed to harden his body to endure the discomfort of racing the marathon distance.

His training is notable because it was a departure from the traditional American approach to marathoning, in which the talented track racers never ran the long race. Moore also emphasized the hard-easy approach to training, compared to the traditional hard training every day. Furthermore, he was able to run a moderately high-level mile (4:02) while training as a marathoner. His shorter interval sessions included the traditional Oregon 16 x 300m in 45 seconds, with 100-meter recovery jogs. It was a training emphasis on quality and recovery (sometimes two easy days for every hard day) that was still rare in the late 1960s and early 1970s. More athletes now realize that truly fast marathon times require the ability to achieve elite marks on the track at 10,000m.

Bill Dellinger's training for Alberto Salazar included training in surging over distances of 800m to a mile to harden him to tactical moves during the marathon. A critical factor in the marathon is to peak properly and avoid over-racing. At the highest levels, no athlete should run more than two marathons during a year. An example of the training load and intensity for an American marathoner (who must peak for the Olympic Trials, then again at the Olympic Games) is shown in Figure 10.9.

David Costill emphasizes the importance of increasing the training load gradually, recommending a load variation from one week to the next. A five-week phase of five microcycles is a good approach to prepare for a marathon. The microcycles involve (in order):

- Test microcycle: Run either a 40 km test effort or a road race of 20-30 km. This test establishes the performance level.
- Restoration microcycle: Recover from the test and establish a base for higher tolerance to training loads. No intensive loads should be used in this microcycle.
- Buildup microcycle: Stabilize the body's performance capabilities with a higher running volume.
- Lead-up microcycle: Establish the tempo and rhythm of the racing pace, again with a relatively high running volume.
- Race microcycle: Unloading, followed by the race.

The phase should not include any work to improve the speed, nor should it increase the number of training runs. Though the training in the third and fourth weeks involves volume, it is not unusually high volume. The primary emphasis is in stabilizing the performance base, then unloading properly to gain the effect of overcompensation.

Table 10.17 shows suggested kilometer paces for training runs for the marathon. There is increasing use of long repetitions at the athlete's 10 km racing pace as a part of training, hardly surprising as the fastest men's races may average a 400m pace

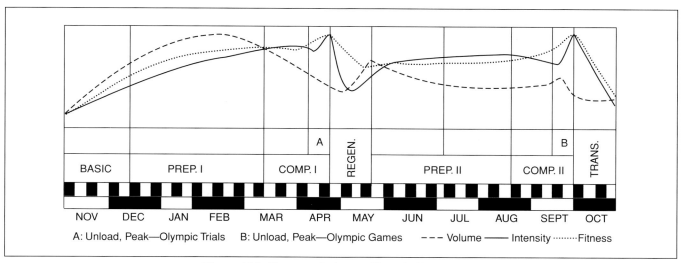

Figure 10.9. Macrocycle for an Olympic Marathoner

of 72-73 seconds.

Women have improved their marathon performances remarkably in the last decade. Preparing for a major race should be based on three training periods followed by a month or more of recuperation. A runner should allow a minimum of six months of preparation for a marathon, with the highest volume in the third (specific training) phase, as most of the energy for a marathon (98%) is aerobic. The ideal pace for training during this phase is based on the runner's anaerobic threshold (the point at which the athlete begins to go into oxygen debt). A non-invasive test allows this threshold to be located by an on-the-track running exercise, with the HR recorded throughout. After the test, the coach can tell the athlete the ideal range of speed and heart rate for their most effective training.

THE MYTH OF THE PERFECT SYSTEM

I feel obligated to add a note here: There is no "magic bullet." There is no "perfect" system or method of training. There is no single factor that will either produce or forecast success.

Sorry about that—it is the most cherished be-

lief in sport. There is always a new system, a new method, a new workout, a new drug that will guarantee success. Except that it is not true.

The human body is unique to its owner. The principles are the same, but every human body has its own peculiarities. Some develop speed more easily, some gain more stamina. Some can reach high levels of performance in a surging race, others cannot develop even a coping ability.

The "secret" to training is discovering exactly what each person needs. The ability to see those needs is what makes the greatest coaches, such as Bill Bowerman. If he had ten milers, they would have ten different training schedules—each adjusted for that person's needs.

Owen Anderson has examined the major approaches to training very critically, and his analysis reinforces these comments. He notes that almost every approach to training has a hidden (and sometimes not-so-hidden) weakness. Whether it is the Lydiard system, the Daniels system, VO_2max training, anaerobic training, heart-rate monitoring, lactate testing, tempo training, or long runs at a slow pace, they all have flaws.

Training systems are not religions, nor are

Table 10.17. Training Paces for Marathon

Individual Anaerobic Threshold Value	Expected Marathon Performance (hr., min)	Slow Endurance Runs (40-50 km)	Medium Pace Endurance Runs (30 km)	Tempo Runs at Marathon Pace (10-20 km)	Long Interval Runs (2-5 km) (min/km)	Short Interval Runs (200-400m) (sec)
2:50	2:08-2:10	up to 3:25	3:02-3:20	2:58-3:00	2:40-2:50	60-64
3:00	2:14-2:15	3:35	3:20-3:30	3:08-3:12	2:50-3:00	62-66
3:20	2;30-2:32	3:55	3:40-3:50	3:32-3:40	3:10-3:20	70-75
3:40	2:47-2:50	4:20	4:00-4:15	3:55-4:05	3:25-3:40	76-81
4:00	3:02-3:06	4:45	4:30-4:45	4:20-4:30	3:45-4:00	82-88

they perfect science. The art of coaching is still a major factor of success. We should never stop experimenting and learning.

REFERENCES

1. NSA Round Table 32: Speed in the 800 metres [Jorge Diaz Gamboa, Ray Elrick, Amarilis Hernández Mora, David E. Martin, Manuel Pascua Piqueras, Matt Paterson, Paul Schmidt & Carlo Vittori]. (1996). *New Studies in Athletics, 11*(4), 7-22.
2. Bernie Dare. (1988). VO₂max, training, and other factors. *Track and Field Quarterly Review, 88*(2), 43-44.
3. Klaus Maulbecker & Jobst Kruger. (1988). Are long distance runners overworked? *Track Technique, 104*, 3328.
4. William H. Freeman. (1975). Distance training methods, past and present. *Track and Field Quarterly Review, 75*(4), 4-11.
5. Dietrich Harre. (1980). Endurance: Classification and development. In Jess Jarver (Ed.), *Long Distances* (pp. 16-19). Mountain View: Tafnews.
6. Jose Manuel Ballesteros & Julio Alvarez. (1979). *Track and Field: A Basic Coaching Manual* (pp. 11, 18). London: IAAF.
7. Norman Brook. (1987). *Endurance Training* (pp. 18-28, 42-45). Ramsbury, Wilts., ENG: Crowood Press.
8. A. Viru, P. Korge & J. Parnal. (1980). Classification of training methods. In *Long Distances* (pp. 32-34).
9. Bill Dellinger & Bill Freeman. (1984). *The Competitive Runner's Training Book*. New York: Collier.
10. Jack Daniels. (1995). Training distance runners. *Track and Field Quarterly Review, 95*(2), 29-33.
11. William H. Freeman. (1985). Concerns in training women distance runners. *Track and Field Quarterly Review, 85*(3), 29-36.
12. Walter Gladrow. (1983). Establishing training loads for women's middle distance. *Track and Field Quarterly Review, 83*(3), 47-50.
13. Vladimir Kuznetsov. (1983). Modern problems of training women for middle and long distance running. *Track and Field Quarterly Review, 83*(3), 51-54.
14. Luiz de Oliveira. (1988). Middle distance training. *Track Technique, 104*, 3319-3321, 3333.
15. Harry Wilson. (1983). Preparation of 1500m runners. *Track and Field Quarterly Review, 83*(3), 14-17.
16. Harry Wilson. (1981). Speed in endurance events. In Vern Gambetta (Ed.), *Track Technique Annual '81* (pp. 56-57). Mountain View: Tafnews.
17. Peter Coe. (1983). Training a world class 800/1500m athlete. *Track and Field Quarterly Review, 83*(3), 19-26.
18. David E. Martin & Peter N. Coe. (1997). *Better Training for Distance Runners* (2nd ed.). Champaign, IL: Human Kinetics.
19. Yuri Tiurin. (1983). A report on the preparation of Ulmasova—3,000m champion of Europe 1982. *Track and Field Quarterly Review, 83*(3), 55-58.
20. John Andersen. (1983). Breaking the thirteen minute barrier. *Track and Field Quarterly Review, 83*(3), 27-34.
21. Pompilio Ferreira. (1983). Experience in Oporto. *Track and Field Quarterly Review, 83*(3), 38-41.
22. William J. Bowerman & William H. Freeman. (1991). *High Performance Training for Track and Field* (2nd ed.). Champaign, IL: Human Kinetics.
23. Enrico Dionisi. (1991). The secrets behind Morocco's running achievements [abstract]. *New Studies in Athletics, 6*(4), 80-82.
24. Antero Raevuori & Rolf Haikkola. (1978). *Lasse Viren: Olympic Champion*. Trans. Matti Hannus. Portland, OR: Continental.
25. Tadeusz Kepka. (1991). Training for long-distance track events—Arturo Barrios [abstract]. *New Studies in Athletics, 6*(4), 73-79.
26. Adam Zajac & Gregory Prus. (1988). Training for middle distance. *Track Technique, 102*, 3250-3253.
27. R. Travin, et al. (1981). Model performances for distance runners. In *Track Technique '81* (p. 127).
28. Frank Dick. (1993). The new Olympiad and the coach [abstract]. *New Studies in Athletics, 8*(3), 102-103.
29. Günter Lange. (1993). Trends in long distance training. *New Studies in Athletics, 8*(4), 23-25.
30. Günter Lange. (1999). Principles of female distance training in Asia—A report from experience. *New Studies in Athletics, 14*(1), 57-66.
31. Felix P. Suslov. (1994). Basic principles of high altitude training. *New Studies in Athletics, 9*(2), 45-49.
32. Manfred Reiss, Olaf Ernest & Dieter Gohlitz. (1993). Analysis of the 1989-1992 Olympic cycle with conclusions for coaching distance running and walking events. *New Studies in Athletics, 8*(4), 7-18.
33. Colm O'Connell. (1996). Environmental conditions, training systems and performance development of Kenyan runners. *New Studies in Athletics, 11*(4), 25-36.
34. P. Shiquin & W. Wenshen. (1995). An analysis of Ma Junren's training methods. *Modern Athlete and Coach, 33*(3), 40-41.
35. Jack Daniels. (1998). *Daniels' Running Formula*. Champaign, IL: Human Kinetics.
36. Tony Benson & Irv Ray. (1998). *Run With the Best*. Mountain View, CA: Tafnews.
37. Arthur Lydiard & Garth Gilmour. (1967). *Run to the Top*. Auckland: Minerva.
38. Joe Vigil. (1996). Training parameters and philosophies in international competition. *American Swimming Coaches Association World Clinic Series, 27*, 315-332.
39. David L. Costill. (1986). *Inside Running: Basics of Sports Physiology*. Indianapolis: Benchmark.
40. J. Velikorondikh, et al. (1988). Marathon training prior to racing. *Track Technique, 103*, 3299.
41. Owen Anderson. (Spring 2000). Ronaldo da Costa's unique marathon training [abstract]. *Track Coach, 151*, 4834-4835.
42. Giampaolo Lenzi. (1983). The women's marathon: Preparing for an important event in the season. *Track and Field Quarterly Review, 83*(3), 58-62.
43. Owen Anderson. (1999). Millennium review: As we reach year 2YK, here's a critical survey of the latest thinking about the ins and outs of training. *Peak Performance, no. 126*, 1-4.

OTHER RESOURCES FOR PERIODIZED DISTANCE TRAINING

Avery, Guy. (1996). A simple but proven way to train for a faster mile. *Track and Field Coaches Review, 96*(2), 10-16.
Bennett, Steve. (Winter 1999). Training for the 800. *Track Coach, 146*, 4649-4656.
Billat, L. Véronique. (2001). Interval training for performance: A scientific and empirical practice. Special recommendations for middle- and long-distance running. Part I: Aerobic interval training. *Sports Medicine, 31*(1), 13-31; Part II: Anaerobic interval training. *31*(2), 75-90.
Bondarenko, Vladimir. (1991) The structure of the last cycle of the training year: 1988 Olympic Champion Olga Bondarenko. *Track and Field Quarterly Review, 91*(2), 51-53.
Bowerman, William J., & William H. Freeman. (1974). *Coaching Track and Field* (pp. 6-84). Boston: Houghton Mifflin.
Burke, Edmund R. (Ed.). (1998). *Precision Heart Rate Training*. Champaign, IL: Human Kinetics.
Burrows, Melonie, & Steve Bird. (2000). The physiology of the highly trained female endurance runner. *Sports Medicine, 30*(4), 281-300.
Christensen, Scott. (Summer 2000). Strength training for endurance runners. *Track Coach, 152*, 4841-4845.
Coffman, Wayne. (1994). Cross country: Theory and training schedule. *Track and Field Quarterly Review, 94*(2), 11-12.
Fallowfield, Joanne L. (Ed.). (1999). *Improving Sports Performance in Middle and Long Distance Running: A Scientific Approach to Race Preparation*. New York: John Wiley.
Fowler, Robert. (1998). A critical analysis of performance trends in distance running. *Modern Athlete and Coach, 36*(4), 3-7.
Gibbons, Tim. (2000). Common characteristics of successful endur-

ance programs. Part I: Factors of success. *Track and Field Coaches Review, 73*(2), 15-17; Part II: Application to U.S. distance running, *73*(3), 24-27.

Gigliotti, Lucia. (1991). Marathon training—Gelindo Bordin's programme [abstract]. *New Studies in Athletics, 6*(4), 72-74.

Gonschinska, Idrill. (1996). The speed and strength training of middle-distance runners from a functional point of view [abstract]. *New Studies in Athletics, 11*(4), 98-102.

Greene, Laurence S., & Russell R. Pate. (1997). *Training for Young Distance Runners.* Champaign, IL: Human Kinetics.

Janssen, Peter. (2001). *Lactate Threshold Training.* Champaign, IL: Human Kinetics.

Jarver, Jess. (Ed.). (1995). *Long Distances: Contemporary Theory, Technique and Training* (3rd ed.). Mountain View, CA: Tafnews.

Jarver, Jess. (Ed.). (1997). *Middle Distances: Contemporary Theory, Technique and Training* (4th ed.). Mountain View, CA: Tafnews.

Koskei, Mike, & Walter Abmayr. (1988). Cross country training in Kenya. *New Studies in Athletics, 3*(4), 53-59.

Litovchenko, M. (1991). High level women's training program: 800, 1500, 3000 meters. *Track and Field Quarterly Review, 91*(2), 54-56.

Lyden, Robert L. (1993). The importance of strength training for middle distance and distance runners. *Track and Field Quarterly Review, 93*(2), 35-59.

Lyden, Robert L. (1994). The sharpening period. *Track and Field Quarterly Review, 94*(2), 39-60.

Lyden, Robert. (2001). *Distance Running.* Moneterey: Exercise Science.

Lydiard, Arthur, & Garth Gilmour. (1999). *Distance Training for Young Athletes.* Aachen, Ger.: Meyer & Meyer Sport.

Martin, David. (1995). Appearances are deceiving: The female athlete triad. *Track Technique, 130,* 4144-4147.

Martin, David. (1994). The challenge of using altitude to improve performance. *New Studies in Athletics, 9*(2), 51-57.

Mikkelsson, Lasse. (1996). How to train to become a top distance runner. *New Studies in Athletics, 11*(4), 37-44.

Mikkelsson, Lasse. (1996). Strengthen the strengths: Annemari Sandell's training. *New Studies in Athletics, 11*(4), 45-50.

Montrucchio, Noel. (Spring 2000). A goal-setting strategy for endurance athletes. *Track Coach, 151,* 4809-4813.

Neuhof, Joachim. (1990). Structure and yearly training build-up in middle and long distance running. *New Studies in Athletics, 5*(2), 69-81.

Newton, Joe, & Joe Henderson. (1998). *Coaching Cross Country Successfully.* Champaign, IL: Human Kinetics.

Popov, Ilia. (1994). Viewpoint: The pros and cons of altitude training. *New Studies in Athletics, 9*(2), 15-22.

Reiss, Manfred. (1999). Guidance and advice in the use and methodology of altitude training for endurance sports. *New Studies in Athletics, 14*(3), 13-28.

Remigino, Lindy. (1994). Coaching the elite 800 meter runner. *Track and Field Quarterly Review, 94*(2), 23-28.

The Running Times Guide to Breakthrough Running. (2000). Ed. Gordon Bakoulis. Champaign, IL: Human Kinetics.

Schaffer, Ray. (1991). Periodization of cross country training for high school women. *Track Technique, 117,* 3725-3727.

Schiffer, Jürgen. (1998). Selected and annotated bibliography 46: Cross country running—Part I. *New Studies in Athletics, 13*(3), 61-88; Part II. *NSA, 13*(4), 55-88.

Schiffer, Jürgen. (1999). Selected and annotated bibliography 50: Steeplechase. *New Studies in Athletics, 14*(3), 75-89.

Shephard, Roy J., & Per-Olaf Åstrand (Eds.). (1992). *Endurance in Sport* [The Encyclopedia of Sports Medicine]. Oxford, Eng.: Blackwell Scientific.

Smith, Richard D. (1992). Insights into the value of strength training and periodized conditioning for runners. *Track Technique, 120,* 3834-3836.

Tanser, Toby. (2001). *Train Hard, Win Easy: The Kenyan Way.* (2nd ed.). Mountain View, CA: Tafnews.

Tegen, Peter. (1994). Middle distance and distance training. *Track and Field Quarterly Review, 94*(2), 21-22.

Usami, Akio. (1988). The development of Japanese marathon runners. *New Studies in Athletics, 4*(4), 61-69.

Walsh, Christopher M. (1990). Bowerman Oregon distance training meets Bompa training theory: Periodized Bowerman mile and 5km training. *Track and Field Quarterly Review, 90*(2), 12-20.

Zelentsova. Tatyana. (Fall 1998). Soviet middle distance training. *Track Coach, 145,* 4637-4638.

SOURCES FOR TABLES

10.1.   Fitness Characteristics of Distance Events: Dick, p. 64
10.2.   Phase Training Ratios for the Distances: Dick, p. 62
10.3.   Phases 1-4 Training: Ballesteros & Alvarez, p. 26
10.4.   Aerobic and Anaerobic Effects: Mathews & Fox, p. 27
10.5.   Contribution of Energy Systems to Performance: Mathews, Donald, & Edward L. Fox. (1976). *The Physiological Basis of Physical Education and Athletics,* 2nd ed. Philadelphia: W.B. Saunders, 27.
10.6.   Performance References: Jarver, *Long Distances* (3rd ed.), p. 39
10.7.   Optimal Training Speeds Based on 10 km. Time: Jarver, *Long Distances* (3rd ed.), p. 86
10.8.   Intensities of Endurance Training Zones: Adapted from Raeburn, Peter, & David Jenkins, (Eds.). *Training for Speed and Endurance.* St. Leonards, Australia: Allen & Unwin, 49.
10.9.   Load Characteristics in Endurance Events: Jarver, *Long Distances,* p. 28
10.10. Training Loads for Endurance Training: Jarver, *Middle Distances,* p. 60
10.11. Estimation of Recovery Times Between Running Intervals: *Track and Field Quarterly Review, 91*(2), 36
10.12. Endurance and Tempo Paces and Controls: Gladrow, 48
10.13. Numbers of Annual Races by Women: Jarver, *Long Distances* (3rd ed.), p. 36
10.14. Single Periodisation: Dionisi, 82
10.15. Direct Competition Mesocycle Load Pattern: Zajac & Prus, 3251-3252
10.16. Races to Peak: *Track Technique, 130,* 4142 (modified by Freeman)
10.17. Training Paces for Marathon: Jarver, *Long Distances* (3rd ed.), p. 77

SOURCES FOR FIGURES

10.1.   Structure of Middle Distance Training: Jarver, *Middle Distances* (2nd ed., 1985), p. 99
10.2.   Middle Distance Training: Dick, p. 46
10.3.   Primary Training Zones of Performance: *Track and Field Quarterly Review, 91*(2), 32
10.4.   Types of Training: Daniels, 32
10.5.   Hill Training (Lydiard System): Jarver, *Middle Distances* (1979), p. 84
10.6.   Graph of Middle Distance Training Year: Ramos, Juan G. Bacallao. (1987). Planning middle and long distance training programs. *Track Technique, #99,* 3155.
10.7.   Main Factors of Training Concepts: Reiss, et al., 18
10.8.   Training Year for Asian Female Runner: Lange (1999), p. 61.
10.9.   Macrocycle for an Olympic Marathoner: Author

CHAPTER 11:
Periodized Training For Sprinters and Hurdlers

Some of the earliest translated articles on periodization in training concerned sprinters. While both sprints and hurdles are explosive effort events, because of their differing technical requirements we will discuss them separately.

SPRINTS

Sample basic training emphases for the phases of sprint training are shown in Tables 11.1 to 11.5.

The changes in load and intensity are shown in Figure 11.1. The general preparation focuses on all-around performance components, while the specific (special) preparation gradually raises the event-specific training to 60-70% of the total training volume. "It [is] completely wrong to believe that the larger the training volume and the wider the methods employed, the better the sprinting results. There is no correlation between 100m performances and the training volume at the various stages of prepara-

Table 11.1. Fitness Characteristics of Sprints and Hurdles

Event	General	Special	Competition-Specific
Sprints, Relays	Aerobic endurance Strength endurance Mobility Maximum strength	Speed endurance Speed Elastic strength Special strength Relative Special endurance 200m, 400m	Sprint technique Start technique Time trials Baton speed technique
Hurdles	Aerobic endurance Strength endurance Mobility Maximum strength	Speed endurance Special mobility Speed Elastic strength Special strength Relative Special endurance 200m, 400m	Hurdles technique Sprint technique Start technique Stride patterns Time trials

Table 11.2. Phase Training Ratios for Sprints

Phase	General	Special	Specific
1	25	55	20
2	15	60	25
3	10	55	35
4	25	55	20
5	10	60	30
6	80	10	10

Phase Training Ratios for Hurdles

Phase	General	Special	Specific
1	35	35	30
2	25	35	40
3	10	40	50
4	20	40	40
5	10	40	50
6	80	10	10

Percent distribution of:
- General Training (mostly compensatory strength and mobility work)
- Special Training (includes aerobic endurance)
- Competition-Specific Training

Table 11.3. Phases 1-4 Training for Sprints

PHASE 1: Improvement of Physical Condition
- 30% Conditioning exercises, circuit training, overall conditioning
- 30% Speed endurance: 4-8 x 200-400m, 3-5 min. recovery, no straining
- 20% Speed work: 2-3 sets of 5 x 20-30m from start, short recovery
- 10% Hill running: 2-3 sets of 5 x 30-60m (steep), 3 min. recovery
- 10% Fartlek: 45 min., on hills and flat, easy and fast mixed

PHASE 2: Increase of Specific Endurance
- 30% Speed endurance: 3-6 x 80-150m, strong rhythm, 6-8 min. recovery
- 30% Full-effort work: 10 x 30-60m from start, on straight or turn at top speed, 3-6 min. recovery
- 20% Power work: jumps, exercises, hill work
- 10% Interval training: 2-3 sets of 5 x 100m, fast but relaxed,1-2 min. recovery
- 10% Fartlek

PHASES 3-4: Improve Speed and Gain Peak Form
- 40% Starts and pace and stride frequency variations, short distances
- 30% Race pace work: 2-4 x 60-80% race distance, 10-12 min. recovery
- 20% Jogging, jumping, exercises to maintain strength and spring
- 10% Speed endurance intervals: 10 x 80m, fast, 2-3 min. recovery
- Meets: One per week, open races and relays

Table 11.4. Training Emphases in the Sprint Macrocycle

* General Preparation I (8 weeks)
  General development: 45%
  General endurance: 40%
  Rest: 15%

* General Preparation II (12 weeks)
  General endurance: 20%
  General ability: 15%
  General strength: 10%
  Special strength: 15%
  Jumping ability: 15%
  Rest: 15%
  Speed endurance: 10%

* Special Preparation (12 weeks)
  General endurance: 20%
  Special strength: 20%
  Speed: 20%
  Speed endurance: 15%
  Rest: 15%
  Technique: 10%

* Pre-Competition and Competition (8-12 weeks)
  Rest: 30%
  General endurance: 15%
  Speed endurance: 15%
  Special strength: 10%
  Speed: 10%
  Technique: 10%
  Competition: 10%

* Transition (8-12 weeks)

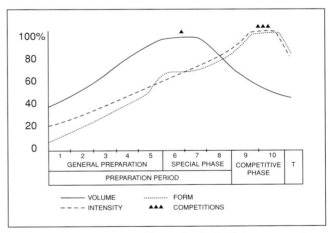

Figure 11.1. Volume and Intensity in Sprint macrocycle

coveries between repetitions, adding extra speed endurance work to the program, the lack of recuperation between training sessions and insufficient maximum-speed development work." (1)

The main physical qualities of an elite sprinter are quickness, strength, and speed endurance. Anaerobic power and endurance are critical to success. The training intervals in Table 11.6 are used to develop anaerobic power, and those in Table 11.7 are used to develop anaerobic endurance.

The training program of 1972 Olympic cham-

tion. On the contrary, the principle of specificity must be applied.

"When the volume of specific work is increased, the volume of non-specific training must be reduced. . . the most common mistakes in sprint training are the shortening and lengthening of re-

Table 11.5. Training Phases for Sprinters, Two Peaks

Phase	Weeks	Dates	Training Emphasis
I	4-5	Sep 21 - Oct 25	1. General conditioning 2. Speed development
IIA	6	Oct 26 - Dec 6	1. Speed 2. Speed endurance 3. Technique 4. Power
IIB	4	Dec 7 - Jan 3	1. Maintenance 2. General conditioning
III	6	Jan 4 - Feb 14	1. Speed endurance 2. Speed and technique 3. Power
IVA	4	Feb 15 - Mar 14	1. Resting phase for indoor peak 2. Speed and technique
IVB	1-2	Mar 8/15 - Mar 21	Transition from Indoor Macrocycle 1. Rest and refreshing cycle 2. Maintenance
V	6	Mar 22 - May 2	1. Speed endurance 2. Speed and technique 3. Power
VIA	2	May 3 - May 16	1. Peaking and resting for conference meet 2. Speed and technique 3. Maintenance
VIB	1	May 17 - May 23	1. Rest and recovery 2. Speed and technique 3. Maintenance
VIC Meet	2	May 24 - Jun 6	1. Peaking and resting for NCAA 2. Speed and technique 3. Maintenance
VID	1	June 7 - Jun 13	1. Rest and recovery 2. Speed and technique 3. Maintenance
VIE	2	Jun 14 - Jun 27	1. Peak 2. Rest for USATF

pion Valeriy Borzov divides the sprinter's training periods into four types, with the following objectives for each period:

- Conditioning Period (Deposit)
    1. Aerobic endurance
    2. Strength endurance
    3. Flexibility
    4. Coordination
- Post-Conditioning Period (Concentration)
    1. Anaerobic lactate capacity
    2. Sprinting qualities
    3. Cadence
    4. Anaerobic alactate power
- Pre-Competition Period (Accumulation)
    1. Sprinting components
    2. Sprinting endurance
- Competition Period (Realization)
    1. Technical perfection
    2. Recuperation.

This program is particularly interesting because Remi Korchemny provides flowcharts that permit the training program to be implemented by developing and refining a computer software program.

A thorough two-peak periodized year for training sprinters at the University of Tennessee concentrates on six major training factors:

1. Speed training: focuses on absolute speed
2. Speed endurance training: uses three types of workout
    - Low anaerobic stress training
    - Medium to high anaerobic stress training
    - High anaerobic stress training
3. Weight training: develops both total conditioning and specific event strength
4. Plyometrics: increases ability to apply force to the ground very quickly
5. Technique work: used more for warmup, developing the holistic movement sense, and muscular strengthening.
6. Relaxation: Includes relaxation both at rest (for calming and visualization) and at speed.

The sprinters take control tests at distances up to 300m, along with related tests and a body fat test by the hydrostatic (underwater) method. The training year is broken into six cycles or phases (Table 11.5) and is an excellent example of applying periodized training to the American college competitive year.

The TAC/USA Level II Coaching Education

Table 11.6. Intervals for Anaerobic Power

Interval Distance	Intensity	Reps	Sets	Rest Between		HR Before Set Begins
				Reps	Sets	
30m	Maximal	4-5	2-3	2-3m.	4-5m.	110
60m	Maximal	3-4	2-3	3-4m.	6-8m.	110
150m	95-98%	2	2-3	8-10m.	12-15m.	120
250m	90-95%	2-3	1	12-15m.	——	120

Note: Reps = Repetitions; HR = Heart rate; m. = Minutes

Table 11.7. Intervals for Anaerobic Capacity

Interval Distance	Intensity	Reps	Sets	Rest Between Reps	Rest Between Sets	HR Before Set Begins
60m	90-95%	4-6	4-6	30-60s.	3-5m.	120
100m	85-90%	5-8	3-4	30-60s.	6-8m.	120
300m	80-90%	2-4	3-4	2-5m.	10-15m.	120
600m	75-85%	2-3	2-3	3-6m.	15-18m.	120

Note: Reps = Repetitions; HR = Heart rate; m. = Minutes; s. = Seconds.

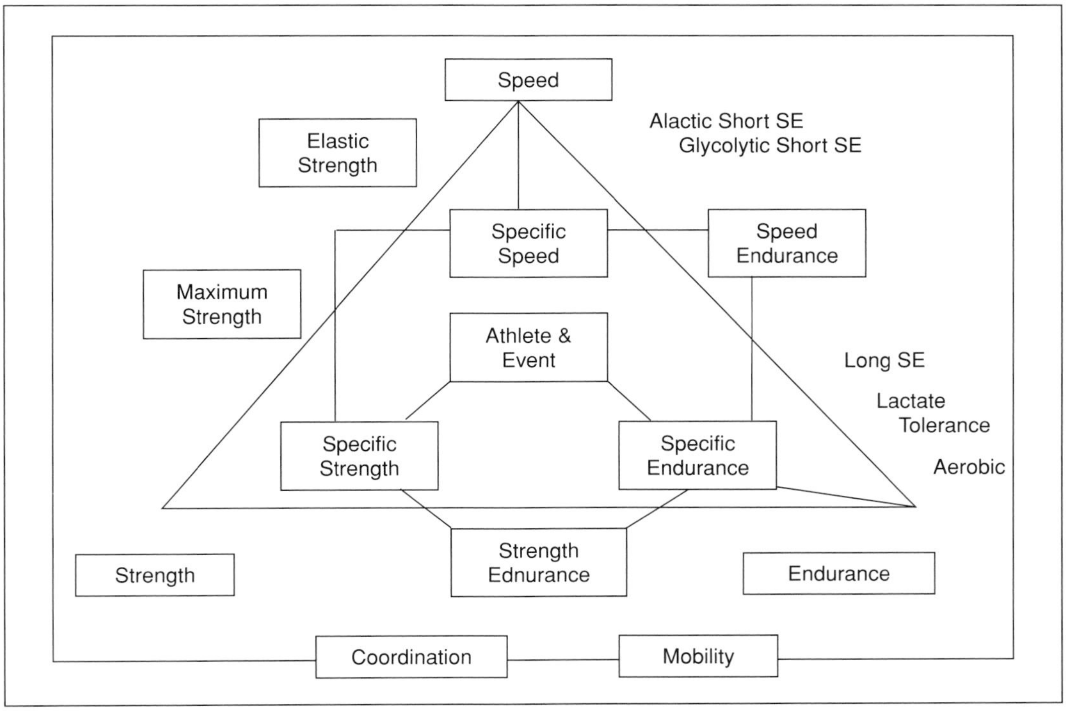

Figure 11.2. Sprint Training Matrix

Curriculum Development Committee on Sprints and Hurdles described the training components of sprinting within two major subgroups: technical components and energy system components. The technical components are:

- Speed Skill (developing effective sprinting mechanics)
- Speed Acceleration (developing effective starting and acceleration techniques.

The energy system components are:

- Speed (absolute speed)
- Speed Endurance
  Short Speed Endurance (alactic and glycolytic)
  Long Speed Endurance
  Lactate Tolerance
- Tempo Endurance
  Extensive (aerobic capacity and aerobic power)
  Intensive (anaerobic capacity)
  Strength Endurance

Gary Winckler describes a training matrix for the sprints, shown in Figure 11.2, while Table 11.8 gives the emphases of an annual training plan for a sprinter. Table 11.9 shows the intervals, intensities, and recoveries needed for developing the different systems needed for elite sprinting.

Tudor Bompa wrote a sample macrocycle for an elite sprinter (Figure 11.3). It is a double-periodized year, aimed at maximizing improvement. The double-periodized year, with two competition cycles, is becoming the preferred model for elite sprinters, while less-advanced sprinter are assisted more by a single-periodized year, which provides more training time.

The direct competition phase (DCP) of the sprinter's microcycle is three successive microcycles (accumulation, intensification, and transformation) lasting for a total of four weeks (Fig. 11.4). The accumulation microcycle is primarily recovery from previous competition. While the volume of training rises, the intensity is generally low. The intensifica-

Table 11.8. Emphases in Annual Sprint Training

GENERAL PREPARATION	SPECIAL PREPARATION	COMPETITION
Major Emphasis	**Major Emphasis**	**Major Emphasis**
General endurance Aerobic capacity Aerobic power General strength Flexibility Coordination	Specific endurance Anaerobic capacity Alactic short speed endurance Speed Specific and general strength	Speed Specific endurance Speed endurance Glycolytic short speed endurance Long speed endurance Lactate tolerance Tactics
Minor Emphasis	**Minor Emphasis**	**Minor Emphasis**
Speed Anaerobic capacity	General endurance Aerobic power Aerobic capacity Flexibility	General and specific strength Flexibility Aerobic power

Table 11.9. Energy System Training for Sprinters

Training Type	Energy* System	Component (Objective)	Distance	% of Best	Recovery Time Reps.	Sets
Speed	AN	Speed [S]	20-80m	90-95%	3-5m.	6-8m.
	AL	Anaerobic Power	20-80m	95-100%	3-5m.	6-8m.
Speed Endurance	AN	Alactic Short Speed Endurance [ASSE]	50-80m	90-95%	1-2m.	5-7m.
	AL	Anaerobic Power	50-80m	95-100%	2-3m.	7-10m.
	AN	Glycolytic Short Speed Endurance [GSSE]				
		Anaerobic Capacity	Under 80m	90-95%	1m.	3-4m.
	GL	Anaerobic Power	Under 80m	95-100%	1m.	4m.
	AN	Speed Endurance [SE]	80-150m	90-95%	5-6m.	
	GL	Anaerobic Power	80-150m	95-100%	6-10m.	
Extensive Tempo	AR	Aerobic Capacity [AC]	Over 200m	Under 70%	Under 45s.	Under 2m.
	AR	Aerobic Power [AP]	Over 100m	70-79%	30-90s	2-3m.
Intensive Tempo	MIX	Anaerobic Capacity [ANC]	Over 80m	80-90%	30s-5m.	3-10m.
Special Endurance	AN	Long Speed Endurance [LSE]	150-300m	90-95%	10-12m.	
	GL	Anaerobic Power	150-300m	95-100%	12-15m.	
	LAT	Lactate Tolerance [LAT]	300-600m	95-100%	Full	

*AL: Alactic; AN: Anaerobic; AR: Aerobic; GL: Glycolytic; LAT: Lactic Acid Tolerance; MIX: Mixed anaerobic and aerobic
**s.: seconds; m.: minutes.

tion microcycle (14 days) requires very high intensity training. The athlete will need a week of transformation training to recover from the intensification process and rise to a higher performance level.

This microcycle, ending with a day of rest followed by the major competition, uses a low training load and short, intensive training sessions mixed with easier sessions to peak the sprinter. Another example of a two-week cycle is shown in Figure 11.5.

Gradual improvement is more important than heavy training that leads to a peak as a junior athlete. Most of the sprinters who reach elite levels as high school performers make little further improvement in college. Most gradually fade from attention as their "less talented" opponents continue to improve during and after their own college years.

The training of Jarmila Kratochvilova, the champion female runner from Czechoslovakia over distances from 200 to 800 meters (11.09, 21.97, 47.99, and 1:53.43) is instructive. Her coach stressed that she was never a "talented" athlete, for she took 15 years of training just to reach world class, beginning her training at age 14. An example of her carefully

DATES	MONTHS	October				November				December					January				February				March	
	WEEKENDS	7	14	21	28	4	11	18	25	2	9	16	23	30	6	13	20	27	3	10	17	24	3	10
CALENDAR OF COMPETITIONS	DOMESTIC														■									
	INTERNATIONAL																■		■		■		■	
	LOCATION																Oregon		NY		LA		WORLDS	
PERIODIZATION	TRAINING PHASE	PREPARATION 1													COMPETITION 1									
	STRENGTH	ANATOMICAL ADAPTATION				MAXIMUM STRENGTH									POWER							MAINTENANCE		
	ENDURANCE	TEMPO																						
	SPEED								DEVELOP FOUNDATION SPEED						MAXIMUM SPEED								

DATES	MONTHS	March			April				May				June				July				August			Sept.	
	WEEKENDS	17	24	31	7	14	21	28	6	12	19	26	2	9	16	23	30	7	14	21	29	4	11	18	24	1	9
CALENDAR OF COMPETITIONS	DOMESTIC								■																	
	INTERNATIONAL										■		■		■		■		■		■			■		
	LOCATION										Seville		Moscow		Berlin		Olso		Zurich					Tokyo		
PERIODIZATION	TRAINING PHASE	TRAIN.			PREPARATION 1								COMPETITION 1												TRANSIT.
	STRENGTH	ANATOMICAL ADAPTATION				MAXIMUM STRENGTH				POWER							MAINTENANCE								
	ENDURANCE	TEMPO																						
	SPEED				DEVELOP FOUNDATION SPEED						MAXIMUM SPEED													

Figure 11.3. Double-Periodized Plan for the Sprinter

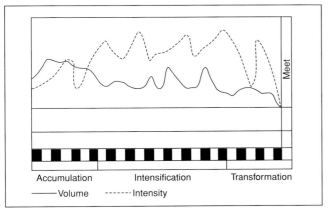

Accumulation   Intensification   Transformation

—— Volume   ------ Intensity

Figure 11.4. Direct Competition Preparation

planned improvement is shown in Table 11.10, which reveals her planned training load increases from 1979 to 1980, during which she improved by 2.01 seconds at 400 meters, rising to world class and winning an Olympic silver medal in Moscow at age 29.

Frank Dick has noted these trends in training sprinters:
- Specific strength units are included throughout the annual cycle, but are reduced or removed during the competition phases.
- Strength units are continued later for women than for men, extending into the competition phase.
- Sub-maximum speed work to super-maximum speed work is used in each microcycle to relate conditioning work to technique development.
- Specific maximum speed work to super-maximum speed work is used mostly in the pre-competition and competition phases, but may be used in some specific preparation blocks of work.
- All systems use a double-periodized year.

He also notes common characteristics of the different training systems or units:
- Specific strength work uses interplay between relevant muscle dynamics and joint actions.
- Where programs use high-intensity strength loadings (90-100%), training units may be continued to the days of competition.
- To ensure the integrity of techniques there is progression from sub-maximum to maximum speed, both intra-unit and inter-unit.
- When working at maximum or super-maximum speeds, there are full recoveries with stimulus duration of 2-3 secs, in sets of 2-4 x 2-4 reps. Note that athletes build gradually to maximum speed, avoiding rapid accelerations.

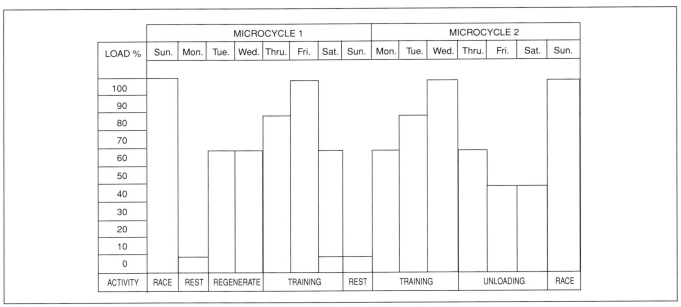

Figure 11.5. Two-Week Sprint Microcycle

Table 11.10. Training Load Increases for 400m

	1979	1980	Change	Percent
Days of training	273	313	+40	+15
Training sessions	388	438	+50	+13
Starting accelerations (km)	19	16	-3	-16
Starting accelerations	379	400	+21	+6
Special running exercises (km)	52	138	+86	+165
Running (km)	2,226	2,459	+233	+10
Running with load and runups (km)	8	122	+114	+1425
Plyometric takeoffs	18,946	7,416	-11,530*	-61*
Barbell work (tons)	530	798	+268	+51
Other sports activities (hrs.)	29	92	+63	+217
Rehabilitation (hrs.)	180	268	+88	+49
Days of competition	28	19	-9	-32
Starts in competition	47	22	-25	-53

* Problems with severe shinsplints on both legs in 1979.

- Units for maximum speed development are are normally separated by 48 hours, with two units per week when other units include starts, acceleration and pickup work.
- Maximum speed work, accelerations, starting and pickup are performed in groups, rather than individually.
- The high-intensity nature of training demands that regeneration units are liberally distributed through the competition microcycles.
- "It is essential that athletes have access to a comprehensive program of medical management."
- Coaches use personally devised tables for contrasts of strength, speed and speed endurance, i.e., control tests (see examples in Figures 7.7 and 7.8, and Table 7.1).

Analyzing sprint trends in the late 1980s, Hartmut Müller suggests these sprint training trends in the 100m and 200m races:

- Increased importance of sprinting strength, especially of maximal speed and speed-strength ability, as a basis for improved speed and acceleration.
- Increase in the proportion of maximal acceleration and speed runs during the training year.
- Greater emphasis on technique in acceleration and speed training, with special emphasis on the individual development of stride rate and stride length.

He makes a few other points for the 400m race:

• The importance of speed is rising faster than that of endurance; that is, the faster runners at 400m are also much faster at 100m and 200m.

• The greatest improvement in 400m times is increased speed over the 400m, with both men and women. This is only possible if the runner is very fast at the 200m distance, thus not running at close to capacity.

• Thus, the main interest is developing the level of maximal velocity. This greatly affects the intensity and effectiveness of the speed-strength training.

As a final note, the training loads of sprinters have risen over the years. An example of the changes in loading and intensity are evident in Table 11.11, based on a theoretical training program developed for elite sprinters by Ukrainian coaches.

THE HURDLES

Sample basic training emphases for the phases of sprint training are shown in Tables 11.1, 11.2, 11.12, and 11.13. A broad picture of the phases of training for women in the 100m hurdles is shown in Tables 11.14 and 11.15. They are useful for both the men's and women's high hurdle race.

The basic periodization process is quite similar to that for sprinting. Janusz Iskra provides a model for technical training in the 110m hurdles in Table 11.16. However, the most detailed book on training for the hurdle races is Brent McFarlane's Canadian text.

Strangely, more articles have been written on

Table 11.11. Distribution of Sprint Training

CYCLES / PERIODS / STAGES	FIRST (20 WEEKS) Fall-Winter			Winter		SECOND (19 WEEKS) Spring-Summer				Summer			TOTAL VOLUME
	GENERAL PREPARATION	STRENGTH ENDURANCE	SPEED-STRENGTH	WINTER PRE-COMPETITION	WINTER COMPETITION	GENERAL PREPARATION	STRENGTH ENDURANCE	SPEED-STRENGTH	FIRST COMPETITION	GENERAL PREPARATION	SPEED-STRENGTH	SECOND COMPETITION	
WEEKS	4	5	5	3	3	2	4	5	6	2	3	7	
Sprinting (km) (0-100% intensity)													
20-80m	-	-	2.2	3.0	3.2	-	0.8	2.4	5.0	-	2.8	5.4	25.0±1.6
100-150m	-	0.4	1.2	1.0	0.6	-	0.4	1.2	1.8	-	1.6	2.8	11.2±2.0
200-300m	-	0.6	1.6	0.8	0.8	-	0.6	1.4	2.0	-	1.2	2.6	11.6±2.2
(80-90% intensity)													
100-150m	-	2.0	2.4	0.8	0.4	-	2.2	3.0	1.4	-	1.2	1.4	14.8±2.8
200-300m	-	1.4	2.0	0.8	-	-	1.4	2.4	1.0	-	1.2	-	10.2±1.5
100-200m	1.6	2.4	-	-	-	0.8	0.8	2.2	-	0.8	-	-	10.8±1.4
300-400m	3.6	8.2	-	-	-	1.8	4.0	1.4	-	1.2	-	-	15.2±2.8
Speed development	-	0.2	0.8	0.6	0.6	-	0.8	1.0	1.4	-	0.8	1.2	7.4±0.8
Hill running 100-150m (km)	2.4	5.4	-	-	-	-	4.8	1.2	-	-	1.2	-	15.0±2.2
Hill running 50-100m (km)	-	-	0.5	0.4	0.3	-	-	0.6	0.8	-	0.4	0.8	8.8±0.4
Running exercises (km)	6.4	6.0	6.0	1.5	1.6	2.0	7.0	6.4	3.6	1.0	1.6	3.8	46.8±3.4
Jumps (km)	5.1	6.2	8.0	1.4	0.8	-	6.8	11.0	3.0	-	12.8	3.0	47.1±4.5
Throwing (no. of throws)	420	510	570	800	240	120	480	660	570	120	220	540	4350±240
Broken running (km)	7.8	8.4	-	-	-	3.6	8.4	-	-	-	-	-	28.0±2.0
Cross country (km)													
Aerobic	7.0	8	18	-	-	12	24	12	-	12	6	-	168±12
Aerobic-anaerobic	6	40	8	-	-	6	24	-	-	6	12	-	102±12
Power cross country	-	20	-	-	-	-	10	-	-	-	-	-	30±5
Strength endurance (tons)	-	68	-	-	-	-	54	-	-	-	-	-	117±14
Maximum strength (tons)	-	30	-	-	-	-	24	-	-	-	-	-	54±7.5
Speed-strength (tons)	-	-	38	6	-	-	-	48	8	-	16	-	111±8.2
Explosive power (tons)	-	-	9	12	12	-	-	10	24	-	6	18	91±4.8
Number of training units	30	38	34	14	12	10	30	34	24	10	16	34	286

Table 11.12. Phases 1-4 Training for High Hurdles

PHASE 1: Improvement of Physical Condition
30%	Technique: drills with low-height hurdles, many repetitions
20%	General conditioning: total training, varied jumps, so forth
20%	Specific conditioning
20%	Speed: 30-50m, many repetitions
10%	General endurance: fartlek or intervals, 100-300m, 75% effort

PHASE 2: Perfecting Technique
30%	Technique: Race pace over 5-6 (to 10) hurdles, few repetitions
20%	Technique: starts over 1-3 hurdles, many repetitions
20%	Speed endurance: 100-150m, few repetitions, short recovery
20%	Speed: 60-80m, long recovery
10%	Specific conditioning: power training and agility

PHASES 3-4: Competitive Pace and Neuromuscular Capacity
40%	Technique: Race pace over 3-5 hurdles from blocks, long recovery
30%	Speed: pace changes over 100m, no straining
20%	Agility: mobility and coordination
10%	Active rest: drills, jumps, jogging, starts from blocks
Meets	

Table 11.13. Phases 1-4 Training for Intermediate Hurdles

PHASE 1: Improvement of Physical Condition and Endurance
30%	General endurance: fartlek or many repetitions over 300-600m at 75% effort, with 100-200m fast intervals included
30%	Technique: drills with low-height hurdles, many repetitions
20%	Speed: 60-80m, many repetitions
20%	General conditioning: total training, varied jumps, so forth
10%	Specific conditioning

PHASE 2: Specific Pace and Endurance
20%	Specific endurance: 200-300m fast, few repetitions, short recovery
30%	Technique: race pace over 5-6 hurdles, few repetitions
20%	Sprints: 100-150m, long recovery
10%	Technique: starts over 1-4 hurdles, many repetitions
10%	Specific conditioning or general endurance

PHASES 3-4: Competitive Pace and Speed
40%	Technique: race pace over 3-5 hurdles from blocks, long recovery
30%	Speed: pace changes over 150-200m, no straining
20%	Slow running or fartlek
10%	Agility: mobility and coordination
Meets	

Table 11.14. Periodization for 100m Hurdles

Phase	Focus	Training Procedures			
		Basic Drills	Speed	3&5-stride	Strength Endurance
I	General adaptation	Heavy	Limited	Moderate	Moderate
II	Specific adaptation	Moderate	Moderate	Heavy	Heavy
III	Competition I (Complete adaptation)	Limited	Heavy	Limited	None
IV	Regeneration	Limited	Moderate	Limited	Moderate
V	Competition II (Final adaptation)	None	Moderate	Limited	None
VI	Transition (Regeneration)	Limited			

Hurdler Gail Devers

Table 11.15. Weekly Training Load for 100m Hurdles by Periods

PREPARATION I
- 300-400 hurdle clearances
- 1,200-1,600m of hurdle exercises
- 800-1,000m of hurdle runs (from crouch or standing start): Begins after two months of Preparation I training
- 2,000-3,000m of repetition runs over 150-300m
- 400-500 foot contacts in jumping/plyometric exercises
- 1-2 hours of strength exercises

COMPETITION I
- 300-400 hurdle clearances
- 800-1,200m of hurdle exercises
- 2,000m of hurdle runs (from crouch or standing start)
- 2,000-3,000m of repetition runs up to 100m
- 800-1,000m of speed runs from a standing start
- 1,000m of repetition runs over 150-300m
- 250-300 foot contacts in jumping/plyometric exercises
- 1 hour of strength exercises

PREPARATION II: 4-day cycle (3 training days, 1 walking or active rest day)
- 600-800 hurdle clearances
- 2,000m of hurdle exercises
- 2,000m of hurdle runs
- 300m sprints (6-10 hours per week)
- 1,000m of hurdle runs (from crouch start)
- 2,500-3,500m of runs over 150-300m
- 1-2 hours of strength exercises

COMPETITION II
- 300-400 hurdle clearances
- 800-1,200m of hurdle exercises
- 2,000m of hurdle runs (from crouch or standing start)
- 300-400m of timed crouch starts (30-60m)
- 800-1,000m of speed runs from a standing start
- 800-1,000m of running exercises and accelerations
- 2 rest days (Thursday and Friday)
- 1 meet day (Sunday)

TRANSITION
- 60 min. of basketball
- 40 min. of handball
- 30 min. of jumping exercises
- 6 x 150m acceleration runs, half effort
- 500m of hurdle exercises
- 30 min. of warming up exercises
- 2 hours of walking in the woods
- 3 rest days

Table 11.16. Model of Technical Training for 110m Hurdles

Element of Rhythm Training	Characteristics
1. Length of the race	• hurdle acceleration • hurdle speed • hurdle endurance
2. Rhythm	• technical rhythm (1-2 strides) • classical rhythm (3 strides) • lengthened rhythm (5,7 strides) • varied rhythm (4,6 strides)
3. Inter-hurdle spaces	• 3-stride rhythm: 8.5-9.14m • 5-stride rhythm: 12.8-13.40m • 7-stride rhythm: 17.3-18.20m
4. Height of the hurdles	• low hurdles: 76-84cm • medium hurdles: 91cm • one-meter hurdles: 100cm • high hurdles: 106.7cm
5. Rest intervals	• maximal: 5-90 min. • optimal: 3-5 min. • shortened: 15 sec. to 3 min.
6. Training intensity	• maximal & submaximal: 90-100% • high: 80-90% • medium & low: 80% and less
7. Length of the approach	• shortened approach: 5-6 strides • standard approach: 7-8 strides • lengthened approach: 8-12 strides
8. Length of the finish	• shortened finish: 2-3 strides • standard finish: 14.02m • lengthened finish: 14.02m & more
9. Type of start	• crouch start • standing start
10. Technical exercises	• trail leg • lead leg

periodized training for the women's hurdle races than for the men's races. This is probably a reflection of the dominance of American male hurdlers, who are rarely exposed to well-planned, periodized training.

While material on periodized training for the intermediate hurdles has been limited, some very good data has now appeared. Max Robertson writes on speed-oriented training in the 400m hurdles, with Table 11.17 as a training example, while Janusz Iskra gives many details of the basic structure of endurance training for the intermediate race. Table 11.18 is Iskra's annual plan for endurance training. Iskra has published a full seven months of training for Pawel Januszewski, winner of the 1998 European Championships in 48.17 secs.

REFERENCES

1. Boris Tabatshnik. (1987). Planning of sprint training. *Track Technique, 101,* 3234.
2. Remi Korchemny. (1984). Sprinting. *Track Technique, 87,* 2774-2779.
3. Bernie Dare & Beverly Kearney. (1988). Speed training. *Track Technique, 103,* 3289-3295.
4. The Level II Coaching Education Curriculum Development Committee on Sprints and Hurdles. (1989). Sprints and relays. In *The Athletics Congress's Track and Field Coaching Manual* (2nd ed., pp. 55-71). Champaign, IL: Human Kinetics.
5. Gary Winckler. (1991). An examination of speed endurance. *New Studies in Athletics, 6*(1), 27-33.
6. Gary Winckler and Vern Gambetta. (1987). Classifications of energy systems for sprint training. *Track Technique, 100,* 3193-3195.
7. Tudor Bompa. (1991). A model of an annual training

Table 11.17. Speed and Speed-Endurance Mesocycles for 400m Hurdles

Period one Starting mid-October	Period two	Period three	Period four	Period five	Period six	Period seven
i) 2 weeks	ii) 2 weeks	6 weeks	8 weeks competition period	6 weeks	6 weeks	competition period for the summer season
4x500 [5'] 2x10x110 [30" & 10'] 3 mile runs	4x500 [4'] as in i) 3 mile runs 3x3x300 [3' & 8']	500/400/300 [3'] [10'] 400/300/200 [3'] 4x150 [w/b] [8'] 3x200 [w/b] 3x(10/8/6)x110 [3' & 10'] 3x3x300 [2'30" & 7']		2x(300 [1'] 250 [5'] 250 [1'] 200) [10'] 3x4x110 [w/b/jog back/30" & 10'] 3x150 [w/b] [10'] 3x200 [w/b] 2x2x300 [3' & 10'] [10'] 1x300 (max.) Hurdle session	100/150/200/150/ 100 [5'] 2x2x300 [3' & 10'] [10'] 1x300 (max.) 2x(250/200) [5' & 10'] 1x7h/1x6H/1x5H [long] 1-7H/2-8H/3-9H/ 4-10H [long]	

Note: The numbers/letters in square brackets indicate the length or type of recovery between repetitions and sets.
w/b = walk back.

Table 11.18. Annual Plan of Endurance Training for 400m Hurdles

Type of endurance	Introduction phase (November)	General preparation phase (Dec-Feb)	Specific preparation phase (Mar-April)	Pre-competition phase (May-June)	Competition phase (June-Aug)
Short alactic speed endurance			■ 4x4x60 92% [2' & 6']	■ 5x4x50 95% [2' & 8']	■ 5x4x40 98% [2' & 8']
Short speed endurance			■ 3x5x40 95% [1' & 4']		
Proper speed endurance: Short rhythm			■ 4x2H/2x4H	■ 3x200 98% [10'] ■ 3x2H/2x4H/2x6H	■ 2x2H/2x5H/2x200 [15']
Special endurance: Medium rhythm, Long rhythm			■ 2x600 98% [15']	■ 350/450 98% [15'] or ■ 2x9H/300 98% adequate	■ 2x300 98% [20'] or 2x10H [20'] or ■ Competition
Stress training: Rhythm stress		■ 300/350/200 95% [4']	■ 350/200h/300 95% [4']		
Intensive interval: Ryhthm interval	■ 2x2x350 80% [2' & 5']	■ 4x(500/250) 80% [2' & 6']	■ 3x(250/250h) [1'30" & 8']	■ 2x6x100 90% [2' & 10']	■ 2x3x120 95% [2' & 12']
Tempo: Rhythm tempo	■ 2x(800/600/400) 85% [6'] or ■ 5x6H [5'] or	■ 6x500 85% [6' & 8'] or ■ 4x200h (alternate) [7']	■ 450/400/350/300 85% [8']		
Strength endurance	■ 5x200 acceleration & 5x150 bounding	■ 3x200 acceleration & 3x100 bounding or ■ 3x50 bounding uphill & 3x100 acceleration	■ 4x(80 acceleration/ 80 relaxed run/ 80 uphill) [jog]		
Interval strength endurance	■ 5x(2x200 acceleration/ 150 uphill bounding/ 100 bunny-hops) [jog & 5']	■ 5x(100 bounding/ 3x100 bunny-hops/ 100 bounding) [jog & 5']			
Extensive interval: elements of rhythm endurance	■ 5x5x100 75% [1' & 5'] or ■ 2x5x300 60% [30" & 1'30"] or ■ 5x2x500 65% [30" & 1'30"]	■ 2x10x150 75% [job & 4']			■ 3x4x100 70% [30" & 2']
Continuous run	■ 3x12' or ■ 2x25'	■ 2x25' ■ 5x4	■ 2x20'	■ 2x15'	■ 2x20'

programme for a sprinter. *New Studies in Athletics, 6*(1), 47-51.

8. NSA Round Table 27: Sprinting. (1995). *New Studies in Athletics, 10*(1), 13-22. [Tudor Bidder, Emperatriz Gonzalez Henao, Victor Lopez, Carlo Vittori, & Gary Winckler].

9. Adam Zajac. (1987). Direct competition preparation for elite sprinters. *Track Technique, 98*, 3114-3115.

10. Miroslav Kvac. (1984). Training of 400m runner Jarmila Kratochilova for the 1980 Moscow Olympic Games. *Track and Field Quarterly Review, 84*(2), 1822.

11. Frank W. Dick. (1989). Development of maximum sprinting speed. *Track Technique, 109*, 3475-3480, 3491.

12. Hartmut Müller. (1991). Trends in the men's and women's sprints in the period from 1985 to 1990. *New Studies in Athletics, 6*(1), 7-14.

13. Alessandro Donati. (1995). The development of stride length and stride frequency in sprinting. *New Studies in Athletics, 10*(1), 51-66.

14. B. Ushko & I. Volkov. (1995). The structure of sprint training. In Jess Jarver, ed., *Sprints and Relays: Contemporary Theory, Technique and Training* (4th ed., pp. 59-62). Mountain View, CA: Tafnews.

15. Janusz Iskra. (1995). The most effective technical training for the 110 metres hurdles. *New Studies in Athletics, 10*(3), 51-55.

16. Brent McFarlane. (2000). *The Science of Hurdling and Speed* (4th ed.). Ottawa: Athletics Canada.

17. Max Robertson. (1990). The merits of speed-orientated as opposed to endurance-orientated training for the 400 metres hurdles. *New Studies in Athletics, 5*(4), 29- 32.

18. Janus Iskra. (1997). Endurance in the 400 metres hurdles. In Jess Jarver, ed., *The Hurdles: Contemporary Theory, Technique and Training* (3rd ed., pp. 104-109). Mountain View, CA: Tafnews.

19. Janus Iskra. (1999). Pawel Januszewski breaks through at the European Championships. *Track Coach. 147*, 4691-2698.

OTHER SOURCES ON PERIODIZATION FOR SPRINTS AND HURDLES

Alejo, Bob. (1993). Weight training for the 400m hurdler. *Track Technique, 123*, 3915-3918.

Alford, Jim. (1995). NSA Interview 8: Malcolm Arnold on Colin Jackson's development. *New Studies in Athletics, 10*(3), 13-15. HH

Baughman, Mark, Mike Takaha & Tom Tellez. (1984). Sprint training: including strength training. *Track and Field Quarterly Review, 84*(2), 9-12.

Bowerman, William J., & William H. Freeman. (1974). *Coaching Track and Field* (pp. 86-157). Boston: Houghton Mifflin.

Bowerman, William J., & William H. Freeman. (1991). *High Performance Training for Track and Field* (pp. 45-84). Champaign, IL: Human Kinetics.

Breizer, Vitaly, & Remi Korchemny. (1993). The preparation of women for the 400 meter hurdles. *Track Technique, 122*, 3895-3897, 3907.

Čoh, Milan, & Aleč Dolenec. (1996). Three-dimensional kinematic analysis of the hurdles technique used by Brigita Bukovec [100mH]. *New Studies in Athletics, 11*(1), 63- 69.

Delecluse, Christophe. (1997). Influence of strength training on sprint running performance: Current findings and implications for training. *Sports Medicine, 24*(3), 147-156.

Delecluse, Christophe, Herman Van Coppenolle, Marina Goris & Rudi Diels. (1992). A model for the scientific preparation of high level sprinters. *New Studies in Athletics, 7*(4), 57-64.

Donati, Alessandro. (1996). The association between the development of strength and speed. *New Studies in Athletics, 11*(2-3), 51-58.

Gambetta, Vern. (1991). Essential considerations for the development of a teaching model for the 100 metres sprint. *New Studies in Athletics, 6*(2), 27-32.

Jarver, Jess, ed. (1997). *The Hurdles: Contemporary Theory, Technique and Training* (3rd ed.). Mountain View, CA: Tafnews.

Jarver, Jess, ed. (1995). *Sprints and Relays: Contemporary Theory, Technique and Training* (4th ed.). Mountain View, CA: Tafnews.

Jarver, Jess, ed. (2000). *Sprints and Relays: Contemporary Theory, Technique and Training* (5th ed.). Mountain View, CA: Tafnews.

Kearney, Beverly. (1993). Sprints & sprint hurdles. *Track and Field Quarterly Review, 93*(1), 29-36.

Kirksey, Brett, & Michael H. Stone. (1998). Periodizing college sprint program: theory and practice. *Strength and Conditioning, 20*(3), 42-47.

Lopez, Victor. (2000). An approach to strength training for sprinters. In Jarver, *Sprints and Relays* (5th ed., pp. 58-63).

Maisetti, Georges. (1996). Efficient baton excange in the sprint relay. *New Studies in Athletics, 11*(2-3), 77-82.

Parjsuk, Vladimir. (1996). The European School in sprint training: the experiences in Russia. *New Studies in Athletics, 11*(2-3), 71-76.

Peters, Darren. (1994). Peaking in sprint events. *Modern Athlete and Coach, 32*(1), 27-30.

Sanderson, Lyle. (2000). Some thoughts on sprint relay racing from a Canadian perspective. In Jess Jarver, ed., *Sprints & Relays: Contemporary Theory, Technique and Training* (5th ed., pp. 157-160). Mountain View, CA: Tafnews.

Schiffer, Jürgen. (1995). Selected and annotated bibliography 34: sprints and relays. *New Studies in Athletics, 10*(1), 99-120.

Schiffer, Jürgen. (1996). Selected and annotated bibliography 39: sprints, relays and speed training. *New Studies in Athletics, 11*(2-3), 169-181.

Seagrave, Loren. (1996). Introduction to sprinting. *New Studies in Athletics, 11*(2-3), 93-113.

Smith, John. (1990). U.C.L.A. 100-400 sprint training. *Track and Field Quarterly Review, 90*(1), 10-15.

Sparrey, Kathleen Raske. (Fall 1997). Identifying and developing elite hurdlers in the United States. *Track Coach, 141*, 4505-4510.

Stepanova, Marina. (Summer 1997). My experiences in the 400m hurdles. *Track Coach, 140*, 4473-4476.

Verhoshansky, Yuri V. (1996). Principles for a rational organization of the training process aimed at speed development. *New Studies in Athletics, 11*(2-3), 155- 160.

Verhoshansky, Yuri V. (1996). Speed training for high level athletes. *New Studies in Athletics, 11* (2-3), 39-49.

Vittori, Carlo. (1991). The development and training of young 400 metres runners. *New Studies in Athletics, 6*(1), 35-46.

Wiemann, Klaus, & Günter Tidow. (1995). Relative activity of hip and knee extensors in sprinting—implications for training. *New Studies in Athletics, 10*(1), 29-49.

SOURCES FOR TABLES

11.1. Fitness Characteristics of Sprints & Hurdles: Dick, Frank W. (1978). *Training Theory.* London: BAAB, 64-65

11.2. Phase Training Ratios for Sprints & Hurdles: Dick, p. 62

11.3. Phases 1-4 Training for Sprints: Ballesteros, Jose Manuel, & Julio Alvarez. (1979). *Track and Field: A Basic Coaching Manual.* London: IAAF.

11.4. Training Emphases in the Sprint Macrocycle: Lopez, Victor. (1982). Analysis about the planification, structure and content of the training and conditioning of sprinters. *Track and Field Quarterly Review, 82*(2), 20-22.

11.5. Training Phases for Sprinters, Two Peaks: Dare & Kearney, 3295

11.6. Intervals for Anaerobic Power: Korchemny, 2774

11.7. Intervals for Anaerobic Capacity: Korchemny, 2775

11.8. Emphases in Annual Sprint Training: Winckler, 32

11.9. Energy System Training for Sprinters: Winkler &

SOURCES FOR FIGURES

CHAPTER 12:
Periodized Training for Jumpers

GENERAL JUMPING TRAINING

Most articles about training for the jumps are concerned with correct technical performance or strength training. Few writings address the range of "what to do and when to do it." An extremely useful, well-illustrated book on training for the jumping events was produced by Derek Boosey. He lists the components of jumping training and performance as:

- Endurance: fartlek and cross country
- Speed: intervals, starts, and approach runs
- Strength/Power: strength training
- Bounding: plyometrics and varied jumping activities

- Technique: from major to minor skill changes.

Boosey's periodization schedule of the changing emphases of each of these components is shown in Figure 12.1. He stresses that as the athlete becomes more experienced and skilled over a period of years, the proportion of training will gradually shift from more general to more specific conditioning.

"Jumping performances depend largely on the power level of an athlete." However, the strength/power program must follow a correct approach if it is to be effective. Simply increasing the volume or load will not necessarily result in improved performances.

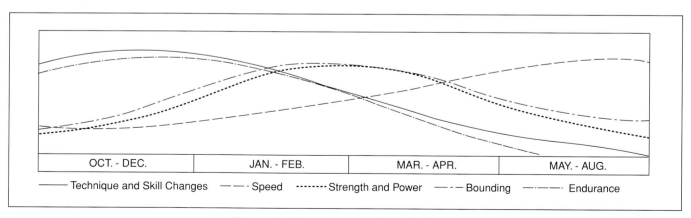

| OCT. - DEC. | JAN. - FEB. | MAR. - APR. | MAY. - AUG. |

——— Technique and Skill Changes   — — · Speed   ········ Strength and Power   — · — Bounding   — — — Endurance

Figure 12.1. Emphases for Jump Training

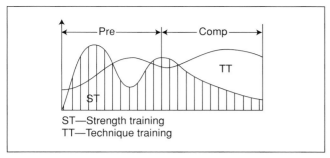

Figure 12.2. Yearly Cycle Strength and Technique

The most effective program uses a varying pattern of loads, intensity, and recovery, resulting in a "wavy but unbroken pattern of improvement in movement speed and explosive power." The training program should not interfere with technique

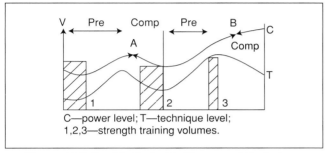

Figure 12.3. Double Period in Power and Technique

development. The pattern of strength and technique training should also change across the macrocycle in a wave-like pattern (Fig. 12.2). The strength training volumes and the resulting power and technique levels are shown in Figure 12.3.

Now we will examine the use of periodized training for specific jumping events.

HIGH JUMP

Examples of periodized training emphases are shown in Tables 12.1, 12.2, and 12.3. A double-periodized year for high jumping, with an indoor and an outdoor macrocycle, is perhaps the most common training year for high jumpers (Fig. 12.4). Bob Myers suggests six phases to the training year, which is consistent with current training trends:

Phase 1: General conditioning (June/July through November)

Phase 2: Specific conditioning [Pre-Competition I] (December through January)

Phase 3: Competition I (February through March)

Phase 4: Specific conditioning [Pre-Competition II] (April)

Phase 5: Competition II (May through last major meet)

Phase 6: Active rest (Transition/Regeneration).

Table 12.1. Fitness Characteristics of Jumping Events

Event	General	Special	Competition-Specific
High Jump	Aerobic endurance Strength endurance Mobility Maximum strength	Speed Special mobility Elastic strength Special strength Jumping Related events	Takeoff technique Flight technique Approach technique Sprint technique Trial meets
Long Jump	Aerobic endurance Strength endurance Mobility Maximum strength	Speed endurance Speed Special mobility Elastic strength Special strength Jumping Related events	Takeoff technique Flight technique Approach technique Sprint technique Trial meets
Triple Jump	Aerobic endurance Strength endurance Mobility Maximum strength Special endurance (jumping, running)	Speed endurance Speed Special mobility Elastic strength Special strength Jumping Related events	Takeoff technique 3 phases Flight technique 3 phases Approach technique Sprint technique Trial meets
Pole Vault	Aerobic endurance Strength endurance Mobility Maximum strength	Speed endurance Speed Special mobility Elastic strength Special strength Upper body-trunk Jumping	Takeoff technique Technique on pole Technique leaving pole Approach and plant technique Sprint technique Trial meets

Table 12.2. Phase Training Ratios for Jumping Events

High Jump and Pole Vault			
Phase	General	Special	Specific
1	35	35	30
2	25	35	40
3	10	40	50
4	20	40	40
5	10	40	50
6	80	10	10

Long and Triple Jumps			
Phase	General	Special	Specific
1	25	55	20
2	15	60	25
3	10	55	35
4	25	55	20
5	10	60	30
6	80	10	10

Percent distribution of:
- General Training (mostly compensatory strength and mobility work)
- Special Training (includes aerobic endurance)
- Competition-Specific Training

Table 12.3. Phases 1-4 Training for High Jump

PHASE 1: Increase Force and Spring
- 30% Technique (learning drills)
- 20% Power training, isometrics, or circuit training
- 20% Sprints and hurdles (3-10 x 30-60m)
- 20% Conditioning in gym (mobility, strengthening, stretching, etc.)
- 10% General conditioning (overall training, jumps, hills, etc.)

PHASE 2: Perfect Technique
- 20% Varied jumps and agility exercises
- 20% Technique (10-20 jumps with full run, increasing heights)
- 20% Technique (20-30 jumps at medium height, correcting faults)
- 20% Gymnasium (specific power exercises, 90 min.)
- 20% Sprints and hurdles (8-10 x 60-80m or 5 hurdles)

PHASES 3-4: Accumulate Neuromuscular Potential
- 40% Technique (10-20 jumps perfecting and combining approach with jump)
- 30% Agility (stretching and relaxation) and low hurdles (no strain)
- 20% Sprint starts (10-20 times)
- 10% Different jumps (varied, intensive, long recoveries)
- Also Competition (one time per week, sometimes rest or other event)

Myers stresses that during heavy load cycles (such as during the general and specific training phases) athletes will break down if all areas of their training have high loads. He recommends alternating the peaks among the strength training, plyometrics and running (Fig. 12.5). The microcycle (week) should also show the wave-pattern of variable loading (Fig. 12.6).

The training year suggested in the *The Athletic Congress's Track and Field Coaching Manual* (2nd ed.) by coaches Berny Wagner, Sue Humphrey and Don Chu is a five-phase, single-periodized program:
- Maximal Loading Base (July through September)
- Power Development (October through January)
- Power Transfer (February through April)

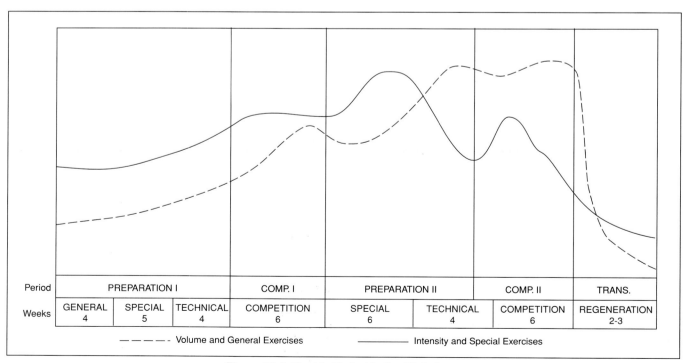

Period	PREPARATION I			COMP. I	PREPARATION II		COMP. II	TRANS.
Weeks	GENERAL 4	SPECIAL 5	TECHNICAL 4	COMPETITION 6	SPECIAL 6	TECHNICAL 4	COMPETITION 6	REGENERATION 2-3

– – – – – Volume and General Exercises   ——— Intensity and Special Exercises

Figure 12.4. Double Period in the High Jump

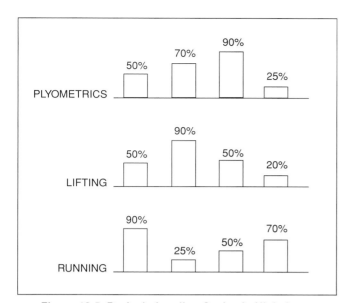

Figure 12.5. Peaks in Loading Cycles in High Jump

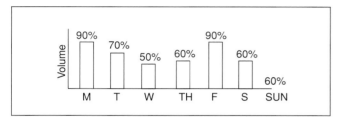

Figure 12.6. Load in the High Jump Microcycle

- Transition/Pre-Competition (2 weeks)
- Power Retention (Competition peak season).

For young male high jumpers, the rapid growth of muscular strength between ages 17 and 19 can hamper proper technique development if conditioning work does not continue along with the technical training. The ages of 19 to 23 are the "high performance development phase" for potential elite jumpers, so jumpers should focus on the improvement of technique and specific fitness components, while gaining competitive experience at a high level.

The fastest development occurs between ages 14 and 15 and between ages 17 and 19, with the "real potential talent" reaching 7'1" to 7'4" during the latter period of improvement. However, athletes should not use maximal loads in resistance exercises before ages 18-19, as a growing athlete is more vulnerable to stress injuries.

LONG JUMP

Examples of periodized training emphases are shown in Tables 12.1, 12.2, and 12.4, with more specific examples of periodized training in Tables 12.5 and 12.6.

Table 12.4. Phases 1-4 Training for Long Jump

PHASE 1: Increase Strength and Spring

30%	Technique (learning drills with 5- to 7-step approach)
20%	Power training, isometrics, or circuit training
20%	Sprints and hurdles (10-12 x 30-90m or 3 hurdles)
20%	Conditioning in gym (strengthening exercises, stretching, etc.)
10%	General conditioning (overall training, jumps, hills, etc.)

PHASE 2: Perfect Technique

20%	Varied jumps and agility exercises
20%	Technique (10-12 jumps with full run)
20%	Sprints and hurdles (6-8 x 60-120m or 5 hurdles, straight and turn)
20%	Gymnasium (power/strengthening exercises, 90 mins.)
20%	Technique (10-20 jumps with short run, correcting faults)

PHASES 3-4: Accumulate Neuro-Muscular Potential

40%	Technique (10-12 jumps perfecting and synchronizing approach & jump)
30%	Sprint starts (10-15 times, on straight and turn)
20%	Agility (stretching and relaxation) and low hurdles (no strain)
10%	Different jumps (varied, intensive, long recoveries)
Also	Competition (one time per week, sometimes rest or other event)

Table 12.5. Main Training Means In Long Jump Phases 1-2

1. Develop power and specific strength (explosive)
2. Develop speed up to 85-90% of potential
3. Develop explosiveness
4. Develop long jumping technique
5. Develop general endurance — aerobic power
6. General and athletic fitness
7. Develop specific endurance — anaerobic power

Weekly Cycle	
Day	**Content**
Monday	Strength + Special endurance
Tuesday	Jumping drills
Wednesday	Speed + Games
Thursday	Strength + Long running
Friday	Jumping drills + Special endurance
Saturday	Speed + General physical conditioning
Sunday	Games

An analysis of world class women long jumpers reveals that despite the American edge in pure talent (seen in sprint performances), that edge does not exist in the long jump. Instead, better planned, more thorough training in Eastern Europe and elsewhere has overcome much of the American advantage. Table 12.7 shows the volume and intensity of work used to improve the jumper's speed quality, as well as the other training means used.

Besides their more intensive training, many European athletes are tested regularly on a battery of control tests designed to assess the specific condi-

Table 12.6. Main Training Means In Long Jump Phases 3-5

1. Develop power and specific strength (explosive)
2. Develop speed 90-95% of potential
3. Develop explosiveness
4. Improve jumping technique
5. Maintain general endurance and fitness
6. Maintain specific endurance

Weekly Cycle

Day	Content
Monday	Strength + Special endurance
Tuesday	General physical conditioning + Jumps
Wednesday	Speed
Thursday	Strength
Friday	Warmup + Jumps
Saturday	Competition
Sunday	Rest

TRIPLE JUMP

Examples of periodized training emphases are shown in Tables 12.1, 12.2, and 12.8, with a more specific example of periodized training in Table 12.9.

Figure 12.7 gives a classic view of periodized training in the triple jump. The basic structure is a classic Matveyevan repetitive pattern of microcycles forming mesocycles forming macrocycles. The example shown is a double-periodized year, allowing a short indoor season and a long outdoor season.

During the preparation (specific conditioning or pre-season) period, a three-week mesocycle may be used. The first week emphasizes jumping power development, the second week stresses strength development, and the third week is a recovery cycle. A

Table 12.7. Volume and Intensity in Long Jump Speed Training

| | Speed Training | | | | Other Training | | |
| | Intensity | | | | Long | | |
Month	100%	About 90%	Runups*	Bounding**	Runs	Games	Flex.
Oct	—	8.2 km.	—	—	25k	10 hr.	5 hr.
Nov	—	12.6 km.	—	—	20k	8 hr.	9 hr.
Dec	1600m	14.2 km.	—	—	16k	8 hr.	12 hr.
Jan	3200m	12.6 km.	38	18	6k	6 hr.	8 hr.
Feb	4600m	13.8 km.	46	28	3k	9 hr.	6 hr.
Mar	1600m	15.8 km.	18	16	12k	8 hr.	15 hr.
Apr	3800m	16.6 km.	24	28	—	10 hr.	10 hr.
May	4800m	15.6 km.	32	30	—	8 hr.	8 hr.
Jun	4800m	14.6 km.	36	32	—	6 hr.	6 hr.
Jul	4800m	13.8 km.	40	32	—	7 hr.	8 hr.
Aug	4600m	12.9 km.	40	32	—	5 hr.	3 hr.
Sep	4200m	12.6 km.	36	28	—	—	—

* Number   ** 50m maximum at a time

tioning and progress in training, with the records kept for year-to-year comparisons of performance and reaction to training.

Elio Locatelli describes six areas of speed training for the improvement of Italian long jumpers:

- Aerobic endurance: circuit training, cross country, and interval training (6 weeks, Oct. to Nov.)
- Anaerobic-alactic capacity: repetition runs of 60-80m at 90-93% maximum (6 weeks, Nov. to mid-Dec.)
- Anaerobic-alactic speed strength: repetitions or series sprints of 30-80m at 95-97% (4 weeks, Jan.)
- Anaerobic-lactic capacity: speed-endurance-oriented repetitions of 100-300m at 80-90% (6 weeks, April to May)
- Anaerobic-lactic speed strength
- Maximal speed: flying sprints, ins-and-outs, downhill sprints, harness runs, approach and takeoff exercises (4 weeks, July).

Table 12.8. Phases 1-4 Training for Triple Jump

PHASE 1: Increase Strength and Spring

30%	Technique (5-7 repetitions of learning drills)
20%	Power training, isometrics, or circuit training
20%	Sprints and hurdles (10-12 x 30-90m or 3 hurdles)
20%	Conditioning in gym (strengthening exercises, mobility, etc.)
10%	General conditioning (overall training, jumps, hills, etc.)

PHASE 2: Perfect Technique

20%	Technique (10-15 jumps with short approach)
20%	Sprints and hurdles (8-10 x 60-120m on turn or 5 hurdles on straight)
20%	Gymnasium (power exercises)
20%	Technique (8-10 jumps with full approach, no strain)
20%	Varied jumps

PHASES 3-4: Accumulate Neuromuscular Potential

40%	Technique (8-10 jumps perfecting technique and rhythm)
30%	Sprint starts (10-15 times, on straight and turn)
20%	Agility (stretching and relaxation) and low hurdles (no strain)
10%	Different jumps (varied, intensive, long recoveries)
Also	Competition (one time per week, sometimes rest or other event)

Table 12.9. Triple Jump Training of Viktor Saneyev

MONTH	10 11 12 1	2 3	4 5	6 7	8 9
Period-ization	PREPARATION PERIOD (I)	COMPETITION PERIOD (II)	PREPARATION PERIOD (III)	COMPETITION PERIOD	TRANSITION PERIOD
Mon.	- Sprinting - Strength	- Rest	Technique - Sprinting	- Rest	- Ball game
Tue.	- Jump power	- Technique - Sprinting	- Jump power - Strength	- Technique - Sprinting	- Rest
Wed.	- Ball game (Active rest)	- Rest	- Rest	- Jump power - Strength	- Ball game
Thu.	- Rest	- Sprinting - Strength	- Rest	- Rest	- Rest
Fri.	- Sprinting - Strength	- Rest	- Technique - Sprinting	- Rest	- Ball game
Sat.	- Jump power - Ball game	- Warmups	- Jump power - Strength	- Warmups	- Ball game
Sun.	- Rest	- Competition	- Rest	- Competition	- Rest

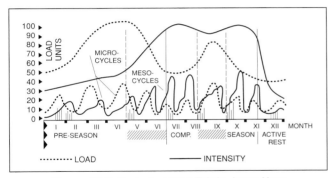

Figure 12.7. Periods of the Triple Jump Year

second type of mesocycle for training during this period is a two-week pattern. The first week emphasizes speed and jumping power development, while the second week focuses on strength development and the recovery cycle. Both of these patterns remind us of the critical importance of allowing a planned recovery after each heavy loading or intensity. Progress is based on the overcompensation that is possible only if the body recovers from the overload created by the training load.

Two important factors about the Soviet training system are the use of training exercises that are a practical simulation of the event-specific skills and the use of control tests that judge the specific fitness as a part of the training process itself. "This control test system has contributed a great deal to giving Russian athletes specific targets for each training schedule component, which is a highly effective factor in judging the progress and physical condition of the athlete during each step of the training process." (10)

Vitold Kreer addresses the growth in women's triple jumping with these training recommendations:

- Encourage continuing development of weak performance links (abdominal, back, ankles).
- Strength development needs daily attention, especially with multiple jumps, bounding, uphill running, and controlled harness work.
- Flexibility needs systematic development.
- Soft surfaces (grass, mats, sawdust) should be used as much as possible.
- While depth jumps should be used periodically, they should not be over 50 cm.
- A planned training year has 300 training and 20 competition days. It includes:
    - 20-25 km of sprinting
    - 1000 takeoffs in multiple jumps
    - 1000 takeoffs in long and triple jumps from a medium runup
    - 2000 reps (500 tons) of strength development exercises.
- The training loads are the same as for men, though 1-2% less intensive.
- Training means and methods should be varied frequently.
- The training structure should be rational:
    - A "wavy" periodization for beginners; a spiral construction of forced blocks for elite athletes.

Pole Vaulter Stacy Dragila

POLE VAULT

The rapid rise of the women's vault has resulted in many studies of training for that event. However, as with the other jumping events, almost all of the material is either biomechanical analyses of the top vaulters or descriptions of proper technique and the best potential candidates for the event. One useful comment is that the top women vaulters are becoming taller (resulting in a higher grip) and lighter, with a focus more on power than on strength. Heavier strength building tends to produce a woman with a heavier lower body, which works against success in the vault.

Examples of periodized training emphases are shown in Tables 12.1, 12.2, and 12.10, with more specific examples of periodized training for vaulters in Tables 12.11 through 12.14.

The preparation phase in the vault (until the first meet) should last at least three months, including at least 120 training sessions, over 200 vaults on a softer pole from short approaches and over 100 full approach vaults with the regular pole. The length of a successful competitive season depends largely on the length of the preparation phase and the vol-

Table 12.10. Phases 1-4 Training for Pole Vault

PHASE 1: Increase Strength and Spring
30%	Technique (learning drills)
20%	Power training, isometrics, or circuit training
20%	Sprints and hurdles (10-12 x 30-60m or 3 hurdles)
20%	Conditioning in gym (specific exercises, trampoline, etc.)
10%	General conditioning (overall training, jumps, hills, etc.)

PHASE 2: Perfect Technique
20%	Varied jumps and agility exercises
20%	Technique (10-15 jumps with full run, increasing heights)
20%	Technique (15-20 jumps with short run, medium height, correct faults)
20%	Gymnasium (power/strengthening exercises, 90 mins.)
20%	Speed work (10-12 x 60-80m carrying pole)

PHASES 3-4: Accumulate Neuromuscular Potential
40%	Technique (perfecting basic technique)
30%	Sprint starts (10-15 times)
20%	Agility (stretching and relaxation) and low hurdles (no strain)
10%	Varied jumps and gymnastic agility
Also	Competition (one time per week, sometimes rest or other activity)

Table 12.11. Periodization of the Pole Vault Year

Period	Length	Task
Preparation I	2 months	1. Develop general conditioning 2. Develop specific conditioning 3. Develop technique
Preparation II	1 months	1. Develop specific conditioning 2. Develop technique
Competition I	6 weeks	1. Develop and stabilize technique
Preparation I	4 weeks	1. Develop specific conditioning 2. Develop general conditioning
Preparation II	4 weeks	1. Develop and stabilize technique 2. Reach competitive form
Competition II	5 months	1. Plan training to meet individual needs
Transition	4 weeks	1. Reduce training volume 2. Take part in enjoyable active rest

Table 12.12. Annual Training Plan for Age 16-17 Pole Vaulter

TASKS:	Development of speed	
	Development of strength	
	Development of technique	
TRAINING:	Total training units:	250-260
	Vaults with 20m run:	650-700
	Vaults with longer run:	380-400
	Transfers, run to hang:	650-700
	Specific drills on pole:	700-750
	Sprints (20-60m):	22-23 km (13-14 miles)
	Sprints (70-100m):	55-60 km (34-37 miles)
	Sprints (over 100m):	55-60 km (34-37 miles)
	Gymnastics and tumbling:	135-140 hours
	Weight training:	80-85 tons
COMPETITIONS:	Pole vault meets:	13-14
	Meets in other events:	8-10
TESTS:	20m from flying start:	2.0-2.1 sec.
	40m from standing start:	4.8-4.9 sec.
	20m flying (with pole):	2.2-2.3 sec.
	60m from crouch start:	7.1-7.2 sec.
	Standing triple jump:	28'11"-29'3"
	Parallel bars uprise:	30 reps in 1:45.0
	Press behind neck:	40-45% of body weight
PERFORMANCES:	100m	11.2-11.4 sec.
	Long jump	20'8"-21'4"
	High jump	5'9"-5'11"
	Pole vault	16'1"-16'9"
	Grip height on pole	14'9"-15'1"

Table 12.13. Annual Training Plan for Age 18-19 Pole Vaulter

TASKS:	Development of power and strength	
	Development of speed	
	Development of technique	
TRAINING:	Total training units:	270-280
	Vaults with 20m run:	600-650
	Vaults with longer run:	500-550
	Transfers, run to hang:	750-800
	Specific drills on pole:	600-650
	Sprints (20-60m):	23-24 km (13-14 miles)
	Sprints (70-100m):	60-65 km (37-40 miles)
	Sprints (over 100m):	60-65 km (37-40 miles)
	Gymnastics and tumbling:	130-135 hours
	Weight training:	100-110 tons
COMPETITIONS:	Pole vault meets:	18-20
	Meets in other events:	4-6
TESTS:	20m from flying start:	1.9-2.0 sec.
	40m from standing start:	4.7-4.8 sec.
	40m from stand (pole):	5.0-5.1 sec.
	80m from crouch start:	9.0-9.1 sec.
	5 hops on takeoff leg: (6-stride approach)	62'4"-65'0"
	Parallel bars uprise:	30 reps in 1:30.0
	Upstart on rings	
	Press behind neck:	50-55% of body weight
PERFORMANCES:	100m	11.0-11.1 sec.
	Long jump	22'4"-22'8"
	High jump	6'1"-6'3"
	Pole vault	17'1"-17'5"
	Grip height on pole	15'3"-15'7"

Table 12.14. Annual Training Plan for Age 20-23 Pole Vaulter

TASKS:	Development of power and strength	
	Development of speed	
	Development of technique	
TRAINING:	Total training units:	310-320
	Vaults with 20m run:	500-550
	Vaults with longer run:	650-700
	Transfers, run to hang:	650-700
	Specific drills on pole:	750-800
	Sprints (20-60m):	20-21 km (13 miles)
	Sprints (70-100m):	55-60 km (34-37 miles)
	Sprints (over 100m):	50-55 km (31-34 miles)
	Gymnastics and tumbling:	100-110 hours
	Weight training:	50-100 tons
COMPETITIONS:	Pole vault meets:	25-30
	Meets in other events:	2-3
TESTS:	20m from flying start:	1.85-1.9 sec.
	40m from standing start:	4.6-4.7 sec.
	40m from stand (pole):	4.9-4.95 sec.
	80m from crouch start:	8.8-8.9 sec.
	5 hops on takeoff leg: (6-stride approach)	65'7"-68'11"
	Gymnastic tests	
	Press behind neck:	55-60% of body weight
PERFORMANCES:	100m	10.8-10.9 sec.
	Long jump	23'0"-23'8"
	High jump	6'5"-6'7"
	Pole vault	17'8"-18'1"
	Grip height on pole	15'7"-15'9"

Table 12.15. Training Loads for the Pole Vault

Component	Annual Load	Microcycles of Emphasis by Periods		
		General	Special	Component
Fartlek	60 miles	1	1	—
PV pop-ups	1600	4-3	3	3-2
PV jumps, short run	1000	3-2	1	—
PV jumps, full run	1000	—	2	3
Acrobatics	1000 reps	3	2	1
Hurdle drills	3500 reps	3-2	2	1
Plyometrics	4000 reps	1	3	1
Sprint starts	5 miles	1	1	1-0
Games	21 hours	4	3-2	2-1
Weightlifting	150-170 tons	3	3-2	2-1
Abdominals	1500 reps	3	3	1-0
Shot & medicine ball	3500 reps	3-2	2	2-1
Knee drills	3600 reps	5-4	3	—
Apparatus drill	600 reps	2	2	1
Speed	8 miles	—	1-2	1
Speed endurance	10 miles	—	1	1/2
Other running	85 miles	6-5	6-5	5

ume of work that is included. During the specific preparation phase, the specific conditioning rises to 60-70% of the total training load.

The training load during competition should be controlled carefully, allowing adequate recovery for good performances. The training volume should drop by about 20-25% per week at this time. However, the training load should not be dropped dramatically, as form may disappear after the next meet is over. A phase of six to eight weeks is used to prepare for a major meet, with the training volume at about 90% of maximum for the first one or two weeks. The emphasis is on quality vaulting, with good rests between vaulting sessions (two days of rest after a session of 15 quality vaults, or three days of rest after a session of 25 quality vaults).

Andrzej Krzesinski has stressed the importance of overall fitness, contrasted to American coaches' emphasis on technique. As he says, "Present vaulters ought to be strong and powerful, fast, with jumping ability, agility and nerve." Table 12.15 summarizes his training loads for a world class vaulter.

Developing vaulters should go through the following stages at about these ages:

- Introductory phase: ages 10-12
- Specialization phase: ages 13-15
- Establishment phase I: ages 16-17
- Establishment phase II: ages 18-19
- Final development phase: ages 20-23.

Examples of their recommended tasks, training loads, number of meets, tests and performance levels are shown in Tables 12.12 to 12.14. They provide an excellent example of how a coach begins planning the annual training program for a vaulter.

Women's pole vaulting has grown rapidly, leading to questions about the necessary differences in training compared to men. The primary weakness lies in the differences in abdominal and shoulder girdle strength, thus limiting full use of proper vaulting techniques. Training of women vaulters should include these elements:

- Development of sprinting and jumping capacities should be similar to the training of long jumpers.
- Gymnastics exercises can be used to improve abdominal and shoulder girdle strength.
- In other respects, training should be similar to that of male vaulters in both methods and means.

REFERENCES

1. Derek Boosey. (1980). *The Jumps: Conditioning and Technical Training*. West Heidelberg, Victoria, Australia: Beatrice.
2. Yuri Verhoshansky. (1981). Specific training for power. In Jess Jarver (Ed.), *The Jumps* (2nd ed., pp. 9-11). Mountain View: Tafnews.
3. Dragan Tancic. (1985). Organization and control of high jump training. *Track and Field Quarterly Review, 85*(4), 17-22.
4. Bob Myers. (1988). Periodization for the high jump. In *The Jumps*. (3rd ed., pp. 46-49).
5. Berny Wagner, Sue Humphrey & Don Chu. (1989). The high jump (Fosbury Flop). In *The Athletic Congress's Track and Field Coaching Manual*. (2nd ed., pp. 105-116). Champaign, IL: Human Kinetics.
6. W. Lonskiy & K. Gomberadse. (1981). Long range training plan for high jumpers. In *The Jumps* (2nd ed., pp. 47-49).
7. Adrian Samungi. (1985). The training of world class women long jumpers. *Track Technique, 92*, 2922-2927.
8. V. Popov. (1994). The organization of training processes in the long jump. In Jess Jarver, ed., *The Jumps: Contemporary Theory, Technique and Training* (4th ed., pp. 80-82). Mountain View, CA: Tafnews.
9. Elio Locatelli. (1993). Sprinting speed as a basis of the men's long jump [abstract]. *New Studies in Athletics, 8*(3), 93-94.
10. Yukito Muraki. (1978). A case study of the selected prominent jumpers. *Track and Field Quarterly Review, 78*(2), 32-45.
11. Vitold Kreyer. (1993). About the female triple jumper [abstract]. *Track Technique, 123*, 3937-3938.
12. Igor Nikonov. (2000). Women become pole vaulters. Trans. Kuulo Kutsar. In Jess Jarver, ed., *The Jumps: Contemporary Theory, Technique and Training* (5th ed., pp. 73-76). Mountain View, CA: Tafnews.
13. Horst Adamczewski & Bettina Perlt. (1997). Run-up velocities of female and male pole vaulting and some technical aspects of women's pole vault. Trans. Jürgen Schiffer. *New Studies in Athletics, 12*(1), 63-76.
14. V. Jagodin & V. Tshunganov. (1981). Periodization in pole vault training. In *The Jumps* (2nd ed., pp. 81-82).
15. Andrzej Krzesinski. (1983). Pole vault: The total program. *Track Technique, 84*, 2679-2682.
16. V. Jagodin, V. Kurbatov & J. Volkov. (1981). Systematic development of pole vaulters. In *The Jumps* (2nd ed., pp. 72-74).
17. V. Jagodin. (1995). Women in the pole vault [abstract]. *Track Technique, 130*, 4162.

OTHER SOURCES FOR PERIODIZED JUMP TRAINING

Adamczewski, Horst, & Dieter Kruber. (1993). Women's pole vault—A technical, conditioning and teaching programme. [abstract] *New Studies in Athletics, 8*(2), 99-101.
Bowerman, William J., & William H. Freeman. (1974). *Coaching Track and Field* (pp. 160-247). Boston: Houghton Mifflin.
Bowerman, William J., & William H. Freeman. (1991). *High Performance Training for Track and Field* (pp. 127-171). Champaign, IL: Human Kinetics.
Godoy, Jose. (1989). Training of Javier Sotomayor up to attainment of his high jump world record. Trans. Richard Westerman. *Track and Field Quarterly Review, 89*(4), 20-22.
Holmes, M. J. (1999). Identifying and developing junior elite athletes [high jump]. *New Studies in Athletics, 14*(1), 31-40.
Homenkova, L.S., ed. (1994). Training for jumping events. *Track and Field Quarterly Review, 94*(4), 44-52.
Jarver, Jess, ed. (2000). *The Jumps: Contemporary Theory, Technique and Training* (5th ed.). Mountain View, CA: Tafnews.
Jeitner, Gerhard. (1993). Training method findings and experiences in the preparation of elite and junior jumpers for competition peaks [abstract]. *New Studies in Athletics, 8*(3), 92-93.
Johnson, Carl. (1993). The elastic strength development of Jonathon Edwards. *New Studies in Athletics, 11*(2-3), 63-69.
Kipreos, Georgios. (1993). Arrangement of weekly training microcycle in the high jump (women). *Track and Field Quarterly Review, 93*(4), 34-37.
Kreer, Vitold. (1981). Training cycles in triple jumping. In *The Jumps* (2nd ed., pp. 116-118).
Lundin, Phil, Bob Myers, Mark Stream, Lore Seagrave, Dan Pfaff, Gary Winckler, Jerry Clayton, George Dunn, & Vern Gambetta. (1989). Theoretical model of long jump training for the American collegiate system. *New Studies in Athletics, 4*(3), 39-42.
Madella, Alberto. (1996). Speed in the horizontal jumps: muscular properties or cognitive treatment? *New Studies in Athletics, 11*(2-3), 127-132.
Myers, Bob. (1991). Restoration for jumpers. *Athletics Science Bulletin, 3*(1), 1-3.
NSA Round Table 31: Speed in the jumping events [Enrique Bianco, David Lease, Elio Locatelli, Yukio Muraki, Dan Pfaff, Efim Shuravetzky & Miguel Velez]. (1996). *New Studies in Athletics, 11*(2-3), 9-19.
NSA Round Table 33: Pole vault [Joël Bailly, Roman Botcharnikov, Leszec Klima, Francisco Martinez Lucia, Peter M. McGinnis, Dave Nielson, Dick Railsback & Julian Shuravetsky]. (1997). *New Studies in Athletics, 12*(1), 23-38.
Schiffer, Jürgen. (1997). Selected and annotated bibliography 41: pole vault. *New Studies in Athletics, 12*(1), 95-107.
Slepica, James. (1991). Training the young athlete for the horizontal jumps. *New Studies in Athletics, 6*(3), 43-48.
Taranov, V., et al. (1995). A cyclic blocks system for jumping events [abstract]. *Track Coach, 133*, 4258.

Wetter, Jochen. (1997). NSA interview: Wanpei Wang. *New Studies in Athletics, 12*(1), 39-40.

SOURCES FOR TABLES

12.1. Fitness Characteristics of Jumps: Dick, Frank W. (1978). *Training Theory.* London: British Amateur Athletic Board, 64-65

12.2. Phase Training Ratios for Jumps: Dick, p. 62

12.3. Phases 1-4 Training for High Jump: Ballesteros, Jose Manuel, & Julio Alvarez. (1979). *Track and Field: A Basic Coaching Manual.* London: IAAF.

12.4. Phases 1-4 Training for Long Jump: Ballesteros & Alvarez

12.5. Main Training In Long Jump Phases 1-2: Samungi, 2924, 2926

12.6. Main Training In Long Jump Phases 3-5: Samungi, 2924, 2926

12.7. Volume & Intensity in Long Jump Speed: Samungi, 2926

12.8. Phases 1-4 Training for Triple Jump: Ballesteros & Alvarez

12.9. Triple Jump Training of Viktor Saneyev: Muraki, 38

12.10. Phases 1-4 Training for Pole Vault: Ballesteros & Alvarez

12.11. Periodization of the Pole Vault Year: Kutman, M. (1981). Planning of pole vault training. In *The Jumps* (2nd ed.) pp. 6667. Los Altos: Tafnews Press.

12.12. Annual Training Plan for Age 16-17 Vaulter: Jagodin, Kurbatov & Volkov, pp. 73-74

12.13. Annual Training Plan for Age 18-19 Vaulter: Jagodin, Kurbatov & Volkov, p. 74

12.14. Annual Training Plan for Age 20-23 Vaulter: Jagodin, Kurbatov & Volkov, p. 74

12.15. Training Loads for the Pole Vault: Krzesinski, 2681-2682

SOURCES FOR FIGURES

12.1. Emphases for Jump Training: Boosey (1980), p. 48

12.2. Yearly Cycle Strength & Technique: Verhoshansky, p. 11

12.3. Double Period in Power & Technique: Verhoshansky, p. 11

12.4. Double Period in the High Jump: Tancic, 18-19

12.5. Peaks in Loading Cycles in High Jump: Myers, 47

12.6. Load in the High Jump Microcycle: Myers, 49

12.7. Periods of the Triple Jump Year: Kreer, p. 117

CHAPTER 13:
Periodized Training For Throwers

As with the jumping events, most writing on the throwing events addresses technique and teaching drills. While this gives little information on how to structure training, some of the advanced biomechanical analyses in *New Studies in Athletics* give key information on the traits found in the top athletes. Recent articles focus more on the value of varied implement weights in (a) helping young athletes make the transition to the adult weights, (b) improving specific strength, and (c) improving the speed of the arm strike.

Most Eastern European programs of periodized training place a strong emphasis on using control tests to measure each athlete's progress toward the year's performance goals. Several excellent examples of Soviet and French control tests are available for the throwing events.

While strength and power training are important to performance in most events, they are especially critical in the throwing events. Chapter 6 reviews the periodization of strength training and gives several sources of training suggestions. Three good sources for the throwing events, especially for developing athletes, are George Dunn and Kevin McGill's book on the throws (*The Throws Manual*), Jess Jarver's compilation of current articles (*The Throws*), and Tony Naclerio's book on teaching progressions in the throws. For the coach who wants more advanced applications of periodization theory

to the throws, Anatoliy Bondarchuk provides a wealth of ideas. Finally, Chapter 4 on training records includes several figures and tables of training for the throwing events.

For the critical peak, the most important events of the year, Bondarchuk provides examples of approaches to perfecting performance, while Zhang Yingbo suggests that the groundwork is laid in the pre-competition phase. Yingbo recommends careful attention to these aspects of training:

1. Technique-oriented training (develop efficiency and stability)
   - Throws with competitive implements and technique, to perfect technique
   - Throws with lighter implements, to increase speed and coordination
   - Imitations of technical movement and speed, to perfect rhythm
   - More competitions, to improve physiological and psychological adaptation
2. Conversion of conditioning into special explosive power
   - Drills in imitative throwing positions
   - Speed-oriented exercises, to develop speed and rhythm sense
   - Plyometrics imitating technical movements
3. Intensity control
   - Limiting throwing intensity (to 90-95%

Table 13.1. Fitness Characteristics of Throwing Events

Event	General	Special	Competition-Specific

Shot Put	Aerobic endurance
	Strength endurance
	Mobility
	Maximum strength
		Speed
		Special mobility
		Elastic strength
		Special strength
		  Absolute
		  Throwing
		  Related events
			Basic put technique
			Entry and shift/turn
			 technique
			Trial meets

Discus Throw	Aerobic endurance
	Strength endurance
	Mobility
	Maximum strength
		Speed
		Special mobility
		Elastic strength
		Special strength
		  Absolute
		  Throwing
		  Related events
			Basic throw technique
			Entry and turn technique
			Trial meets

Javelin Throw	Aerobic endurance
	Strength endurance
	Mobility
	Maximum strength
	Special endurance
	 (jumping, running)
		Speed endurance
		Speed
		Special mobility
		Elastic strength
		Special strength
		  Absolute
		  Throwing
		  Related events
			Basic throw technique
			Entry and approach
			 technique
			Trial meets

Hammer Throw	Aerobic endurance
	Strength endurance
	Mobility
	Maximum strength
		Speed
		Special mobility
		Elastic strength
		Special strength
		  Absolute
		  Throwing
		  Related events
			Basic throw technique
			Turns technique
			Swings technique
			Trial meets

max.) slightly for 3-7 days before major competitions
- At the same time, limiting intensity of other exercises slightly
- These combine with lowered volume for physiological and psychological peaking
4. Psychological preparation
- Competition simulation of conditions, including atmosphere
- Visualization techniques, to establish automatic control system and stabilize technique.

Table 13.2. Phase Training Ratios for Throwing Events

Phase	General	Special	Specific
1	25	35	40
2	15	45	40
3	10	40	50
4	20	40	40
5	10	40	50
6	80	10	10

Percent distribution of:
- General Training (mostly compensatory strength and mobility work)
- Special Training (includes aerobic endurance)
- Competition-Specific Training

SHOT PUT

General suggestions for objectives and training emphases during the phases of the year are given in Tables 13.1, 13.2, 13.3, and 13.4. Current training trends for the shot suggest that the strength training program should change after every three to four microcycles, while emphasizing the parts of the body in proportion to their contribution to the throw (50% legs, 30% trunk, and 20% arms). Figure 13.1 shows the pattern of volume and intensity for strength training during the year.

The pattern of training phases is:
- General Fitness (July, 4 weeks)
  Low weight (50%), high volume lifting
  5 sets of 10 reps, 4-5 days per week

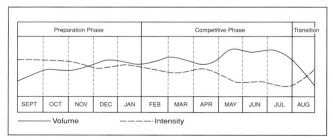

Figure 13.1. Periodization of Shot Put Strength

Table 13.3. Phases 1-4 Training for Shot Put

PHASE 1: Increase Strength and Physical Condition
- 30% Technique (learning drills or throws with heavy weights)
- 20% General conditioning (strength, mobility, circuits, varied throws)
- 20% Power work (weight training: high weight and low repetitions)
- 20% Power work (weight training: moderate weight and more repetitions)
- 10% Speed work (20-40m), low hurdles, jumping, and agility

PHASE 2: Perfect Technique and Maintain Strength
- 20% Technique (25-30 throws without strain, sometimes 9 kg. weights)
- 20% Power work (weight training: moderate weight and many repetitions)
- 20% Technique work (3-5 sets of 3-5 throws (15-20), good effort)
- 20% Speed work: Starts, accelerations, low hurdles, jumping, and agility
- 20% Power work (3-1 reps of 2-3 exercises at max. load, good recoveries)

PHASES 3-4: Accumulate Neuromuscular Potential
- 30% Technique work (12-15 throws at competitive rhythm, good effort)
- 30% Technique work (20-25 throws below maximum effort, perfect technique)
- 20% Jumping and loosening exercises, mixed with jogging
- 20% Different sprints and jumps
- Also Competition (one time per week, sometimes rest or other event)

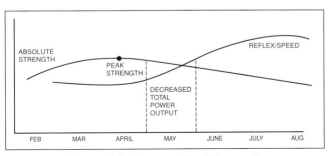

Figure 13.2. Recuperation Microcycle

- Specialized Strength (August-September, 8 weeks)
  - Extreme overload, so general skills decline temporarily
  - 5-10 reps at 75-88% (nothing heavier)
  - No maximum throwing; technique drills, flexibility work
- Pre-Competition Technique (October-November, 8 weeks)
  - Training emphasis shifts to throwing technique
  - High volume of throws, maximum about once a week
  - Lifting tonnage drops 30-50%; increased rest
- Pre-Competition Strength (December-January (4-6 weeks)
  - Length depends on date of first meet
  - High-intensity, low-volume lifting (Strength level should pass previous year's limit)
  - Good throwing performance, but too early to peak
- Competition (mid-January through May)
  - Focus on high-level throwing performance
  - Throws slightly shorter for 4-6 weeks
  - Lifting peaks at 85-90% of maximum from last phase
  - Recovery days use lifting of 5-8 reps at 60-75%
  - Top performance period is about 6-8 weeks long
- Active Rest (June, 4 weeks)
  - Active rest, with no throwing or lifting.

During the competition period, the Recuperation Microcycle (Fig. 13.2) is a training pattern for a week that falls between two major meets. For the microcycle leading to a major meet (Fig. 13.3), the following training pattern is recommended:

Table 13.4. Periodization of Shot Put Training

MACROCYCLE			
Period	Oct.4-Dec.9	Dec.10-Mar.6	Mar.7-May 9	May 10-Aug.30
Mesocycle	10 weeks	10 weeks	10 weeks	Competition
Intensity	65%	100%	85%	50%

MESOCYCLE									
Week	I	II	III	IV	V	VI	VII	VIII	IX	X
Intensity	100%	85%	50%	100%	85%	50%	100%	85%	50%	REST

MICROCYCLE						
Day	MON	TUE	WED	THU	FRI	SAT	SUN*
Intensity	100%	85%	50%	REST	100%	85%	50%

* Active rest

133

Sunday: Light technique work, or Rest (if meet on Saturday)

Monday: Rest, or Light technique work (if rested on Sunday)

Tuesday: Mixed program: moderate volume and low intensity

Jumps, sprints, light technique work

    Perhaps 1-2 strength exercises (instead of Wednesday)

Wednesday: Special tests (not with regular implement)

    10-15 throws with light shot

    Special exercises (standing LJ, standing TJ) and 30m sprints

    2-3 strength exercises (such as snatch, squats, incline bench), 3-4 reps. at 85-95%

Thursday: Rest

Friday: 2-3 barbell exercises, 3-4 reps. at 85-

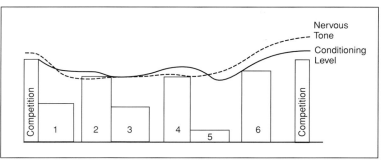

Figure 13.4. Shot and Discus Strength Macrocycle

95%. This stimulates the neuromuscular system. No throwing of any kind

Saturday: Major Meet.

DISCUS THROW

General suggestions for objectives and training emphases for the discus during the phases of the year are given in Tables 13.1, 13.2, 13.5, 13.6, and 13.7. The shot put training also applies to training for the discus throw, as most throwers below the elite level will compete regularly in both events.

These training emphases are appropriate for young male throwers in the 155'-180' range with the college discus:

- Phase 1: Quantity training, moderate intensity

    80-85% conditioning: 70% general, 30% specific

    15-20% technique

- Phase 2: Quantity training, higher intensity

    65-70% conditioning: 60% general, 40% specific

    30-35% technique

- Phases 3-4: Low-quantity, high-intensity training

    50% conditioning: primarily specific or special

    50% technique.

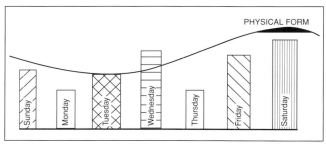

Figure 13.3. Peaking Microcycle

Table 13.5. Phases 1-4 Training for Discus Throw

PHASE 1: Increase Strength and Physical Condition

- 30% Technique (learning drills or throws with heavy weights)
- 20% General conditioning (gym work, mobility, circuits, varied throws)
- 20% Power work (weight training: high weight and low repetitions)
- 20% Power work (weight training: moderate weight and more repetitions)
- 10% Speed work (30-60m), low hurdles, and jumping

PHASE 2: Perfect Technique and Maintain Strength

- 20% Technique (30-35 throws without strain, sometimes 1.5 kg. discus)
- 20% Power work (weight training: many repetitions)
- 20% Technique work (4-5 sets of 3-5 throws (20-25), good effort)
- 20% Speed work: Starts, accelerations, low hurdles, and jumping
- 20% Power work (3-1 reps of 2-3 exercises at max. load, good recoveries)

PHASES 3-4: Accumulate Neuromuscular Potential

- 30% Technique work (15-20 throws at competitive rhythm, strong effort)
- 30% Technique work (25-30 throws below maximum effort, perfect technique)
- 20% Relaxation and jumping exercises, mixed with jogging
- 20% Different sprints and jumps
- Also Competition (one time per week, sometimes rest or other event)

Table 13.6. Training Proportions for Discus (Mac Wilkins)

Season	Throwing	Drills	Lifting
Fall	65%	0%	35%
Winter	40%	15%	45%
Early Spring	40%	20%	40%
Late Spring	50%	10%	40%
Summer	70%	0%	30%

Table 13.7. Training Proportions for Discus (John Powell)

Season	Throwing	Drills	Lifting
Fall	25%	25%	50%
Winter	25%	25%	50%
Early Spring	40%	10%	50%

A top-level thrower should take 5,000 to 6,000 high-intensity throws in a year, compared to 2,500 to 3,000 for a 17 to 18-year-old thrower and 3,700 to 4,500 for a young (ages 18-19) collegian throwing 160'.

A high school thrower should take at least 75-100 full throws per week, while college throwers should take at least 100 full throws per week. Only 65% of the throws in Phases 1-3 should be with the regulation-weight discus.

Table 13.8 is one example of the progression in training loads of a World Champion thrower (Imrich Bugar). Another example of training loads at the elite level is the great Cuban thrower, Luis Delis (233'2"). He was able to train very intensively only by devoting his full-time energies to training. His training year fell into four periods (the figures are weekly):

- Phase 1: General Physical Preparation
  Includes 600 general throws and 40 specific throws
  Includes 360 general jumps, sprinting, gymnastics, swimming, and special endurance activities
- Phase 2: Absolute-Strength Preparation
  Includes 170 general throws and 375 specific throws
  Includes 450 jumps, sprinting, and 6 sessions of absolute-strength training
- Phase 3: Special-Strength Preparation

Hammer Thrower Lance Deal

Includes 270-325 specific throws
Includes jumping, sprinting, and 3 sessions of fast-strength training
- Phases 4-5: Competition
  Includes 60-130 specific throws
  Includes jumping, sprinting, and 2 sessions of competitive-strength training.

Edward Harnes and Peter Rachmanliev explain the training of elite women throwers in Bulgaria, which emphasized speed over strength. Table 13.9 shows a one-year training plan for women throwing 67-71m (220'-233'), revealing the annual training load in numbers.

HAMMER THROW

General suggestions for objectives and training emphases for the hammer during the phases of the year are given in Tables 13.1, 13.2, and 13.10. The Soviet men dominated the hammer throw in the 70's and 80's, but with the breakup of the Soviet Union, the Hungarians and Germans have emerged as the world's best. Anatoliy Bondarchuk, the most successful Soviet hammer coach, divides the devel-

Table 13.8. Training Loads for Discus (Imrich Bugar)

Year	1975	1977	1980	1982
Age	20	22	25	27
Best Mark	176'9"	205'2"	217'9"	225'1"
				(232'0" in 1983)
Training days	163	222	236	249
Sessions	177	258	319	323
Tons lifted	738	1491	1861	1646
Throws	2620	1640	2729	2195
Jumps	2960	5770	6270	5790
Stomach/back repeats	3020	4770	5715	6220
Meets	27	25	26	25
Body Weight	229	238	258	265
CONTROL TESTS:				
20m sprint	3.10	3.10	3.00	3.05
StJ	29'6"	30'8"	30'2"	30'2"
Snatch	209	265	309	309
Bench press	253	320	419	441
Clean	265	320	386	397
Squat	375	441	529	529
5 kg. shot (discus style)	68'10"	77'9"	88'7"	89'10"
Overhead shot	—	—	72'6"	70'6"
4 kg. shot, with turn (discus style)	—	—	122'0"	123'6"
Note: All weights are in pounds.				

135

Table 13.9. Training Plan for Female Discus Throwers (67-71m)

Throwing Implements and Their Weights	X	XI	XII	I	II	III	IV	V	VI	VII	VIII	IX	PER YEAR TOTAL
Heavy implements 1.6-2.0kg		200	250	210	300	150	70						1180
Heavy implements 1.2-1.5kg	200	280	450	500	600	500	130	100		200	100		3060
Competition implements 1.0kg	380	810	800	600	570	1100	800	680	600	800	740	420	8300
Lighter implements 0.75kg						220	160	140					
General throws with implements other than the discus (3-6kg shot; medicine balls, dumbbells up to 8kg)	870	1020	820	440	360	280	260	260	290	540	260	240	5640
Sum per month	1450	2310	2320	1750	1830	2250	1420	1180	890	1540	1100	660	18700
Sum per week	362	577	580	437	457	562	355	295	222	385	275	165	
Amount of competitions						1	2	2	3		3	3	14

opment of hammer throwers into three stages:

- Initial Preparation Level: Ages 12-14
  3-4 sessions per week, 90-120 minutes each
  All-around development exercises, sprinting, jumping
  Use light implements (3-5 kg.)
  Shot putting (4-6 kg.) from different positions

Table 13.10. Phases 1-4 Training for Hammer Throw

PHASE 1: Increase Strength and Physical Condition
- 30% Technique (learning drills and throws with heavy implements)
- 20% General conditioning (gym work, mobility, circuits, varied throws)
- 20% Power work (weight training: high weight and low repetitions)
- 20% Power work (weight training: moderate weight and more repetitions)
- 10% Speed work (30-60m), low hurdles, and jumping

PHASE 2: Perfect Technique and Maintain Strength
- 20% Speed work: starts, accelerations, low hurdles, and jumping
- 20% Technique (25-30 throws at full effort, sometimes 6 kg. hammer)
- 20% Technique work (20-25 throws with power and range)
- 20% Power work (weight training: specific exercises, many repetitions)
- 20% Power work (3-1 reps of 2-3 exercises at max. load, good recoveries)

PHASES 3-4: Accumulate Neuromuscular Potential
- 30% Technique work (15-20 throws at competitive rhythm, strong effort)
- 30% Technique work (25-30 throws below full effort, perfecting technique)
- 20% Jumping and loosening exercises, mixed with jogging
- 20% Different sprints and jumps
- Also Competition (one time per week, sometimes rest or other event)

Weight training
Maximum training load for single session:
  2 tons of weight lifted
  15-20 hammer throws
  25 throws with the shot
  500 meters of sprinting
  Most training in first (50-80%) and second (80-90%) zones of intensity
  5% of training load in higher zones

- Special Fundamental Preparation Level: Ages 14-18
  5-8 sessions per week, 120-150 minutes each
  All-around development exercises, sprinting, jumping
  Use light (5-6 kg.), normal, and heavy (8 kg.) hammers
  Shot putting (6-16 kg.) from different positions
  Weight training and special exercises
  Maximum training load for single session:
    5-6 tons of weight lifted
    25 hammer throws
    25 throws with the shot
    1,000 meters of sprinting
    60-70% of weights in second zone (80-90%)
    25% of weights in first (50-80%) zone of intensity
    10-15% of training load in higher zone (90-100%)

- Perfecting Acquired Skill Level: Ages 18 and over
  Can reach 200 throws a day, but found that 30-40 (sometimes 50-60) throws are sufficient.

A series of figures illustrates the general Soviet hammer training plan. Figure 13.5 shows the pattern of power training, peaking at 120 kg. (265 lbs.) in the snatch in February, with the hammer performance level beginning in late February at the 70-meter (230') level. This is the training for world record holder Yuriy Syedikh, with a PR of over 280'.

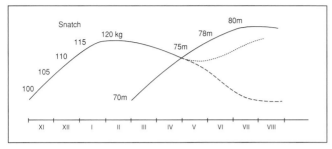

Figure 13.5. Hammer Power Training Macrocycle

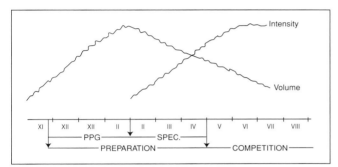

Figure 13.6. Hammer Training Volume and Intensity

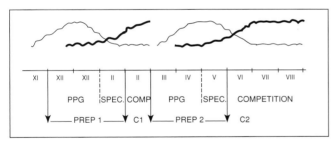

Figure 13.7. Hammer Training Doubled-Periodized

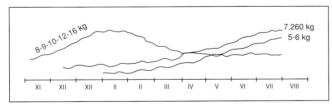

Figure 13.8. Varied-Weight Hammer Macrocycle

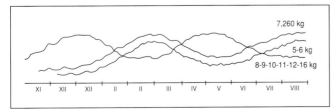

Figure 13.9. Double-Period Varied Weight Hammer

This is not the start of his throwing; it is his technical level as he completes the heavy focus on power (so his throwing technical level will be diminished).

The mix of volume and intensity are shown in both single- (Fig. 13.6) and double-periodized (Fig. 13.7) form. Figure 13.7 is appropriate for American athletes who throw the 35-pound weight indoors.

The Soviet throwers mix light and heavy implements with the regulation-weight implement in all of their throwing events. Figure 13.8 shows a single-period macrocycle and the changing training emphasis of the different weights. Figure 13.9 shows a double-period pattern, again one that is appropriate for athletes competing indoors. Figure 13.10 shows the relative emphasis of the types of training across the year, while Figure 13.11 shows a more general model based on East German training.

For all the differences that appear from one plan to another, the similarities are striking. The focal points of each phase, with the relative training

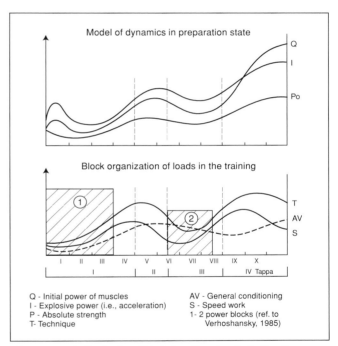

Figure 13.10. Periodized Training Emphasis in the Hammer

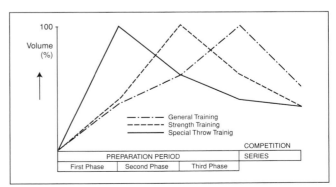

Figure 13.11. Periodized Training Year for Hammer

emphasis at each point, are remarkably similar. The great difference is from the broad curves of the training pattern for young athletes to the more complex mix used by experienced elite throwers.

JAVELIN THROW

General suggestions for objectives and training emphases for the javelin during the phases of the year are given in Tables 13.1, 13.2, and 13.11. Writing for the USATF, Bill Webb and Bob Sing suggested four training periods of three months each for the javelin thrower:

- Foundation (June through August)
    Develop strength and stamina base
    High repetition, low resistance exercises
    Weight training, running, basic skill work
- Power Development (September through November)
    Develop power for specific throwing motion
    Alternate-day weight training with pyramid method
    Quality throwing with balls and shortened javelins
    Distance runs, sprints, bounding, and jumping
- Competition I (December through February)
    Refine technique
    Continue power training with reduced loads
    Physical and mental training exercises
    Sprinting and bounding exercises
    Early meets used for rehearsal
- Competition II (March through May)
    Emphasis on throwing, flexibility, and speed training
    Regular mental imagery and rehearsal exercises.

Esa Utriainen describes the differences in training men and women throwers. He mentions the following differences (compared to men) that affect women's training and performance:

Weaknesses:
- Smaller relative proportion of muscles to body weight, 27% to 40%, and greater percent of body fat
- Lower testosterone production (10-11 times less)
- Weak middle and upper trunk (generally)
- Natural slowness because of small, weak muscles
- Poorer technical skills and weaker implement control (generally)
- Mechanical disadvantages: shorter (4"/10 cm), lighter (10 kg),and legs are 25%

Table 13.11. Phases 1-4 Training for Javelin Throw

PHASE 1: Increase Strength and Physical Condition
- 30% Technique (drills and throws with clubs, balls and weighted balls)
- 20% General conditioning (gym work, mobility, circuits, varied throws)
- 20% Power work (weight training: high weight and low repetitions)
- 15% Power training and mobility work
- 15% Speed work (40-60m), low hurdles, and jumping

PHASE 2: Perfect Technique and Maintain Strength
- 20% Technique (25-30 throws with half run or last 5 strides)
- 20% Power work and mobility work
- 20% Technique work (15-20 full-run throws at good effort)
- 20% Speed work: starts, accelerations, low hurdles, and jumping
- 20% Power work (weight training: fast medium load, pullies, isometrics)

PHASES 3-4: Accumulate Neuromuscular Potential
- 30% Technique work (10-15 throws at competitive rhythm, "heel running")
- 30% Technique work (20-25 throws easy throws, perfecting technique)
- 20% Jumping and loosening exercises, mixed with jogging
- 20% Different sprints, jumps, and agility
- Also Competition (one time per week, sometimes rest or other event)

shorter, along with a low, broad, weaker hip.

Strengths:
- Greater training capacity
- Better mental balance
- Able to stand intensive training at an earlier stage
- "A woman is tougher and she stands more pain than a man" (p.56).

He suggests that an average training year would include about 10,000 throws (from 7-13,000), but only 30-50% are performed with a javelin. Women more often use lower weights, which allows better control and the perfection of technique, along with increased speed. He notes that the throwers have moved to a double-periodized year, with about three weeks of indoor competition with blunt-pointed javelins in a large indoor facility. It is also, in part, because the throwers tire of continual indoor training during the long winter and need a challenge.

REFERENCES

1. Jean-Paul Baert. (1985). Shot put. In Jess Jarver (Ed.), *The Throws* (3rd ed., pp. 74-77). Mountain View, CA: Tafnews.
2. Kevin McGill (Trans.). (1984). Tests of equivalence. *Track and Field Quarterly Review*, 84(1), 50-53.
3. George D. Dunn, Jr., & Kevin McGill. (1994). *The Throws Manual* (2nd ed.). Mountain View, CA: Tafnews.
4. Jess Jarver, ed. (2000). *The Throws: Contemporary Theory, Technique and Training* (5th ed.). Mountain View, CA: Tafnews.
5. Tony Naclerio. (1988). *The Teaching Progressions of the Shot Put, Discus and Javelin*. Rockaway, NJ: Author.
6. Anatoliy Bondarchuk. (1988). Constructing a training system,

Parts 1 and 2. *Track Technique, 102*, 3254-3259, 3268; *103*, 3286-3288.

7. Anatoliy Bondarchuk. (1994). About the development of form. *Track Technique, 129*, 4120-4121, 4132.
8. Zhang Yingbo. (1992). Successful pre-competitive preparation for throwers. *Track Technique, 121*, 3854-3855.
9. George Dunn. (1987). Current trends in shot put training. *Track Technique, 98*, 3118-3123.
10. Richard Marks. (1985). Specialized strength and technique training for shot and discus. *Track Technique, 91*, 2898-2899.
11. Freidhelm Endemann. (1981). Discus training program. In *Track Technique Annual '81*, Vern Gambetta, ed. (pp. 31-33). Los Altos: Tafnews Press.
12. Vern Gambetta. (1986). TT interview: Mac Wilkins. *Track Technique, 96*, 3053-3055.
13. Max Jones. (Ed.). (1984). The training of Imrich Bugar. *Track Technique, 89*, 2831-2833.
14. Hermes Riveri. (1986). Discus training periodization. *Track Technique, 96*, 3058-3059.
15. Edward Harnes. (1989). Training plan for advanced female discus throwers in Bulgaria. Trans. Freidhelm Endemann. *Track Technique, 106*, 3371-3375, 3393- 3395.
16. Peter Rachmanliev & Edward Harnes. (1990). Long-term preparation for advanced female discus throwers. *New Studies in Athletics, 5*(1), 69-92.
17. Anatoly Bondarchuk. (1987). Secrets to Soviet hammer throw achievement. *Track and Field Quarterly Review, 87*(3), 27-28.
18. Kevin McGill. (1984). Hammer clinic. *Track and Field Quarterly Review, 84*(1), 42-49.
19. Bill Webb & Bob Sing. (1989). The javelin throw. In *The Athletic Congress's Track and Field Coaching Manual* (2nd ed., pp. 189-199).
20. Esa Utriainen. (1987). Difference in men's and women's training for javelin. In *Amicale des Entraîneurs Français d'Athlétisme*, ed. *The Throws: Official Report of the XIVth Congress, European Athletics Coaches Association* (pp. 55- 68). Paris: European Athletics Coaches Association.

OTHER SOURCES FOR PERIODIZED TRAINING IN THE THROWS

Auvinen, M., & K. Ihalainen. (1995). Junior World [javelin] Champion Taina Uppa's training, 1993-1994. *Track Coach, 134*, 4284-4287.

Badon, Tommy. (1990). Adapting training plans for the prep discus thrower. *Track Technique, 110*, 3503-3505, 3524.

Bakarinov, Juri. (1990). Theoretical aspects of training control for highly qualified throwers. *New Studies in Athletics, 5*(1), 7-15.

Bakarinov, Yuri. (1990). The hammer throw: evolution and perspectives. *Soviet Sports Review, 25*(3), 113-116; *25*(4), 184-185.

Bartonietz, Klaus, Lawrie Barclay & Dean Gathercole. (1997). Characteristics of top performances in the women's hammer throw: Basics and technique of the world's best athletes. *New Studies in Athletics, 12*(2-3), 101-109.

Bosen, Ken O. (1994). Recent trends in technique and training in javelin throwing. *Track and Field Quarterly Review, 94*(3), 53-56.

Bowerman, William J., & William H. Freeman. (1974). *Coaching Track and Field* (pp. 250-331). Boston: Houghton Mifflin.

Bowerman, William J., & William H. Freeman. (1991). *High Performance Training for Track and Field* (pp. 173-218). Champaign, IL: Human Kinetics.

Burke, Ed, Ladislav Pataki & Ken Doherty. (1989). The hammer throw: fundamental technique and strength plan. *National Strength & Conditioning Association, 11*(4), 8-10, 77-81.

Cissik, John M. (2000). Conditioning for hammer throwers. *Track and Field Coaches Review, 73*(1), 32-34.

Escamilla, Rafael F., Kevin P. Speer, Glenn S. Fleisig, Steven W. Barrentine & James R. Andrews. (2000). Effects of throwing overweight and underweight baseballs on throwing veloc-ity and accuracy. *Sports Medicine, 29*(4), 259-272.

Freeman, William H., & Arne Nytro. (1994). Training theory of the hammer throw. In Jarver, *The Throws* (4th ed., pp. 96-101).

Jianrong, Chen. (1992). Load variations of elite female javelin throwers in a macrocycle. *Track Technique, 119*, 3788-3792.

Judge, Larry W. (1992). Designing a strength & conditioning program for the thrower. *Track and Field Quarterly Review, 92*(3), 48-60.

Lawler, Peter. (1994). The javelin throw—the past, present and future. *Track and Field Quarterly Review, 94*(3), 47-52.

Lenz, Gudrun, & Hans-Jürgen Frolich. (1994). Strength and power-orientated training of young throwers. In Jarver, *The Throws* (4th ed., pp. 8-11).

NSA Round Table 30: The role of speed in the throws [Ekkart Arbeit, Anders Borgström, Carl Johnson & Yuriy Sedykh]. (1996). *New Studies in Athletics, 11*(1), 11-16.

NSA Round Table 34: Hammer throw [Teodoru Agachi, Yuriy Bakarynov, Lawrie Barclay, Guy Guérin, Boris Rubanko, Allan Staerck, Sergey Ivanovich Sykhonosov & Ernö Szabó]. (1997). *New Studies in Athletics, 12*(2-3), 13-27.

Schiffer, Jürgen. (1997). Selected and annotated bibliography 43: hammer throw. *New Studies in Athletics, 12*(2-3), 140-157.

Schiffer, Jürgen. (1998). Selected and annotated bibliography 45: javelin throw. *New Studies in Athletics, 13*(1), 65-86.

Schiffer, Jürgen. (1997). Selected and annotated bibliography 44: rotational technique of shot putting. *New Studies in Athletics, 12*(4), 81-98.

Wirth, Allan. (1995). The integration of competitive Olympic weight lifting with discus and hammer throwing. *New Studies in Athletics, 10*(3), 23-28

Venegas, Art. (1989). U.C.L.A. shot put-discus conditioning program. *Track and Field Quarterly Review, 89*(3), 6-8.

SOURCES FOR TABLES

13.1. Fitness Characteristics of Throws: Dick, Frank W. (1978). *Training Theory*. London: British Amateur Athletic Board, 64-65

13.2. Phase Training Ratios for Throws: Dick, p. 62

13.3. Phases 1-4 Training for Shot Put: Ballesteros, Jose Manuel, & Julio Alvarez. (1979). *Track and Field: A Basic Coaching Manual*. London: IAAF.

13.4. Periodization of Shot Put: Baert, *Track Technique, 88*, 2812

13.5. Phases 1-4 Training for Discus: Ballesteros & Alvarez

13.6. Training Proportions for Discus (Wilkins): Bullard & Knuth, *Discus: Wilkins vs. Powell* (p. 55). San Jose: LK Publications.

13.7. Training Proportions for Discus (Powell): Bullard & Knuth, p. 55

13.8. Training Loads for the Discus: Jones, 2831-2832

13.9. Training Plan for Female Discus Throwers (67-71m): Harnes (1989), 3372

13.10. Phases 1-4 Training for Hammer: Ballesteros & Alvarez

13.11. Phases 1-4 Training for Javelin: Ballesteros & Alvarez

SOURCES FOR FIGURES

13.1. Periodization of Shot Put Strength: Dunn, 3118

13.2. Recuperation Microcycle: Dunn, 3123

13.3. Peaking Microcycle: Dunn, 3123

13.4. Shot and Discus Strength Macrocycle: Marks, 2899

13.5. Hammer Power Training Macrocycle: McGill, 48

13.6. Hammer Training Volume and Intensity: McGill, 48

13.7. Hammer Training Doubled-Periodized: McGill, 48

13.8. Varied Weight Hammer Macrocycle: McGill, 49

13.9. Double-Period Varied Weight Hammer: McGill, 49

13.10. Periodized Training Emphasis in the Hammer: Freeman & Nytro, p. 99

13.11. Periodized Training Year for Hammer (East Germany): Freeman & Nytro, p. 99

CHAPTER 14:
Periodized Training For The Combined Events

Table 14.1 gives the fitness characteristics needed for success in the combined events. We will look briefly at training for the men's decathlon, then the women's heptathlon. Sergio Etcheverry did a detailed analysis of the top 50 decathletes. It yields much useful information for modeling the performance and training the athlete, though it holds no surprises. For the women's event, Lyle Sanderson did a detailed study of heptathlon performances. It, too, has implications for training.

The training for the individual events within the combined contests follows the same patterns discussed in the chapters on those events. However, the sequence of performing the events in a com-

bined meet affects the performance of the events that follow. For example, going from the shot put to the high jump is not the same as warming up and competing in the high jump as the first or only event of the day.

American dominance in the combined events is a thing of the past (it never existed in the women's event). The reason lies in two major changes, first seen in Soviet and Eastern European training. Compared to American training, their programs showed:

- Carefully planned and recorded training plans and results
- Increasing training loads for both men and women

Table 14.1. Fitness Characteristics for Combined Eventers

General	Special	Competition-Specific
Aerobic endurance	Speed endurance	Individual techniques
Strength endurance	Special mobility	Time trials
Mobility	Speed	Trial meets
Maximum strength	Elastic strength	Individual events
Special endurance (jumping, running)	Special strength Relative Jumping Throwing	Groups of events

Table 14.2. Recommended Training Loads for Soviet Combined Eventers

	Women	Men
Training days	280	280
Training sessions	420	220
Training hours	1,120	1,120
Running at max. speed (km)	35	40
Repetition runs, 100-600m (km)	85	75
Steady running (km)	1,100	1,200
Hurdling (number of hurdles)	4,000	3,100
Long jumps	900	700
High jumps	1,100	800
Shot puts	2,600	2,300
Javelin throws	3,100	3,000
Weight training (tons)	240	300
Jumping exercises (takeoffs)	11,000	11,000

The result is a superiority in the strength and technical events, which reflect effective training methods.

Table 14.2 gives an example of the increasing training loads by showing the recommended annual training load for Soviet combined event athletes, both men and women.

DECATHLON

The long-range training of decathletes falls into three stages:
- Beginning Training: ages 14-17
- Development of Specialized Motor Foundation: Ages 18-20
- Specialized Training: after age 20

The first stage is concerned with general physical training, emphasizing aiding the body's growth and development with effective training, rather than overloading it and interfering with the growth process. Endurance (rather than speed) receives special attention, as it provides a base for the development of speed and strength in the later stages. The development of flexibility and dexterity through a wide range of coordinated motion (motor skills) is emphasized. The emphasized individual events are the hurdles and pole vault, as they are the most complex skill events in the decathlon.

During the second stage the foundations for elite-level motor skills are developed. The work volume becomes very high, with optimal volumes in running, jumping, strength training, and the mastery of the skills of each individual event. Speed training exercises are added to the annual program in January, with much use of intervals of 170-200 meters, along with cross country intervals of 800-1,000 meters.

The strength emphasis is on absolute strength, using 75-90% of maximum in most exercises. Jumping exercises are used, both single- and double-legged, as well as jumps from a run and over hurdles. Jumping

control tests for decathletes at this stage are:
- Standing long jump: 9'10"-10'6"
- Standing triple jump: 30'6"-32'2"
- 5-jumps from a stand: 51'10"-54'2".

The overall training program uses more intense, complex training methods and higher volume to improve the athlete's capabilities in:
- Speed-strength preparation
- Endurance
- Flexibility
- Technique
- Coordination
- Reactiveness
- Ability to relax.

The ability to relax is needed because of the length of decathlon competitions. The athlete must conserve his reserves during the intervals between peak efforts.

The third stage uses strength training to develop speed-strength qualities, jumping exercises, and technical training with more advanced skills. Psychological preparation increases in importance. The coach and athlete must be cautious not to overuse jumping exercises or plyometrics, otherwise the athlete may suffer frequent injuries.

Coaches are not agreed on all aspects of decathlon training. A common view suggests trying to balance inexperienced athletes' performances across the events, until a stable performance level is possible in every event. At that point, the athlete will begin to emphasize special "big-point" events. Though the scoring tables were revised in 1985, they still favor the sprinter-jumper.

The most common approach to daily training is to train for the events in competition order, as some events have negative effects on the events that follow them. The athlete must be accustomed to those conditions in competition. However, coaches are moving toward training that uses more general skills common to more than one event. For example, aspects of speed training and technique are used in seven events, the start from blocks is in three events, and the three jumps all have similar aspects of take-off traits.

We still have much to learn about effective training methods in the decathlon, as it involves the interaction of training for events whose major performance traits are not completely compatible. The strength needs for the shot put clash with the body size need for jumping and vaulting, as an example. The periodization pattern will follow that of the individual events, though the coach and athlete might prefer to plan a wave-like pattern that places the emphasis upon only two or three events during a given phase, allowing more concentrated skill development.

The practice of competing in a large number

of individual events during the early season should be limited carefully. The athlete should compete in no event that doesn't allow a proper warmup and concentration on achieving the athlete's goal for that single event for the meet. Rushing from one event to the next results in poor habits of concentration, less effective technique, and an unrealistic sense of what the decathlon is like. In most combined events, the athlete will have from 30 minutes to an hour or more between events (the Olympic Games takes a two-hour "lunch break" after the second event each day). Competition in individual events should simulate the specific needs of the decathlete, not the needs of a team for an extra few points.

HEPTATHLON

The points just made about periodization and competing in individual events for the decathlon also hold for the heptathlon. Again, there is the tendency for coaches to use the talented multi-event athlete as a "big points-man" (or woman) for the team, but it is detrimental to their chances to become truly elite combined event athletes.

The developmental process in the heptathlon divides into two stages:
- Learning Stage: emphasizes performance balance across the events and the improvement of conditioning, speed, strength, and endurance
- Specificity Stage: emphasizes increasing the speed, specific strength, speed endurance, and specific endurance.

These training components should be stressed in planning the training program:
- Speed training: needed for four of the seven events
- Technique training: stress common technique factors, as mentioned in the decathlon
- Strength training:
  1. General strength: Olympic lifts and power lifts
  2. Specific strength: power or speed-strength. Includes plyometrics and high-volume technique drills.
- Endurance training: base for 800 meters and work capacity for extensive training and competition
- Mobility (flexibility): increases the range of motion, improving technique and decreasing the risk of injury
- Recovery: extremely important because of high training volume. Includes mental and physical recovery, restoration, active rest, and complete rest. Active rest is preferred.

All training should be classified and recorded.

FIONNBAR CALLANAN

Decathlete Chris Huffins

An example is the classification of work for combined events shown in Table 14.3. American heptathletes tend to be deficient in special endurance and strength (both general and specific), compared to their foreign opponents.

Younger athletes should have four training periods, as they are less prepared for extensive competition and will usually need a single-periodized year:
- Off-Season (Phases 1-2): training to train, or general development (August through November)
  Focus on sprinting technique, strength, speed endurance and training endurance
- Early Season (Phases 2-3): preparing to compete (November to March)
  Focus on technique and speed endurance
  Highest work load of year
- In-Season (Phases 4-5): training to compete (April through June)
  Focus on developing peak speed, special endurance, and refining technique

- Transition (Phase 6): regeneration, or active rest (July).

A plan for intermediate and advanced athletes is aimed at the collegiate competitor, with a double-periodized year that allows indoor meets or prepares for an early season qualifying meet. It has six phases:

- Phase 1: Foundation I (July through October)
    Focus on overall conditioning
    Build the physical and mental foundation for the year
- Phase 2: Pre-Competition I (November through January)
    Specific preparation, focusing on power, speed endurance, and speed
- Phase 3: Competition I (February through March)
    Indoor meets or first outdoor heptathlon
    Focus on technique work, special endurance, and peak speed
- Phase 4: Pre-Competition II (April)
    Re-establish high volume and basic conditioning (a condensed form of Phase 2)
- Phase 5: Competition II (May and June)
    Focus on competition-specific training, peak results

- Phase 6: Transition June to July, 2-4 weeks)
    Focus on enjoyable fitness activities, unrelated to track and field.

Each phase is divided into mesocycles of three to six weeks (ending with control testing) and subdivided into single-week microcycles, using this training pattern:

Monday and Tuesday: High-volume training
Wednesday and Thursday: Lower-volume training (sprinting)
Friday and Saturday: Medium-volume training
Sunday: Total rest or restoration.

Gertrud Schäfar, writing on Sabine Braun's training, notes that her microcycles vary from five to ten days, with 3-9 training sessions per week. She uses a sequence of four microcycles:

- Introductory microcycle
- Basic load microcycle
- Performance microcycle
- Active regeneration microcycle.

Sanderson writes that the throwing events are not as effectively used in practice, which likely costs the athletes more lost points than coaches realize. At the same time, the decline in 800m performances suggests that athletes are spending too little time training for that event also. Training for the women's event still emphasizes the sprint/jump events at the

Table 14.3. Classification of Work for Combined Events

Type of Training	Intensity	Notes
1. Speed 1-4 sets of 1-4 x 20-60m 1-5 min. recovery per rep 5-10 min. recovery per set	95-100%	Run on track from different starting positions
2. Speed-endurance 1-3 sets of 2-5 x 60-150m (400-600m total) 2-5 min. recovery per rep 8-10 min. recovery per set	90-100%	Run on track
3. Special endurance 1-5 x 150-600m (300-1,800m total) 5 min. to full recovery per rep	90-100%	Run on track
4. Plyometrics	80-100%	Do on track for multiple contacts, or on track for high intensity
5. Intensive tempo 1-4 sets of 2-6 x 100-1,000m recovery to 110-115 HR	80-90%	Run on grass, if possible
6. Extensive tempo 1-3 x 1-3 km, recovery to 120 HR	40-80%	Run on grass
7. Technique	Varies	
8. Circuit training	Varies	
9. Weight lifting	Varies	

cost of true balance of performance.

We should see the women's event become the same decathon as the men's (except for standard weight/distance differences) within a very few years. As I noted in a research study of heptathlon performances, "A willingness to train our women more at the level of the men in intensity, with loadings in proportion to their relative body sizes, will pay many benefits in the coming years; for in the revolution in women's track and field, the United States has been largely content to follow sluggishly along some distance behind the leaders. The talent has always been there; it is time for American coaches to work at a more thorough development of it."

REFERENCES

1. Sergio Guarda Etcheverry. (1995). Profile of the decathlete. *New Studies in Athletics, 10*(2), 23-27.
2. Lyle Sanderson. (1995). Trends in women's combined events. *New Studies in Athletics, 10*(2), 13-22.
3. A. Rudski & B. Aptekman. (1986). Stages in the training of decathloners. *Track and Field Quarterly Review, 86*(2), 16-17.
4. William H. Freeman. (1986). Decathlon performance success: progress and age factors. *Track Technique, 96*, 3050-3052.
5. Andrzej Krzesenski. (1984). The specific features of the decathlon. *Track Technique, 89*, 2828-2830.
6. Bob Myers. (1986). Periodization for the heptathlon: a practical training theory. *Track and Field Quarterly Review, 86*(2), 34-36.
7. Bob Myers. (1989). Heptathlon. In *The Athletic Congress's Track and Field Coaching Manual* (2nd ed., pp. 209-218). Champaign, IL: Human Kinetics.
8. Gertrud Schäfar. (1995). The overall planning of Sabine Braun's heptathlon training and competition. *New Studies in Athletics, 10*(2), 57-61.
9. William H. Freeman. (1986). An analysis of heptathlon performance and training. *Track and Field Quarterly Review, 86*(2), 30-34.

OTHER SOURCES OF COMBINED EVENT TRAINING

Berndt, Axel, & Helmar Hommel, eds. (1995). Report: XIX Congress of the European Athletics Coaches Association: Combined events. *New Studies in Athletics, 10*(2), 87-103.
Bowerman, William J., & William H. Freeman. (1974). *Coaching Track and Field* (pp. 334-353). Boston: Houghton Mifflin.
Bowerman, William J., & William H. Freeman. (1991). The combined events: decathlon and heptathlon. In *High Performance Training for Track and Field* (2d ed., pp. 219-240). Champaign, IL: Human Kinetics.
Freeman, William H. (1976, April). Decathlon competition organization. *Scholastic Coach, 45*, 34ff.
Freeman, William H. (1986). Factors of decathlon success. *Track and Field Quarterly Review, 86*(2), 4-11.
Higgins, Andy. (1990). Beyond speed in the decathlon. *Track Technique, 111*, 3544-3546, 3556.
Kersee, Bob. (1989). Philosophy of running training and methodology: Women sprinters and heptathlon. *Track and Field Quarterly Review, 89*(1), 3-5.
Kunz, Hansruedi. (1989). Long term planning of combined event training. *New Studies in Athletics, 4*(2), 8-13.
Maksimenko, G. (1992). The final preparation phase in the decathlon. *Modern Athlete and Coach, 30*(4), 30-33.
Marra, Harry. (1986). The decathlon. *Track and Field Quarterly Review, 86*(2), 12-15.
Marra, Harry, & Freeman, Bill. (1989). The decathlon. In *The Athletic Congress's Track and Field Coaching Manual* (2nd ed., pp. 203-207).
McGuire, Rick. (1992). Concentration for the field event athlete: an application of Cook's Model of Concentration. *Track and Field Quarterly Review, 92*(1), 49-51.
McStravick, Brad. (Fall 1997). Long-term planning for combined events [abstract]. *Track Coach, 141*, 4512-4513.
Myers, Bob. (1989). Training for the jumps and multi-events. *Track Technique, 108*, 3449-3452; *109*, 3492-3493 [corrections].
Panteleyev, Viktor. (1998). Preparation of decathletes. *Modern Athlete and Coach, 36*(3), 35-38.
Sanderson, Lyle. (1988). The systematic development of talent for heptathlon. *New Studies in Athletics, 3*(3), 53-59.
Shuravetzky, Efim. (1995). An outline of the Australian decathlon coaching programme. *New Studies in Athletics, 10*(2), 43-47.
Tolsma, Brant. (1984). A scientific view of decathlon training. In George G. Dales (Ed.), *Proceedings of the International Track and Field Coaches Association IX Congress* (pp. 121-124). Kalamazoo, MI: USCTFCA.
Zarnowski, Frank, Dorothy Doolittle & Fred Samara. (1991). Multi-event panel. *Track and Field Quarterly Review, 91*(4), 42-46.

SOURCES FOR TABLES

14.1. Characteristics for Combined Eventers: Dick, Frank W. (1978). *Training Theory,* London: BAAB, 64-65
14.2. Recommended Loads for Soviet Combined Eventers: Kudu, Fred. (1984). Training load in the heptathlon. *Track Technique, #89*, 2883
14.3. Classification of Work for Combined Events: Myers (1989), p. 214

CHAPTER 15:
Periodized Training for Walkers

Unfortunately, little training information for race walkers is in print. While race walking is popular in areas such as Eastern Europe and Mexico, it receives limited interest in the United States, being treated more as a "funny" event. Fortunately, several states have added short walking events to the high school track schedule, exposing more young athletes to this Olympic event. We should see more progress now that the women's walking has been added to the Olympic program, just as the longer women's running events were added after such an extended delay.

Table 15.1 lists the general, special, and competition-specific fitness characteristics of race walking. Table 15.2 suggests how to distribute the training for those characteristics during the different phases of the macrocycle. Table 15.3 gives a more

Table 15.1. Fitness Characteristics for Walkers

General Specific	Special	Competition
Aerobic endurance technique	Speed endurance	Walking
Strength endurance	Speed	Time trials
Mobility	Special mobility	Tactical trials
Maximum strength	Special endurance Event distance	

Table 15.2. Suggested Training Ratios for Walkers

Phase	General	Special	Specific
1	20	75	5
2	20	70	10
3	10	70	20
4	10	85	5
5	10	80	10
6	55	40	5

Percent distribution of:
• General Training (mostly compensatory strength and mobility work)
• Special Training (includes aerobic endurance)
• Competition-Specific Training

specific set of periodic emphases for training in the walks.

Fortunately, Bob Kitchen reproduced his earlier chapter on technique and training for the walks in *The Athletics Congress's Coaching Manual* (2nd ed.). He recommends training aimed at improving the endurance capacities (cardiovascular), expanding both the aerobic and anaerobic components. Because of the peculiar "rolling" gait and motion required by the event, an athlete needs to develop considerable flexibility throughout the body, with emphasis on the shoulders, trunk, hips, and legs. The exaggerated arm action of race walking requires good upper body strength.

A training program for race walking should

Table 15.3. Periodic Emphases for Walk Training

BASIC CONDITIONING: Increase General Strength and Basic Endurance

25%	Organic endurance (walking 1-1/2 to 5-1/2 times race distance)
20%	Muscular development (weight training, 15-20 reps at 20-40% max.)
20%	Speed endurance (2-4 x 1/3rd racing distance)
20%	Fartlek (walk or run, long distance or 10-20 x 800m)
15%	Muscular endurance (4-6 x 500m hill runs; 5-7 x 800-1,000m walks)

SPECIFIC CONDITIONING: Develop Specific Endurance

30%	Endurance: General, physical, and mental (Long walks, 2-5 hours)
20%	Organic endurance (1-2 x 2/3rds to 3/4ths race distance)
20%	Speed work for long races (2-5 x 6-10 km at pace, 12-15 min. rests)
15%	Muscular endurance (6-12 x 500-1,000m at 95% effort, 4-6 min. rests)
15%	Competition speed (5-8 x 2-5 km at goal pace)

COMPETITION CONDITIONING: Final Speeding Up

40%	Competition pace (3-6 x 2-4 km at pace, 10-12 min. rests)
25%	Event pace (Test effort at 2/3rds of racing distance)
20%	Speed endurance (1-2 x 1/2 racing distance, 15-20 min. rest)
15%	Speed work (6-10 x 500-800m at 90-95%, long recoveries)
Also	Competition (spaced)

include the following components:

- Drills (technique, specific strengthening, and endurance)
- Strength training
  Includes weight training, hill work, and flexibility
- Endurance work: 90% aerobic distance walks, both long-slow (9:00-11:00 per mile) and long-fast (7:30-9:00 a mile)
- Speed work: both anaerobic speed work and pace work
- Running and other sports: cardiovascular benefits from running for younger athletes
  Cross country skiing is good
  Record how outside activities affect training, then decide what to use and what to avoid.

A two-peak year for the junior athlete's race, the 10,000-meter walk, will look like this:

- Phase 1: General Preparation (August through September)
- Phase 2: Specific Preparation (October to Thanksgiving)
- Phase 3: Pre-Competition I (Late November and December)
- Phases 4-5: Competition I (January to March)
  Indoor meets, with races of 1-2 miles
- Phase 3: Pre-Competition II (March)
  Re-establish base conditioning before races begin
- Phases 4-5: Competition II (April and May Annual peak, with races of 5-20 kilometers
- Phase 6: Transition (Summer: June and July)
  Some races or active rest, with slow- to moderate-paced walking

Weight training, static stretching, and stamina training continue.

Sample weeks of training for each phase are provided in Kitchen's chapter. More advanced training information is in a book on race walking by Martin Rudow.

Roger Burrows and John Fitzgerald discussed the development of the women's 10 km race, noting the rapid improvements that result from increased training focus on speed-endurance. They particularly note that successful walkers often move to the walks from other events in which they were successful, generally those requiring the "ability to maintain rhythm and composure under considerable anaerobic fatigue."

They note that training conforms to patterns of the middle distance track races, though they consider speed and skill the most important training factors. The need to walk in a somewhat unnatural manner at a high stride frequency for 45 minutes or more requires considerable skill, as well as endurance. This leads to the need to work on rhythm; they recommend developing a target rhythm, "a parameter combining race pace and correct technique which shapes the design of those workouts and gives the coach a guideline for what is productive and what is not" (p. 42).

Julian Hopkins discussed training for the men's 50 km walk, starting with the recommendation that a walker concentrate on a single distance for the best results. He notes that the most successful racers compete at that distance 3-4 times each year. He breaks the training into three types of walking:

- General endurance: Slower than racing speed
  Hopkins suggests long walks, up to 4-5 hrs. once a week

- Specific endurance: At racing speed

  This includes medium-length walks (up to 30 km) at race pace, which improves both conditioning and pace judgement

- Speed: faster than racing speed

  This may include shorter tempo walks, as well as competing in shorter races.

Hopkins cautions against too much speed work, or walking too quickly, as it may develop the habit of starting races at too high a rate of speed.

REFERENCES

1. Bob Kitchen. (1989). Racewalking. In *The Athletics Congress's Track and Field Coaching Manual* (2nd ed., pp. 219-227). Champaign, IL: Human Kinetics.
2. Martin Rudow. (1994). *Advanced Race Walking* (4th ed.). Seattle: Technique.
3. Roger Burrows & John Fitzgerald. (1990). The women's 10 kilometres race walk event. *New Studies in Athletics, 5*(3), 39-44.
4. Julian Hopkins. (1990). Improving performance in the 50 kilometres walk. *New Studies in Athletics, 5*(3), 45-48.

OTHER SOURCES

Arcelli, Enrico. (1996). Marathon and 50km walk race: physiology, diet and training. *New Studies in Athletics, 11*(4), 51-58.

Marín, José. (1990). Controlling the development of training in race walkers. *New Studies in Athletics, 5*(3), 49-53.

Reiss, Manfred, Olaf Ernest & Dieter Gohlitz. (1993). Analysis of the 1989-1992 Olympic cycle with conclusions for coaching distance running and walking events. *New Studies in Athletics, 8*(4), 7-18.

Strangman, Denis. (1990). *An annotated bibliography of race walking and related subjects, with particular reference to the young athlete*. National Sports Centre, Australian Sports Commission.

Yukelson, David, & Rick Fenton. Psychological considerations in race walking. *Track and Field Quarterly Review, 92*(1), 72-76.

SOURCES FOR TABLES

15.1. Fitness Characteristics for Walkers: Dick, Frank W. (1987). *Training Theory.* London: IAAF, 64-65

15.2. Suggested Training Ratios for Walkers: Dick, pp. 62

15.3. Training Emphases for Walkers: Ballesteros, Jose Manuel, & Alvarez. (1979). *Track and Field: A Basic Manual.* London: IAAF, 24